THE ADULT SAFEGUARDING PRACTICE HANDBOOK

Second Edition

Kate Spreadbury with Rachel Hubbard

T0340671

P

First published in Great Britain in 2024 by

Policy Press, an imprint of
Bristol University Press
University of Bristol
1–9 Old Park Hill
Bristol
BS2 8BB
UK
t: +44 (0)117 374 6645
e: bup-info@bristol.ac.uk

Details of international sales and distribution partners are available at policy.bristoluniversitypress.co.uk

© Bristol University Press 2024

British Library Cataloguing in Publication Data
A catalogue record for this book is available from the British Library

ISBN 978-1-4473-7481-7 paperback
ISBN 978-1-4473-7482-4 ePub
ISBN 978-1-4473-7483-1 ePdf

Cover design: Andrew Corbett
Front cover image: iStock/paul_june
Bristol University Press and Policy Press use environmentally responsible print partners.
Printed and bound in Great Britain by CPI Group (UK) Ltd, Croydon, CR0 4YY

FSC
www.fsc.org
MIX
Paper | Supporting
responsible forestry
FSC® C013604

Contents

List of figures and tables

Figures

Tables

Acronyms and abbreviations

ABH	actual bodily harm
ADASS	Association of Directors of Adult Social Services
AMCP	Approved Mental Capacity Professional (Liberty Protection Safeguards)
AMHP	Approved Mental Health Professional
BASW	British Association of Social Workers
BCP	Antisocial Behaviour Crime and Policing Act 2014
BIA	Best Interest Assessor (Deprivation of Liberty Safeguards)
BIHR	British Institute of Human Rights
CHC	Continuing Health Care (NHS funded community healthcare)
CICA	Criminal Injuries Compensation Authority
CLDT	Community Learning Disabilities Team
COP	Court of Protection
COSHH	control of substances hazardous to health
COVID-19	Coronavirus Disease
CPS	Crown Prosecution Service
CQC	Care Quality Commission
CRPD	United Nations Convention on the Rights of Persons with Disabilities
CTO	community treatment order
DAPN	domestic abuse protection notice
DAPO	domestic abuse protection order
DASH	domestic abuse, stalking and 'honour'-based violence
DH	Department of Health (to 2018)
DHSC	Department of Health and Social Care (since 2018)
DoLS	Deprivation of Liberty Safeguards
ECHR	European Convention on Human Rights
ECtHR	legal citation used for the European Court of Human Rights
EHRC	Equality and Human Rights Commission
EWCA	legal citation used for the Court of Appeal
EWCOP	legal citation used for the Court of Protection
EWHC	legal citation used for the High Court
EWHC Family	legal citation used for the Family Court
FGC	family group conference
FGM	female genital mutilation
GBH	grievous bodily harm
GP	general practitioner
HRA	Human Rights Act 1998
IDVA	Independent Domestic Violence Advocate

IMCA	Independent Mental Capacity Advocate
IMHA	Independent Mental Health Advocate
ISVA	Independent Sexual Violence Advocate
LeDeR	Learning from Deaths Review
LGA	Local Government Association
LGBTQ	Lesbian Gay Bisexual Transgender Queer/Questioning
LPS	Liberty Protection Safeguards
MAPPA	Multi-Agency Public Protection Arrangements
MARAC	Multi-Agency Risk Assessment Conference
MASH	multi-agency safeguarding hub
MCA	Mental Capacity Act 2005
MEAM	Making Every Adult Matter
MEH	multiple exclusion homelessness
MHA	Mental Health Act 1983 (2007)
MoJ	Ministry of Justice
MSP	Making Safeguarding Personal
NHS	National Health Service
NICE	National Institute for Health and Care Excellence
OPG	Office of the Public Guardian
PACE	Police and Criminal Evidence Act
PCSO	Police Community Safety Officer
PTSD	post-traumatic stress disorder
RAG	Red amber green
RIDDOR	reporting injuries, diseases and dangerous occurrences
RiPfA	Research in Practice for Adults
RJ	restorative justice
RPR	Relevant Person's Representative
RSPCA	Royal Society for the Prevention of Cruelty to Animals
SAB	Safeguarding Adults Board
SAMHSA	Substance Abuse and Mental Health Administration
SAR	Safeguarding Adults Review (post-Care Act 2014)
SARC	Sexual Assault Referral Centre
SCIE	Social Care Institute for Excellence
SCR	Serious Case Review (pre-Care Act 2014)
SSWWA	Social Services and Well-being (Wales) Act 2014
UDHR	Universal Declaration of Human Rights
UKHL	legal citation used for decisions made by the House of Lords
UKSC	legal citation used for the Supreme Court
UKUT	legal citation used for the Upper Tribunal
UN	United Nations

About the authors

Kate Spreadbury is an independent social worker specialising in adult safeguarding. She is a lead reviewer for Safeguarding Adults Reviews (SARs) and the current coordinator of the national SAR reviewer network.

Rachel Hubbard is Senior Lecturer in Social Work and Programme Leader for Social Work Continuing Professional Development at the University of the West of England Bristol. She is an experienced social work practitioner and educator with experience of adult safeguarding and human rights practice and training.

Acknowledgements

The authors would like to thank the hardworking staff at Policy Press, especially Isobel Bainton, Laura Vickers-Rendell, Rich Kemp, Ruth Wallace and Inga Boardman, as well as Polly Chester at Bourchier.

Kate Spreadbury would like to thank everyone who has contributed to developing the evidence base for adult safeguarding, whether through sharing practice experience, contributing to Safeguarding Adults Reviews or research. We have come a long way in the last 20 years. Kate would also like to thank another Kate Spreadbury, her grandmother, whose wisdom about community and compassion grows clearer with age.

1

Introduction

Chapter aim

In this chapter we will introduce the handbook, its purpose and structure. We will look at the behaviours of 'professionally curious' practitioners; the theme of professional curiosity recurs throughout the book. We describe the concept of 'well-being' and present a summary of preventative approaches. Lastly, we will consider taking care of your own well-being as an essential precursor to engaging in the development of good practice.

This chapter Includes:

- What is adult safeguarding?

- *The Adult Safeguarding Practice Handbook*

- The principle of well-being

- What is professional curiosity?

- Supporting and developing our practice

What is adult safeguarding?

If you were to google 'What is adult safeguarding in the UK?', you would collect a wide range of definitions. Is adult safeguarding a multi-agency procedure? A way of reducing risk? A means to promote well-being? A legal framework? We would argue that the central purpose of adult safeguarding is to promote and support the human and civil rights of adults who are unable to claim, and are sometimes prevented from claiming, their own rights. The practice of adult safeguarding is about working alongside adults to solve problems, to challenge discrimination, to give the same right of access to protection that all citizens can claim and to enjoy the same quality of life. Our role as practitioners is to promote these rights in every aspect of health and social care, indeed in our society, so there will be less need for adult safeguarding approaches.

This rights approach is what has motivated us through years of practice. We have been social workers, trainers and leaders in safeguarding roles. You will have your own perspectives and, as you gain more practice experience, your own wisdom. We hope that you enjoy dipping in and out of this handbook. You could read it chapter by chapter, but having had the comfort of handbooks in moments of doubt and bewilderment during our practice, we wanted to create one for you based on our learning, and hope that it is of help.

Adult safeguarding post-2014

> Safeguarding means protecting an adult's right to live in safety, free from abuse and neglect. It is about people and organisations working together to prevent and stop both the risks and experience of abuse or neglect, while at the same time making sure that the adult's wellbeing is promoted including, where appropriate, having regard to their views, wishes, feelings and beliefs in deciding on any action. This must recognise that adults sometimes have complex interpersonal relationships and may be ambivalent, unclear or unrealistic about their personal circumstances. (DHSC, 2014, 14.7)

Adult safeguarding in Scotland, Wales and England is underpinned by legislation. Scotland passed legislation in 2007 (the Adult Support and Protection (Scotland) Act) while England (the Care Act) and Wales (Social Services and Well-being (Wales) Act) legislated in 2014. Northern Ireland works to the Adult Safeguarding Prevention and Protection in Partnership (2015) Policy, with legislation recommended for the future (Commissioner for Older People in Northern Ireland, 2014).

Adult safeguarding practice demands the use of excellent practice skills, many drawn from the social work knowledge base, together with the ability to reflect on and resolve ethical dilemmas. Practitioners must be able to use a range of approaches to make relationships with people and involve them in their own safeguarding enquiries and plans, working with people who may be in crisis, afraid and anxious or very unwell. We must be legally literate, understanding the application of legislation to real-life situations. Practitioners must be able to undertake risk assessments and make person-centred effective plans with adults to address risk and recover from the trauma of abuse. We must also take time to form positive and creative working relationships with practitioners and managers from other organisations; effective safeguarding is based on good inter-agency work. Adult safeguarding practice is at the core of all social work practice with adults.

Adult safeguarding work presents us with practice and ethical dilemmas: whether to respect the adult's wishes that we should not interfere, or to continue in the knowledge that the harm the adult is experiencing is having a serious impact on their well-being and could lead to injury or death, or that the influence of a controlling third party is preventing the adult from living a fuller, fulfilled life. Our respect for the self-determination of an adult must be balanced with confidence in understanding the duty of care we have to the adults we work with. We can feel powerless or frustrated, anxious or despairing in the face of the misery of another human's experience and our own inability to support them towards a better quality of life. We can also feel the satisfaction of knowing that an adult is now free of abuse and developing their own life in the way they have long wished for. Adult safeguarding work challenges us: we need to understand our own values, biases and prejudices, be confident enough to work in risky situations without feeling we must be experts, but also know where and when to get the support we need to practice well.

The Adult Safeguarding Practice Handbook

The Adult Safeguarding Practice Handbook is designed as a practical guide to adult safeguarding for those new to practice, as well as those looking to develop their skills and knowledge. We hope to support students and practitioners with a range of professional and practice backgrounds to develop their skills, knowledge and value base in order to undertake the role of an adult safeguarding practitioner across the full range of adult safeguarding activities. Although much of adult safeguarding practice is undertaken by social workers working in local authorities, there are other roles and settings where adult safeguarding work is conducted. Whether you are a social worker or not, this practice handbook can offer you insights and ideas for more person-centred and rights-based safeguarding practice. This handbook contains plenty of practice examples to illustrate legislative, policy and practice developments that you can use to reflect on in order to extend your competence in the complex area of adult safeguarding. The practice examples are based on real-life case studies, anonymised and changed to reflect common themes in practice. We also use narratives and findings from Safeguarding Adults Reviews (SARs) as illustrative examples. SARs are a good source of learning, but because of their nature will reflect on what has gone wrong rather than what good practice looks like. Social workers are reported to respect the SAR process, but also find that reading a SAR will 'scare' them into practising differently (O'Reardon, 2022). It is not our intention to scare our readers into learning; we will sometimes, therefore, rewrite the SAR story to illustrate what could have happened. We suggest further reading at the end of each chapter so that you can take a deeper look at some of the topics we have introduced.

The focus of the legislation and statutory guidance in the handbook is on England. We are both English social workers with extensive experience of working in this part of the UK. However, we will compare legislation and policy across the four UK nations and use research undertaken across the UK to help us to explore the different aspects of adult safeguarding.

The six government principles of adult safeguarding (DH, 2011, 2013) and the Making Safeguarding Personal (MSP) approach are explored in detail in some chapters. These approaches also underpin everything within the handbook. Good safeguarding practice is about using the rights-based, person-centred, strengths-based approach of MSP and we will not explicitly reference MSP or the six principles as if they were separate from good practice. In this second edition we will also refer to using professional curiosity as an approach to making relationships and striving for a deeper understanding of the adult's situation. We also introduce trauma-informed approaches and the impact of these on how practitioners work with people with whom they struggle to engage.

Terminology

We will use the following terms within the handbook:

- *Adult* refers to a person with care and support needs who is alleged to be at risk of abuse or being harmed.
- The terms *harm* and *abuse* are used interchangeably. We generally use the convention that abuse is something that a third party or person does to an adult, whereas harm is what is experienced by the adult.
- We will use the term *statutory guidance* to refer to the Care and Support Statutory Guidance that was originally published in 2014 and revised on a number of occasions since then and is used to support the implementation of the Care Act 2014 in England (see DHSC, 2014).
- We refer to those undertaking adult safeguarding enquiries and other roles as *adult safeguarding practitioners*. Though we are aware that the majority of this work is undertaken by social workers in the UK, there are others who undertake elements of these roles, including those working in all provided services and safeguarding specialist nurses working in mental health or acute trusts, and community organisations.

What is in the handbook?

We have used the English Care and Support Statutory Guidance (DHSC, 2014) and subsequent 'suggested' guidance (LGA, 2019a, 2020) together with the English Care Act 2014 as a framework for considering the statutory adult safeguarding duties. This handbook attempts to clarify and illustrate the statutory guidance but is not a substitute for either this or the policies and procedures in use in your local area. You should always refer to your local policies and procedures and, if in any doubt, consult your manager.

The Care and Support Statutory Guidance (DHSC, 2014) is being updated at regular intervals, hence we recommend that you always access the guidance online and do not rely on a 2014 copy. Much has changed since the guidance was first published, including the deletion of the role of 'designated adult safeguarding manager' in the local authority and the interpretation of self-neglect as a Section 42 enquiry.

The handbook has been designed to consider some of the main practical elements of adult safeguarding, including the context for practice, the challenges of ethical decision making and the necessity for ongoing learning in the role. As well as case studies, we have included summaries of key information and wider reading together with reflective questions to help you consider important issues and support your development as a practitioner.

This introductory chapter sets out the structure of the handbook and introduces some of the key ideas and themes that will be considered. The handbook is divided into two parts: *The context of adult safeguarding*, covering key contextual frameworks and themes and *Good adult safeguarding practice*, which explores the skills and practical application of ideas and frameworks for positive adult safeguarding practice.

Part I: The context of adult safeguarding

The first part of the handbook outlines the principles underpinning adult safeguarding, the legislation and statutory guidance within which contemporary practice is located and the definitions used in adult safeguarding work.

Chapter 2: Human rights: the principles that inform adult safeguarding

We will describe how aspects of the European Convention of Human Rights and the United Nations Convention on Rights for Disabled People underpin adult safeguarding practice and give case studies of human rights in action. Human rights, as both a legal framework and a values-driven approach, are essential to person-centred adult safeguarding practice. How can adult safeguarding practice address oppression and recognise the intersectional nature of discriminatory abuse? We detail each of the six principles of adult safeguarding (DH, 2011, 2013) and illustrate how good practice should adhere to each of the principles. The statutory guidance (DHSC, 2014) accompanying the Care Act recommended a culture change in adult safeguarding practice, currently promoted by the sector-led, person-centred MSP programme. We describe the principles of MSP and examine its relationship to human rights and anti-oppressive practice.

Chapter 3: Adult safeguarding legislation

This chapter examines adult safeguarding legislation and how it defines the parameters of practice in England, mostly focusing on the Care Act 2014. Differing legal frameworks for practice in Scotland, Northern Ireland and Wales are briefly considered in comparison to practice under the Care Act 2014 in England. Other significant legislation and legal frameworks will be explored including the High Court and its inherent jurisdiction, use of the provisions of domestic abuse legislation and responses to forced marriage and modern slavery. Finally, we detail how practitioners can develop legal literacy to keep their practice up to date and legally compliant.

Chapter 4: Mental capacity and adult safeguarding

This chapter explores the role played by the Mental Capacity Act 2005 (MCA) in adult safeguarding practice, including its role in forming decision making and protecting rights within the safeguarding process. We explore what is meant by executive function and how this relates to mental capacity. What other factors may also impact on a capacitated adult's decision making? We also illustrate the use of the MCA 2005 to support autonomous decision making, especially in the context of risk and the role of the Court of Protection in supporting the rights of those assessed as lacking capacity to make a specific decision.

Chapter 5: Definitions in adult safeguarding

Adult safeguarding legislation applies to a small section of the population: adults in need of care and support. We begin this chapter with an analysis of who adults in need of care and support might be, and the challenges faced by different groups in protecting themselves and claiming the right to protection. We describe how abuse is defined and how harm may be identified if it is not disclosed. Key ideas about power, exploitation and coercive control inform our descriptions of abuse.

These themes are explored again in Chapters 6 to 10, where we focus on adult safeguarding practice.

Part II: Good adult safeguarding practice

The second part of the book focuses on adult safeguarding practice. Each chapter explores the knowledge, skills and values needed to undertake practice in adult safeguarding. The themes of anti–discriminatory practice, the six adult safeguarding principles, professional curiosity and the person–centred MSP approach appear throughout this section.

Chapter 6: Relationships, values and ethics

This chapter explores building working relationships with the adult and those who are close to them, including, when necessary, the person who has abused them. We detail the essential precursors to forming a relationship that will support an adult through the process of identifying, acknowledging, addressing and recovering from harm. This includes the ability to use professional curiosity in the creation of a relationship, and to understand trauma, discrimination, the dynamics of power and how these can change through the life course. Case studies are used to illustrate how practitioners can use relationship-building skills to engage with and empower people to change the dynamics of harm. We consider building relationships with colleagues from other organisations and reflect on the need to understand common organisational cultures and values, the impact of differences in these on adult safeguarding work, and how these can be resolved. Lastly, we reflect on challenges to personal, professional and organisational identity, values and ethics, and how an understanding of one's own and others' value base provides a rich context for the development of good practice in adult safeguarding.

Chapter 7: Assessment of risk

We provide an overview of how risk assessment is used in adult safeguarding practice and explore how we use professional curiosity to understand and incorporate the adult's perception of their risk. We discuss the influence of organisations' attitudes towards risk and how multi-agency perspectives on risk contribute to assessment. Models of adult safeguarding risk assessment currently used in practice are presented in usable formats. We introduce other useful risk assessments; for example, those used in domestic abuse situations, or in organisational abuse.

Chapter 8: Decision making in adult safeguarding

We describe the decisions that must be made in the course of adult safeguarding, and who makes them. In this chapter, we clarify decisions that must be made by a local authority as part of its statutory duty, and those that must be made by the adult at risk, or by using the best-interest decision-making process if the adult has been assessed as lacking the capacity to make those specific decisions. We ask: 'What gets in the way of making objective decisions?' Adult safeguarding practitioners will encounter decision makers in other organisations – for example, criminal justice – who make decisions that influence adult safeguarding enquiries and plans. We discuss how other agencies make decisions, the criteria and processes used.

Chapter 9: Adult safeguarding enquiries

We will describe the function of an enquiry and detail each component, from effective planning to quality assurance. The way in which the six principles of adult safeguarding are enacted throughout an enquiry is explored. We will look at examples of 'proportionate enquiry', observing the elements that must be part of any enquiry, no matter how brief or complex, or who is undertaking the enquiry. We will explore the involvement of adults at risk, how adults are involved in an enquiry, and how advocates support adults who have 'substantial difficulty' in being involved. We will explore how to support organisations that can be asked or 'caused' to undertake a specific enquiry on behalf of the local authority. We suggest actions that can be taken to promote partnership working, including the use of escalation pathways as necessary.

Chapter 10: Recovery and resolution

The Care Act requires that an enquiry should consider redress, how the adult will recover from harm and/or achieve a resolution of the experience. This element of adult safeguarding is often neglected, perhaps because harm has occurred within a family setting and practitioners are unsure how to support recovery and resolution between people, or because the long-term or traumatic impact of harm on the well-being of adults is inadequately considered, or because services who might assist adults to recover are unknown. We will use research studies to consider the long-term impact of harm on adults at risk through different stages of the life course and in different settings. We will compare and illustrate approaches to recovery and resolution, including mediation, restorative justice and family group conferences together with access to counselling and other supportive interventions. Compensation and redress through the criminal courts are also considered.

The principle of well-being

We will frequently refer to an adult's 'well-being' in the handbook. Local authorities have a duty under Section 1 of the Care Act 2014 to promote an individual's well-being in all care and support functions. 'Well-being' encapsulates all aspects of an adult's life. Whenever we work with adults, we must pay attention to their:

- personal dignity, including treatment of the individual with respect;
- physical and mental health and emotional well-being;
- protection from abuse and neglect;
- control by the individual over day-to-day life;
- participation in work, education, training or recreation;
- social and economic well-being;
- domestic, family and personal life;
- suitability of living accommodation; and
- the individual's contribution to society (DHSC, 2014, 1.5).

As each individual is unique, some areas of well-being will be more important to one adult than others, but if we are mindful of an adult's well-being during every contact, assessment or review, we can make sure that we engage in conversations with a view to preventing harm. This may be about reducing isolation, making sure an adult is happy with their accommodation and in the community they live, that they have agency over their lives, that they have access to medical help as needed, or any other aspect of life that will contribute to a quality of life and desired level of safety. The observation of the well-being principle underpins both the prevention of harm and actions taken in response to harm.

 ESSENTIAL INFORMATION: LEGISLATION

Care Act 2014 Section 1 Promoting Individual Well-being

In exercising a function under this Part in the case of an individual, a local authority must have regard to the following matters in particular:

(a) the importance of beginning with the assumption that the individual is best placed to judge the individual's well-being;

(b) the individual's views, wishes, feelings and beliefs;

(c) the importance of preventing or delaying the development of needs for care and support or needs for support and the importance of reducing needs of either kind that already exist;

(d) the need to ensure that decisions about the individual are made having regard to all the individual's circumstances (and are not based only on the individual's age or appearance or any condition of the individual's or aspect of the individual's behaviour which might lead others to make unjustified assumptions about the individual's well-being);

(e) the importance of the individual participating as fully as possible in decisions relating to the exercise of the function concerned and being provided with the information and support necessary to enable the individual to participate;

(f) the importance of achieving a balance between the individual's well-being and that of any friends or relatives who are involved in caring for the individual;

(g) the need to protect people from abuse and neglect; and

(h) the need to ensure that any restriction on the individual's rights or freedom of action that is involved in the exercise of the function is kept to the minimum necessary for achieving the purpose for which the function is being exercised.

How can we work in a way that reduces the possibility of harm to adults while respecting the elements of life that can serve as protective factors, especially the adult's self-determination about how they will live their life? Evidence on the effectiveness of preventative approaches is hard to obtain: how can we measure something that has not occurred? However, we can use the evidenced best practice available to reduce the likelihood of harm occurring wherever possible and to promote an adult's ability to self-protect.

How can individual practitioners prevent harm?

We have explored the well-being duty, as described in Section 1 of the Care Act 2014. Section 2 of the Care Act addresses the local authorities' prevention duty; the statutory guidance (Chapter 2) explicitly requires local authorities to work with partner agencies to actively promote people's independence and well-being (2.24), and not to only focus on responding to crises when they occur (2.1 and 2.7). 'Prevention' is one of the six principles of adult safeguarding; our aim in everything we do as practitioners must be to prevent abuse and neglect from occurring or recurring wherever possible.

How can we promote prevention as part of everyday practice? A starting point for practitioners is to ask adults with care and support needs how they want to live their lives, helping people to develop their resilience and retain their independence. The focus should be on all aspects of the person's well-being, not just their safety. Adults should be encouraged to think about their strengths, existing resources and any informal support networks they have around them. Such conversations can help adults to identify their particular needs, what complex situations may exist in their lives and whether they believe there are risks to their well-being. Carers assessments and services are vital in supporting those caring for the adult, who may themselves be at risk of poor mental and physical health.

Isolation and loneliness have been identified as presenting a risk to the physical and mental health of older people (Age UK, 2011) and can also increase the vulnerability to abuse of all adults with care and support needs, whether through engaging with exploiters in order to experience 'friendship' or by being unable to discuss feelings of concern or dilemmas with their peers. Coercive control is about isolating the adult from any source of support so that the controller can impose their wishes and version of reality. If an individual has a connection to others, this will maintain their physical and mental health and will also reduce the likelihood of harm.

Some adults do not feel comfortable in the company of others; we need to respect this but can discuss what level of connection they are engaged with or are interested in creating.

REFLECTIVE ACTIVITY

Case study: Roberta

Roberta lived on her own and did not willingly talk to other people. In order to calm her intrusive thoughts, she walked for miles each day, having a regular circuit that encompassed shops and cafes. The people who ran those businesses got to know her and looked out for her. Without intruding into her life, they provided her with sufficient companionship and connection, and when she later became ill, offered practical support to her through her daily perambulation.

Reflective question
- How can you ensure that communities will support the people for whom they are a significant social support?

> *Our thoughts* are that we need to promote the knowledge of shopkeepers, cafe owners and others about who to contact for advice should they have concerns. Your local authority and local Safeguarding Adults Board will have community engagement strategies; have a look on their websites or ask your Principal Social Worker. You should see evidence of this in GP surgeries, hospitals, libraries, police stations and in the press. Get to know the community you work in, who frequents the local cafes, what the churches provide. Is there a community hub you can promote and engage with?

Some adults may prefer one-to-one regular contact rather than a group; a befriending volunteer may help. Others may be keen to extend or create a wider support network; practitioners may be able to identify opportunities in their community for the adult to connect with and may build the facilitation of these connections into the support plan. Understanding an adult's cultural needs may open up new opportunities to connect with social or religious groups. An adult who identifies with people in the LGBTQ community can be facilitated to find a social group, or an adult with a particular interest can be facilitated to join a group sharing their interests, whether that be birdwatching, trainspotting or fitness. You may be able to find creative ways of 'building bridges' between the isolated person and their community. Ideas from the 'circles of friends' who work with people who have learning disabilities may also be valuable for people who have experienced long-term isolation from community and friendships for different reasons.

 ESSENTIAL INFORMATION: PRACTICE GUIDANCE

What is a circle of friends?

A 'circle of friends' is the intentional building of relationships around a person who may have become disempowered because of disability or difference. It is a group of people that care and come together at the request of the individual or 'focus person' to help them think about their life. Circles were developed to support individuals to become connected in the community, and to make friendships and relationships, and are a valuable tool for creating networks of friends and relationships and promoting empowerment and inclusion.

The circle meeting is facilitated by another but chaired by the focus person who is respected as an individual with gifts and capacities, someone with their own views, beliefs and opinions; someone with the right to self-determination and a lot to offer to the community. It takes seriously the focus person's vision of how they want their life to be and helps them to become connected with people who can support them to achieve that vision.

The first step in creating the circle is to map existing relationships with the focus person. They will identify who should be invited to the circle and the meeting will be held at a venue where they feel most comfortable. Participants can be paid staff or advocates as these are sometimes the only people the adult has in their community. Family members and advocates may also be circle members as may neighbours, community volunteers or anyone the focus person wants to invite into their circle.

The circle creates an action plan to fulfil the focus person's vision, however small or large that may be. The experiences of being part of the circle, which can continue to evolve through time, contribute to the development of confidence and self-esteem, the focus person experiences the ability to make changes in their lives, to be assertive and valued, and to be supported by a community of their choosing.

(Adapted from Burke, 2006)

Adults and their families can be alarmed by the media attention to harm in provided services or from exploitative individuals, especially if the only knowledge the adult has of care services is a TV documentary depicting cruelty to people using services. The challenge to practitioners is how to promote awareness of potential harm or poor quality without confirming an already bleak vision of care services. A positive approach can be taken by providing information about what a person can expect from services: what does good care look like, what should the adult expect? South Gloucestershire Safeguarding Adults Board (2019) have published a short guide 'What Makes a Good Care Home' emphasising the principle that everyone – practitioners, adults and their families – should ask themselves the question 'would I want to live here?' and 'if not, why not?' What does good care mean to all of us? The standard should be an environment in which anyone would be happy to live. Encouragement and contact details are useful if the adult has any concern, however small, about their service.

Raising awareness about what abuse is also has a place; one of the challenging aspects of exploitation is the ease with which an exploiter can prepare an adult to be coerced and harmed. It can be difficult for anyone to spot the initial signs of potential abuse. The skills of those perpetrating internet and postal scams and frauds evolve so quickly that it is hard to tell the difference between safe and unsafe approaches. Isolated people had no one to check worries out with during the COVID-19 pandemic, online fraud or scamming targeted people who were vulnerable and isolated (National Crime Agency 2020) and as the pandemic progressed, health-related, financial and romance scams increased. Adults can still be targeted via their everyday lives. There is a range of accessible information available to support such conversations via Take Five to Stop Fraud (2024) or from your local Safeguarding Adults Board (SAB), Trading Standards or the police.

It is good practice to make sure that people are aware of the provisions of the Mental Capacity Act 2005 that are available to them. We can provide adults with information about the role of the Court of Protection and the Office of the Public Guardian as well as the mechanisms available (such as power of attorney, deputyship, Department of Work and Pensions appointee-ship) to ensure their best interests are protected and to safeguard against financial exploitation in the future.

Recent SARs (Somerset Safeguarding Adults Board 2018; South Gloucestershire Safeguarding Adults Board 2018) have highlighted the preventative role individual practitioners and commissioners can play in ensuring a care home or other setting is unlikely to cause harm to the adult living there.

- **Pre-placement:** visit the setting, with the adult if possible, and consider: is the building suitable for the adult? Can you observe person-centred care from a well-supported staff team? Will the adult be able to maintain existing networks of support if the placement is far from friends and family? How will connections be maintained?
- **Who else lives in the setting?** Are the needs of others who are living there compatible with those of the adult you are placing? How will adults be supported to live together? How will any tension or risk be managed?
- **After the adult begins to live in the setting:** do visit and review thoroughly and regularly. How does the adult feel about where they are living? How is their quality of life developing? What do they feel good about? Who do they get along with? What upsets them?

Do use the skills discussed in Chapter 6 to create a relationship with the adult to support them to tell you how life is for them. In the reflection below, Mr Ralph shares his thoughts on the importance of having reliable contact with a social worker who is interested in your well-being.

REFLECTIVE ACTIVITY

Case study: Mr Ralph

Mr Ralph had lived in institutions for most of his adult life. He had social workers who were interested in how he was experiencing the care home he lived in; he also had social workers who he never saw. He lived in 'good places' where he felt at ease and useful, and places where he was ill-treated, sometimes not having enough to eat or being cold in bed at night.

Mr Ralph said that in care homes other people have power over you; what you need is to have someone on your side who is also powerful, because you have no power in the situation at all. Mr Ralph thought that having a social worker who was interested in what happened to you and who could be relied on was vital in making the difference between having to tolerate poor care and abuse and being able to live in a comfortable place where you felt at home.

Reflective questions

- How do the adults you work with experience the care setting they live in?
- How can you make sure their experiences, thoughts and feelings are always understood, and that they have recourse to a 'powerful person' who is 'on their side' if needed?

Our thoughts are that all service users in institutional settings should be offered and supported to engage with outside advocacy, including development of their understanding of what is OK and what is not when being cared for. Advocacy and service user training on adult safeguarding should both be explored alongside working with organisations running institutions to develop positive, open and accountable working practices.

Some care settings are open to advocates having a presence in the service, or regular 'befrienders'. Openness to outside scrutiny is an essential trait to encourage in institutional settings to address the power imbalances that were identified in the case of Mr Ralph. An adult with no external connections in a care setting can be left in a vulnerable position regarding the need to confide concerns or in having no external person who cares about them to support them.

What is professional curiosity?

The term 'professional curiosity' can be understood as a development of the term 'respectful uncertainty' used by Lord Laming in his enquiry into the case of Victoria Climbié, a child murdered by her great-aunt and her great-aunt's partner in 2000:

> While I accept that social workers are not detectives, I do not consider that they should simply serve as the passive recipients of information, un-questioningly accepting all that they are told by the carers of children about whom there are concerns. The concept of 'respectful uncertainty' should lie at the heart of the relationship between the social worker and the family. (Lord Laming, 2003, p 205)

Professor Eileen Munro later talked about the importance of 'curiosity' in her Review of Child Protection (2011) and the importance of critical thinking augmented by creativity and curiosity.

The concept of 'professional curiosity' is now referenced widely in SARs. In the national analysis of English SARs undertaken between April 2019 and March 2023, Preston-Shoot et al (2024a,b) noted that the use of professional curiosity was a finding of good practice in 3 per cent of the 652 SARs analysed but a 'practice shortcoming' in 44 per cent of the SARs.

> One key omission in practice, noted in multiple SARs, was the absence of professional curiosity. In many cases practitioners had not sought sufficient information to provide an understanding of what was happening beneath the surface in many circumstances of abuse and neglect. There was a failure to look beyond the presenting circumstances, and to interrogate the superficial features in order to reach for a deeper understanding. (Preston-Shoot et al, 2024b, pp 40–1)

It has been argued that the term professional curiosity lacks a clear definition and has been used to blame practitioners for failing to identify harm, while the systems in which they work are not considered (Burton and Revell, 2018). In order to develop and use professional curiosity, we must be supported by the culture and working practices of the organisation in which we work.

The most commonly found definition of professional curiosity in adult safeguarding is 'the capacity and communication skill to explore and understand what is happening within a family rather than making assumptions or accepting things at face value' (Norfolk Safeguarding Adults Board, 2021).

Professional curiosity is much more than a skill in the toolbox. Professionally curious practitioners develop attitudes that permeate their practice, they seek out and enjoy acquiring knowledge, enjoy new ideas, can express positive emotions and can tolerate uncertainty. They are not defensive or negatively critical of self or others. They are unafraid of exploring their own biases and prejudices, they are interested in people, wanting to understand the person's story and hear the voice of lived experience (Research in Practice, 2020).

 ESSENTIAL INFORMATION: PRACTICE GUIDANCE

What does a professionally curious practitioner do?

It is more helpful to describe what a professionally curious practitioner does than attempt to produce a brief description of what professional curiosity is.

The professionally curious practitioner:

- knows how to create collaborative relationships with individuals, families and partner organisations, and also knows how to have difficult conversations;
- seeks out the knowledge necessary to understand the situation, including legal literacy;
- is self-aware, they are aware of the impact of their personal biases and prejudices;
- is observant, they listen and analyse, they can identify themes, incongruities, strengths and the emotion being experienced by the person;
- triangulates information from different sources to gain a better understanding of the individual or family situation;
- gets an understanding of the history of the person or family, hears the person's story, looks at cumulative risk, what has worked in the past? Why is there a concern now? What has emerged or changed?; and
- tests out their initial hypothesis and does not make assumptions (avoids confirmation bias).

We will return to professional curiosity in Chapters 6, 7 and 8.

Supporting and developing our practice

Taking care of yourself

We can experience stress because of the context in which we work as well as the empathy we feel for the adults we work with. Recent surveys (Social Workers Union 2024) across all social work services found that 58 per cent of responding social workers said their caseloads were unmanageable, with almost all (92 per cent) saying that vulnerable children and adults would be better protected if caseloads were lighter. The UK is currently experiencing high rates of poverty, with disabled people and informal carers experiencing particularly high levels of poverty alongside people from minority ethnic groups and those living in rented accommodation (Joseph Rowntree Foundation, 2024). People living in poverty find it harder to live healthy lives, harder to access NHS services, live with greater illness and die earlier than the rest of the population (Kings Fund 2024). Public services are struggling to respond to social need, including the needs arising from the COVID-19 pandemic, in an environment where real-term spending is limited. Fewer resources mean less funding of the third sector, traditionally the sector that can prevent crises, or for social care providers who are struggling to recruit and retain staff post Brexit and post pandemic (Migration Advisory Committee 2022). It has perhaps never been a harder time to work in services and do our best to support adults at risk of abuse. How can we make sure we remain able to do our best and retain our commitment to ensure the rights of the adults we work with?

The culture of the organisation we work in is important. Practitioners must have access to reflective supervision that supports as well as challenges our thinking. We need access to our peers; peer support is a key mitigator against stress, while a well-functioning team will also have a protective effect. We need access to good legal and practice advice. Organisations need to have a willingness to learn and encourage learning; a defensive culture takes away our opportunity to be professionally curious or enable positive risk-taking. There should be flexibility around workflows: if we have agreed a break in seeing an adult who is overwhelmed by our intervention, then that case should not be closed to us. Pressure on resources can mean that an adult's case is closed quickly, but this can mean they will return in a worse situation than before, so taking up even more precious resources.

We have a professional and personal responsibility to take care of ourselves. Eating, sleeping well and taking regular exercise improves our practice as does practising mindfulness or making time to lose ourselves in a hobby. Greer (2016) describes the idea of a sanctuary space, a time when you can absorb yourself in something totally different from your working life. If our workloads mean we are not doing this, we need to pay attention: what is going on? Think about your fundamental beliefs about your job and your own well-being; your well-being is paramount and while there will be crises that eat into your own time occasionally, you cannot live on adrenaline for longer periods of time. Is your work enabling you to pursue what you feel passionate about, or has it become something else, more onerous and less fulfilling?

Adult safeguarding means encountering people at very difficult times in their lives. Do acknowledge your anger, sadness or whatever emotion your empathy leaves you with. Experiencing negative emotion is a healthy response to the pain we witness. However, continual exposure can leave us with compassion fatigue, an overwhelming mental and physical exhaustion brought on by feeling the pain, stress and other emotions of the people we are helping. There is a possibility that you can experience a sudden trauma reaction to a situation. This can be a triggering of a trauma you have experienced or a vicarious trauma (trauma caused by exposure to the trauma of others). Your organisation should provide counselling support or fund external counselling as needed. Many of us have taken up this opportunity.

Learning from experience as a practitioner

No one theory, no matter how well you can intellectually grasp it, will apply to all the situations you will encounter as a practitioner. Individuals are unique, as are the circumstances that they live in; their situations can be complex and may challenge everything you have previously understood. Social work skills and knowledge are largely context-specific; you must adapt and extend what you know to address each situation. You must also be wise enough to understand how your personal value base may lead to bias in thinking and decision making, you must recognise your own ignorance, together with the expertise of the adults and others you are working with.

Thompson and West (2013) capture this element of practice wisdom:

> Wise professionals recognize not just their own knowledge and procedures in practice, they also recognize their own ignorance and the client's expertise. Thus, wisdom lies in intuitively recognizing when deficiencies present a need for further theoretical and procedural knowledge and when there is a need for deference to client or other knowledge. (p 125)

Dybicz (2004) emphasises how we use the power of our knowledge in helping relationships, and how awareness of our value base will provide a welcome compass as we descend into the unknown.

We are sometimes asked how long it will take to develop 'practice wisdom'. If you are wise enough to know that experience is not enough and are already engaging in reflection, then you are already on the pathway to becoming wise. Most of us can never sit back and feel truly 'wise' as every day can bring a different 'unknown'. Perhaps the real wisdom is knowing that you cannot know all the answers and indeed it is unhelpful to think that you should.

Reflection on practice

Reflecting on our emotions, our feelings of discomfort, shock or despair, is vital to keep us healthy when working in sad and at times seemingly hopeless situations. Practitioners who believe they must behave as if they are not affected by an adult's situation or distress often do not allow themselves to deeply reflect on their work. There are many ways of reflecting and several reflective models to use. The organisation you work for must support reflection via supervision and support for group learning, it may also have an agreed framework for supporting reflective practice. You may also find your own framework for reflection that suits your learning style.

There are areas within this handbook that you can use as a reflective basis for the analysis of events. You could use one of the six principles of adult safeguarding, the five MCA principles, MSP approaches, pondering curious questions, research into what works when working with people who self-neglect or whatever you want to focus on at that time. For example, if you use the adult safeguarding principle of 'empowerment', you could evaluate how you used your professional power in an interaction: how did you work with the adult to make sure that their views were respected and that they were able to make their own decision? Consider how effective your approach was. Where were the gaps in your understanding, or conflicts with your value base?

Reflecting on mistakes or what could have gone better can be productive, and the wish to do better provides the motivation to reflect (Sicora, 2017). Reflecting on the errors of practice can create feelings of inadequacy without a reflection partner to provide context; you may find that reflecting with a colleague or manager is supportive. A 'critical friend' in your organisation can help you make sense of your reflections by contextualising your experience from an external perspective. While learning from our mistakes can generate the motivation to change, it is also important to reflect on what has gone well, and how this positive practice can be extended to other areas of work. Ghaye (2008, p 203) poses three questions to help think through and extend positive practice:

Think of a success that you achieved at work this week:

- What contributed to the success?
- What do you need to keep doing to create further success?
- What is the one behaviour you need to keep, and how will you keep doing it?

Opportunities for learning

Reflecting on everyday practice provides a regular opportunity to develop but sometimes we grow stale and need to be challenged and inspired, or we must understand a new way of practising that is consistent with new legislation or case law. Learning events, including training, are precious in providing opportunities to focus on a particular aspect of adult safeguarding practice, meet with other safeguarding practitioners and extend our own knowledge and understanding. We need to be active in making the most of these opportunities as it is often hard to get away from the 'day job'. The Social Care Institute for Excellence (SCIE) has a wealth of webinars available on the 'Social Care TV' YouTube channel, Research in Practice for Adults (RiPfA) offer webinars and videos on current topics. Your learning will be maximised if you discuss and analyse these programmes with colleagues afterwards.

SARs provide powerful learning opportunities. The purpose of a SAR is to identify lessons that can be learned from examining the case that will apply to similar cases in the future or will generally improve the systems and ways that organisations work together. That knowledge does not prevent practitioners and managers being initially fearful of a SAR in their area; it is sometimes only by experiencing a SAR process that treats practitioners respectfully and results in useful learning that we will stop being afraid. While learning from mistakes can be effective (Sicora, 2017) it can also be painful and, if poorly managed, creates stress in practitioners and teams. SARs can be commissioned to learn from good practice (DHSC, 2014, 14.164) but at the time of writing no such SAR has been commissioned.

The national SAB Chairs network hosts an indexed SAR library containing a wide range of published SARs and is a less stressful way of learning lessons from tragic circumstances. You can find a link at the end of this chapter together with more information about where to find learning from SARs.

📖 FURTHER READING

- **You can find the latest version of the Care Act Care and Support Statutory Guidance on this link. Always refer to the online version as it is often updated: www.gov.uk/government/publications/care-act-statutory-guidance/care-and-support-statutory-guidance [Accessed 12 July 2024].**

- For a comprehensive and practical guide to reflection, and learning from our mistakes, read Sicora, A. (2017) *Reflective Practice and Learning from Mistakes in Social Work*, Bristol: Policy Press.

- Maclean, S. (2010) *The Social Work Pocket Guide to Reflective Practice*, Lichfield: Kirwan Maclean Associates is also a simple and enjoyable guide to reflective practice.

- Stay up to date with research by subscribing or asking your organisation to subscribe to a regular e-journal such as *The Journal of Adult Protection*.

- Published SARs in England are available via the National Chairs network website, https://nationalnetwork.org.uk/search.html [Accessed 3 January 2024].

The following are useful compilations of SARs around a particular topic:

- Alcohol Change (2019) 'Learning From Tragedies: An Analysis of Alcohol Related Safeguarding Adults Reviews Published In 2017'. Available from: https://alcoholchange.org.uk/publication/learning-from-tragedies-an-analysis-of-alcohol-related-safeguarding-adult-reviews-published-in-2017 [Accessed 4 April 2024].

- Manthorpe, J. and Martineau, S. (2019) 'Mental Health Law Under Review: Messages From English Safeguarding Adults Reviews', *Journal of Adult Protection*, 21(1): 46–64.

- Martineau, S., Cornes, M., Manthorpe, J., Ornelas, B. and Fuller, J. (2019) Safeguarding, Homelessness And Rough Sleeping: An Analysis of Safeguarding Adults Reviews. NIHR Policy Research Unit in Health and Social Care Workforce: The Policy Institute. London: King's College London. Available from: https://kclpure.kcl.ac.uk/ws/portalfiles/portal/116649790/SARs_and_Homelessness_HSCWRU_Report_2019.pdf [Accessed 4 April 2024].

Part I
The context of adult safeguarding

2

Human rights: the principles that inform adult safeguarding

Chapter aim

In this chapter we will explore the context for human rights that informs adult safeguarding practice. We will consider how anti-discriminatory practice plays a crucial part in ensuring that adult safeguarding practice is truly person-centred while acknowledging how diverse experiences and intersectionality may interact with risk and abuse. We consider two fundamental aspects of adult safeguarding work – the six adult safeguarding principles and person-centred approaches, known as 'Making Safeguarding Personal'.

This chapter includes:

- Human rights and adult safeguarding in practice

- Discrimination, anti-discriminatory practice and identity

- Applying the six adult safeguarding principles of the Care Act 2014

- Making Safeguarding Personal in practice

Human rights and adult safeguarding in practice

All adult safeguarding practice must be informed by a human rights perspective and consider the legal framework that supports human rights. Fundamentally, adult safeguarding practice is about promoting and protecting the human rights of adults whose care and support needs make it difficult for them to exercise their autonomy and will.

To use a human rights perspective, we must understand:

- what human rights are as set out in law;
- where we might see abuses of the human rights of adults with care and support needs; and
- how our decisions must be informed by values based on the principles of human rights.

The first national policy framework for addressing the abuse of vulnerable adults in England, 'No Secrets' (Home Office and Department of Health, 2000) described abuse as 'a violation of an individual's human and civil rights by any other person or persons' (para 2.5), placing human and civil rights at the centre of adult protection practice. This was replaced by the Care Act 2014 which barely references the Human Rights Act 1998 (HRA) or UN Rights Conventions (for example, the United Nations Principles for Older Persons (1991)). The Equality Act 2010 is referenced only with regard to accessible information and in one chapter of the Care and Support Statutory Guidance (DHSC, 2014, 16.78) with reference to discrimination in schools for disabled people. The statutory guidance chapter on adult safeguarding does include the statement 'safeguarding means protecting an adult's right to live in safety, free from abuse and neglect' (DHSC, 2014, 14.7) but gives no further context for these rights. The lack of reference to human and civil rights is troubling, and indicates a different perspective, one of principles rather than rights; a subtle but important distinction. Collingbourne (2014) finds that, while many of the provisions of the Care Act correspond with the UN Convention on the Rights of Persons with Disabilities 2006 and are an improvement on previous legislation, the Care Act legislates for welfare, not rights:

> successive governments have chosen to view international socio-economic rights not as 'rights' but as principles and objectives to guide politicians in the allocation of scarce resources. They argue that these 'principles and objectives' are implemented through the policies, laws and practices of the British welfare state – such as, for example, the Care Act 2014. Under this argument, rather than being identified as constitutional rights of equal importance to and indivisible from the civil and political rights they enable, support services become 'welfare entitlements' subject to the gift (or denial) of the State. (p 5)

On 14 December 2021 the UK government launched a consultation on proposals to replace the HRA with a 'Bill of Rights' (MoJ, 2021). The consultation was difficult for anyone without a constitutional law background to understand and no accessible version was initially published. A wide range of people and organisations wanted to engage in the consultation. People First, a UK user-led self-advocacy organisation, along with two hundred other organisations, wrote to the Parliamentary Joint Committee on Human Rights to tell them that the consultation was not accessible to people with learning disabilities or communication needs (People First, 2022). An 'Easy Read' accessible version was published just 12 days before the consultation was due to end; this version did not meet the standards for accessible information and People First and other groups made more representations. A new accessible version along with an audio guide was published and the consultation deadline extended by six weeks. Alongside the lack of accessibility for all UK citizens, the consultation made a number of statements about the need for reform of the HRA, including the idea that public services experience legal uncertainty, confusion and risk aversion in using the HRA in operational work (MoJ, 2021), the prohibitive cost to public services of expensive 'human rights litigation' and, of great concern to adults with care and support needs, the proposal that there should be a 'permissions stage' to identify which claims to the UK Courts are 'genuine' and which are not. The consultation received almost 13,000 responses, from individuals, charities, academics, legal experts and others. In total, 80–90 per cent of respondents rejected the proposed human rights reforms (Law Society, 2024). While not everyone could answer the set questions about constitutional law, there was a good deal of what the government called 'sentiment analysis' about the value of human rights. The British Institute of Human Rights (BIHR, 2022) submission illustrates this. A 'Bill of Rights' Bill was introduced to Parliament in June 2022 but dropped the following year. The responses to the government consultation demonstrated that the legal framework for human rights in the UK is understood and valued by people with care and support needs and those who work with or represent them. But is one of the central arguments of the reform consultation true? Are public services 'confused' by the HRA? We will now explain the legal framework, and the human rights we think about most in adult safeguarding.

The legal framework: human rights law in the UK

Human rights law has evolved over centuries round the world, with key developments, like Magna Carta, being created in the UK. The HRA sets out the fundamental rights and freedoms that every citizen in the UK is entitled to. It incorporates the rights set out in the European Convention on Human Rights (ECHR) into domestic British law. The HRA came into force in the UK in October 2000.

All citizens of a country where human rights laws apply (for example, nations who are signatories to human rights conventions such as the Universal Declaration of Human Rights (UDHR), the ECHR and the United Nations Convention on the Rights of Persons with Disabilities (CRPD)) can use these laws to challenge the decisions made by representatives of the state. These protections are available to all those in the care of public bodies; for example, local authorities, the NHS (including hospitals, GPs and other community health and ambulance services), the police and criminal justice system, as well as those acting on behalf of the state. Those acting on behalf of the state include care and support providers commissioned by local authorities or the NHS to provide care and support in the adult's home, community or in institutions like care homes, and those commissioned using public funds, such as Direct Payments and Continuing Health Care (CHC).

There is a gap in the provisions of the HRA for people funding their own care, whether in a care home setting or when using domiciliary support. If there is no 'state involvement' in these cases, either by the regulator, the Care Quality Commission (CQC) or any other mechanism, then the HRA may not apply. It must be remembered that if a person is not funded by a public authority, they cannot use a local authority complaints system or the Local Government

Ombudsman. CQC does not investigate individual complaints. The Care Act did not address this gap; Section 73 states that the HRA would only apply if the person's care was arranged by 'the local authority'. Self-funders are again left unprotected by the HRA.

The regulator, the CQC, will inspect against human rights standards in all regulated services. 'Our role is to make sure people have safe, high-quality care. Care that does not respect and promote human rights is neither safe nor high-quality' (CQC, 2023). Breaches of human rights will result in a poor quality rating and a monitored action plan.

The CQC can provide a measure of protection via the regulation of services. However, self-funders using carers who are self-employed and may be sourced via an online platform will have no protection via CQC regulation.

It is very important to note that local authorities still have statutory duties to undertake enquiries under Section 42 of the Care Act 2014, no matter how care arrangements have been made.

Section 6 of the HRA gives public bodies the duty to ensure that their actions do not infringe a citizen's human rights unlawfully, known as a *negative obligation*. Public bodies also have a *positive obligation* to act to prevent human rights abuses, in all functions including operational practices; for example, assessment, to commissioning or quality assuring care from public and non-public bodies. In addition, public bodies must also ensure that there are systems in place to protect human rights, known as the *procedural obligation* (BIHR, 2013, p 7).

This range of obligations means that the actions of those responsible for the care, support and treatment of adults must protect from, address and prevent human rights abuses. The role of an adult safeguarding practitioner is to support people to claim their human and civil rights because, by reason of their care and support needs, they have been unable to do so by themselves. Human rights law remains an essential underpinning to the rights and freedoms violated when adults are abused by others.

Values in action: which rights most relevant to adult safeguarding are protected under human rights law?

Consideration of human rights should inform the decisions we make in adult safeguarding as well as the risk assessments and other activities we undertake. Key human rights for adults at risk of harm and abuse set out within the ECHR and the HRA include the following.

Article 2: right to life

This right is absolute as – except in states where lawful execution may be legally sanctioned – it cannot be removed. This right also gives states the positive obligation to protect life, though this obligation is not absolute, as the state may make decisions that may lead to the person's death, for instance by choosing not to provide certain life-sustaining but expensive medical treatments. This right also means that decision making by state bodies should act to protect life; for example, by taking efforts to prevent suicide (Johns, 2014, p 31) or providing care to an acceptable standard so that a person's life is maintained. When we explore the impact of risk in a person's life, we must understand whether the person's right to life is endangered and how to balance this with the other rights they have.

Article 3: freedom from torture and inhuman and degrading treatment

Article 3 is also an absolute right.

The United Nations Torture Convention (United Nations Human Rights, 1984) (Article 1) defined torture as:

- the intentional infliction of severe mental or physical suffering;
- by a public official, who is directly or indirectly involved;
- for a specific purpose (Association for the Prevention of Torture, 2017).

The implication here is that torture is sanctioned by the state and is carried out for a purpose, either to gain information or to punish. This first part of the right is rarely relevant in terms of adult safeguarding, but the second part – 'freedom from inhuman and degrading treatment' – is a more common theme seen in adult safeguarding concerns.

Examples of potential breaches of Article 3 include:

- Adults who are not incontinent being forced to wear incontinence pads because staff do not have time to take them to the toilet.
- Adults left in soiled beds or clothes for long periods of time.
- Adults shouted at or called names by those supporting them.
- Adults living in squalid undignified accommodation, either as result of neglect or self-neglect.

Article 5: right to liberty and security of person

This right protects people from unreasonable detention. It is a limited right: there are circumstances in which detention may be necessary and so Article 5 sets out the circumstances when lawful action can be taken to infringe this right. Of particular interest in adult safeguarding are the provisions for detention under a legal framework for people who have a medically diagnosed mental disorder, which underpins the necessity for legal frameworks such as the Mental Health Act 1983 (as amended in 2007) (MHA), and the current Deprivation of Liberty Safeguards (DoLS) amendment to the Mental Capacity Act 2005 (MCA). DoLS arrangements were revised in the Mental Capacity (Amendment) Act passed in 2019, but at the time of writing the Liberty Protection Safeguards (LPS) in England and Wales have not yet been implemented.

Deprivation of Liberty Safeguards

People who have been assessed as lacking mental capacity to make these decisions are considered to be deprived of this right when their care and treatment meets the three criteria for deprivation of the Article 5 right to liberty. The three elements are:

- *Objective*: detention in a specific place for a not-negligible period of time. The 'acid test' defined the threshold as 'under continuous supervision and control and not free to leave' the establishment where they are residing for care and treatment in the *P v Cheshire West and Chester Council* and *P and Q v Surrey County Council* (2014) Supreme Court cases (known as the *'Cheshire West'* judgement).
- *Subjective*: consent to reside in the location for care and treatment amounting to a deprivation of liberty, including deciding that the person lacks mental capacity to make this decision.
- *Imputable to the state*: responsibility for deciding on the care and treatment in the location can be attributed to the state in some way; for example, through planning, providing, funding, monitoring or supervising the care or treatment.

The Mental Health Act 1983

For people who have a diagnosed mental illness, the criteria for detention under two of the most commonly used sections of the MHA are as follows.

Section 2: an application for admission for assessment may be made in respect of a patient on the grounds that

- they are suffering from mental disorder of a nature or degree which warrants the detention of the patient in a hospital for assessment (or for assessment followed by medical treatment) for at least a limited period; and
- they ought to be so detained in the interests of their own health or safety or with a view to the protection of other persons.

Section 3 is an application for treatment, made on the grounds that

- they are suffering from a (mental disorder) of a nature or degree which makes it appropriate for them to receive medical treatment in a hospital;
- it is necessary for the health or safety of the patient or for the protection of other persons that they should receive such treatment and it cannot be provided unless they are detained under this section; and
- appropriate medical treatment is available for them.

Current practice within DoLS has intersected with adult safeguarding, especially where Best Interests Assessors (BIAs) scrutinise care practice for individuals. The BIA can identify and draw attention to decision making that does not respect the adult's right to autonomy or organisational abuse during their assessment, facilitate safeguarding reporting and develop monitoring; for example, with conditions attached to DoLS authorisations (McNichol, 2016).

REFLECTIVE ACTIVITY

Case study

A BIA assessment noted that an older man with a dementia diagnosis was being kept in bed for much of the day because the care staff were concerned about him repeatedly lying on the floor whenever he moved around the care home independently. In order to stop him doing this, the home had decided to restrict him to his bed. An occupational therapy assessment identified little risk to him from lying on the floor when he chose to, but greater risks to him in preventing him from leaving his bed: the risks of pressure sores, muscle wastage, frustration and boredom. The BIA assessment noted the restriction to his bed as unnecessary and recommended a DoLS authorisation with the condition that he be supported to move freely within the home and to choose how he spent his time. The involvement of the local authority safeguarding team encouraged the home to reconsider their approach to risk management in this case and to see the importance of noting the severity of risks inherent in the range of potential options for managing his care in the context of his right to live a life as free from restrictions as possible.

DoLS cannot be used to protect or restrict other rights. There have been cases in the past when DoLS was used by a local authority to restrict Article 8 rights; for example, by limiting contact with family and placing the adult in residential care in order to safeguard from alleged harm (reported cases include *MK v Somerset County Council*, 2014, *Milton Keynes Council v RR and Ors*, 2014, *Essex County Council v RF and Ors*, 2015). The judgements in each of these cases clearly show that using DoLS to infringe Article 8 rights offers no legal protection to practitioners as DoLS was designed solely as a legal framework for lawful deprivation of the right to liberty. DoLS is also about the restriction of a person's liberty; it is not a substitute for other decisions the person needs to make that may require subsequent assessments of mental capacity.

Article 5 does not just offer a right to protection to those subject to restrictions amounting to deprivation of liberty in institutional settings like care homes and hospitals. People without decision-making capacity regarding their care and treatment can be considered to be deprived of their liberty where there is any state involvement in decision making about, or funding of, their care and treatment in supported living, residential schools or Shared Lives arrangements or when receiving care in their own home. These circumstances can be relevant to adult safeguarding because unnecessary restrictions that interfere with the person's right to liberty can also be seen as abusive (physically or psychologically).

REFLECTIVE ACTIVITY

Case study: Safeguarding Adults Review

While **Stephen** was a long-term patient in a neurological centre, he was diagnosed with terminal cancer. His discharge was arranged as it was thought he would enjoy a better quality of life in his own accommodation and near his family. Stephen had complex needs that needed the skilled support of a multidisciplinary team. He was disabled after sustaining head injuries, he also experienced epilepsy and diabetes, and had been diagnosed with Korsakoff's syndrome. Stephen had been assessed as lacking capacity to make decisions about his own care and treatment, and while in the neurological centre, decisions were made in Stephen's best interests.

Stephen's transfer from a mental health hospital to his own tenancy had been carefully planned, but no application for a Community Deprivation of Liberty Safeguard was progressed as part of the planning. Stephen met the criteria for application as he was not free to leave his flat and was 'under continuous supervision, monitoring and control'. An application could have been made before he was discharged, or afterward, and would have prompted more thought about the restrictions of the placement on Stephen and the impact of these, whether these could be reduced and if they were in his best interests. His rights would be taken into consideration and the limits to his restriction understood. Stephen would have had a 'voice' as part of the assessment and best-interest discussions, and an advocate to enable a focus on his past and present wishes (Solihull SAB, 2020).

ESSENTIAL INFORMATION: LEGISLATION

Protections for Article 5

The legal **safeguards** available for people with mental disorders in England and Wales with regard to their Article 5 rights at the time of writing include:

- A range of procedures prescribed by law including the Mental Health Act 1983 (2007) (MHA), the Deprivation of Liberty Safeguards (2007) amendment to the Mental Capacity Act 2005 (DoLS) and application to the Court of Protection for what may be called 'community', 'domestic' or 'judicial' deprivation of liberty under Section 16 of the Mental Capacity Act 2005 (MCA). DoLS and community deprivation of liberty frameworks may be replaced by the Liberty Protection Safeguards (LPS) through the implementation of the Mental Capacity (Amendment) Act 2019; at the time of writing, the date for this is unknown.
- These legal frameworks each include the **right to appeal** (to meet ECHR Article 5(4)) via the managers of the hospital where the person is detained or the two-tier tribunal system under the MHA, via the Court of Protection for DoLS authorisations and via the Court of Appeal where the Court of Protection has made the decision to deprive the adult of their liberty.
- Each legal framework includes support to the right to appeal through **advocacy** whether via the rights of access to an Independent Mental Health Advocate (IMHA) and free representation by a solicitor for appeals to those detained under the MHA, to a Relevant Person's Representative (RPR) and Independent Mental Capacity Advocate (IMCA) under DoLS or appropriate person or advocate under LPS to a litigation friend for Court of Protection applications and appeals. Appeals under each of these legal frameworks attract Legal Aid and the applications for Legal Aid funds can be signed off by IMCAs.
- The MHA offers **specific safeguards** to those in institutional care. For example, it stipulates that 'the local safeguarding team should be made aware of any patient being supported in longer term segregation' (Code of Practice, 26.153 in Department of Health (DH) 2015a) as an extra layer of scrutiny when a patient is confined to one area on a ward and prevented from mixing with other patients on a long-term basis.

Each of these legal frameworks has been criticised regarding how they are used as safeguards for people deprived of their Article 5 human rights.

Deprivation of Liberty Safeguards:

- *Complexity*: DoLS and the Court of Protection (COP) have been criticised for the complexity of assessment, language used and ability to be understood by lay people. Guidance for professionals, families and people subject to these legal frameworks is available from user organisations such as Age UK or government run/funded organisations such as the Social Care Institute for Excellence (SCIE) or the Office of the Public Guardian (OPG) but this does not solve the inherent complexity of the decisions being made and the language used in law to describe them, which is alienating to health and social care providers applying for a deprivation of liberty as well as other practitioners across public services.
- *Inability to meet the demand*: the impact of the *Cheshire West* (2014) Supreme Court judgement caused a massive increase in the number of DoLS applications. The

impact of COVID-19 reduced the number of applications made (CQC 2022) as providers became uncertain about whether the pandemic restrictions they were introducing under government guidance also constituted a deprivation of liberty. The demand for DoLS authorisation is still above what local authority services can offer. This demand has also limited *appeal processes*: DoLS and community deprivation of liberty applications to the COP have been criticised regarding access to appeal. The demand for appeals against DoLS decisions has grown in line with the increased number of people subject to these detentions. The ability of the COP to respond in a speedy manner to applications for appeal is limited.

- *Availability of advocacy*: the increase in numbers of DoLS and community deprivation of liberty applications to the COP since the *Cheshire West* judgement, together with the judgement in the *Re AJ* (2015) case, that promoted the importance of Relevant Person's Representatives (RPRs) to aid access to appeals, have both led to increased pressure on local authority funded advocacy services. These services are commissioned to provide IMCAs and where needed are also acting as paid RPRs. There is insufficient resource to commission the number of advocacy services needed to meet the increased demand, and so advocates are not always able to respond as needed.

The UK government was prompted to consult and draft new legislation by the House of Lords (2014) report on the implementation of the MCA, which recommended that DoLS be scrapped and replaced by a simpler and more rights-based version, and the *Cheshire West* (2014) Supreme Court judgement, which caused the massive increase in the number of DoLS and COP applications. The Mental Capacity (Amendment) Act 2019 was given Royal Assent in May 2019. At the time of writing, the new legislation has not been implemented and appears unlikely to be for some years yet. The preparation for LPS undertaken by organisations working with adults with care and support needs has sharpened understanding of the MCA for some, but for others (CQC 2022), focus on DoLS has waned and training in some areas has stagnated as the new systems are delayed.

 ESSENTIAL INFORMATION: LEGISLATION

Liberty Protection Safeguards

Who?
Adults from *16* years of age, with a *mental disorder* that means they *lack capacity* to make decisions about their care and whose care plan amounts to a *deprivation of liberty* (defined via case law, as defined in the *Cheshire West* (2014) judgement regarding the 'acid test'). The assessment must

note: whether the arrangements are *necessary and proportionate* '(without defining what the arrangements are proportionate to)'; whether detention would be more appropriate under the *MHA*; that those interested in their care have been *consulted*; how *representation* is available to the person; and whether additional scrutiny from a specialist *Approved Mental Capacity Professional* (AMCP) assessor is required.

Where?

The Safeguards apply in England and Wales to people living in their own home, sheltered or supported housing, residential schools, extra care housing, care homes and hospitals. Scotland and Northern Ireland have their own legal frameworks.

How long?

Up to one year, renewal for up to one year then up to three years.

How is it organised?

Responsible bodies manage the LPS processes with relevant NHS bodies responsible for people in hospital or with CHC funding and local authorities responsible for everyone else, including inpatients in private psychiatric hospitals.

What is the process?

- *Assessments*: those conducting health and social care assessments will identify those whose care is likely to amount to a deprivation of liberty and will complete an LPS necessary and proportionate assessment. LPS assessments can be conducted by anyone with relevant experience and knowledge, although the mental capacity and mental health elements of the assessment are likely to need a professionally qualified practitioner.
- *Pre-authorisation check*: the responsible body identifies a person not involved in the assessed person's care to scrutinise the written assessments. If the assessed person is objecting, or they reside in a private psychiatric hospital or for another reason at the responsible body's discretion, the reviewer can ask an AMCP to review the assessments, including visiting the person and consulting those involved in their care.
- *Authorisation*: the responsible body authorises the LPS detention.

What safeguards does LPS offer?

As with the MHA and DoLS, the LPS offers access to *appeal* (via the COP), *representation* by an Appropriate Person or advocate and right to *review*.

Summarised from Edge Training, 2019

The Mental Health Act 1983

Criticism has also been made of the Mental Health Act (MHA) 1983. Broadly, this centres around the use of detention and Community Treatment Orders (CTOs), the disproportionate impact of detention on black people and the inappropriate, and often lengthy, detention of autistic people and those with learning disabilities (DHSC, 2018). The draft Mental Health Bill was introduced to parliament in June 2022. The draft Bill contains a number of amendments to the Mental Health Act 1983, which would bring in changes such as:

• redefining 'mental disorder' so autistic people and people with a learning disability cannot be treated under Section 3 without a coexisting psychiatric disorder;
• raising the threshold for detention and reviewing the need for detention more frequently;
• replacing the Nearest Relative with a Nominated Person, chosen by the patient;
• expanding access to advocacy services;
• removing prisons and police cells as places of safety; and
• for patients in the criminal justice system, introducing a 'supervised discharge' and a statutory 28-day time limit for transfer from prison to hospital.

Pre-legislative scrutiny by a Joint Committee was completed by January 2023 (UK Parliament Committees, 2023). The Committee noted 'collective failure' on racial disparity with CTOs representing 'the starkest racial disparity' (para 65) in the use of the Act, with evidence of an increase in their disproportionate use for black and ethnic minority patients; around 11 times higher than for white individuals. The Joint Committee had concerns that, without improvement of community services, people with autism and learning disabilities would continue to be detained long-term in inappropriate mental health settings using different legal powers from the MHA Section 3 or be diverted into the criminal justice system. The Joint Committee made detailed proposals on stronger duties for health and care bodies to identify those in need of community care, 'safeguards' including those that could mitigate the loss of funding for preventative services through MHA Section 117 entitlements.

At the time of writing, the MHA reforms have not been enacted, leaving a very out-of-date piece of legislation to protect the rights of people with mental health conditions.

Article 8: respect for private and family life, home and correspondence

When considering intervention to safeguard an adult from the risk of harm and abuse, we must consider the adult's right to respect for their private and family life, home and correspondence. This right is designed to protect the individual from unnecessary intervention in their right to live their life as they choose. It is not an absolute right – as suggested by the use of the phrase 'respect for' – but something that all those representing the state in their work must consider and balance with any risks to the adult's other human rights and well-being before intervening in their life.

The legislation and regulations used in the UK during the 2020 COVID-19 pandemic illustrate how human rights may need to be balanced against each other. The Coronavirus Act 2020 was emergency legislation subject to a fast-track procedure through Parliament. It contained wide, sweeping powers to enable the government and the NHS to deal with the COVID-19 pandemic. These powers supplemented existing powers available under the Public Health (Control of Diseases) Act 1984 and the Civil Contingencies Act 2004. The Coronavirus Act initiated a wide range of restrictions on human rights in the UK. The right to life (Article 2 ECHR) was central to the UK government's response to COVID-19. It gives the government a positive duty to take appropriate steps to safeguard the lives of those within its jurisdiction. In order to fulfil this positive duty, other human rights were displaced, in particular Article 8. People could not enjoy their Article 8 rights while family gatherings and visits to care homes and hospitals were forbidden. This restriction caused misery (SCIE, 2022) as people living in care homes or hospitals, families and friends were separated, often for months. The impact on people with dementia (Alzheimer's Society, 2020) and learning disabilities (Learning Disability England, 2022) was particularly profound; unable to grasp the cause of the restrictions, adults felt abandoned and depressed and their mental and physical health suffered. Relatives formed campaign groups (Rights for Residents 2020; now Care Rights UK 2023) to challenge the restrictions and, in the longer term, create new roles and ways of working to ensure that Article 8 rights would be supported in the future. At the time of writing, the Care Supporters Bill, giving people the right to a Care Supporter while using health or care services, has not yet been passed by Parliament. For adults with care and support needs still living in the community, the displacement of Article 8 rights meant the loss of protective networks, self-neglect, and an increase in psychological and domestic abuse concerns (LGA, 2021b).

When we make decisions in adult safeguarding, whether about the outcome of an enquiry for an adult with care and support needs or a best-interest decision about an adult who lacks capacity, we will be balancing a range of rights and responsibilities towards the individual. Adults have Article 8 rights, and underpinning these is the right to individual self-determination (ECHR). Local authorities have a positive duty to uphold Article 2 and 3 rights, taking action to prevent harm that may lead to a risk to life or to dignity. Balancing these rights and duties causes some of the key dilemmas in adult safeguarding decision making. We will explore these further in Chapter 7.

REFLECTIVE ACTIVITY

Case study: Article 8 rights, Jay and Daisy

Jay Jones and Daisy Smith have been engaged to be married for ten years. Their parents have opposed their marriage for all of this time, saying that as they both have learning disabilities and live in supported living, they have no idea what marriage is and have no right to marry. Jay and Daisy's support workers are convinced that both do understand marriage and what this entails but are worried about what the parents' reactions would be if they were to bring this up with them.

The support workers became concerned about the breach of the couple's Article 8 rights in not supporting their right to choose to marry and contacted the local adult safeguarding team who arranged a number of interventions. These included conversations with Jay and Daisy about the nature of marriage, where each demonstrated their understanding and desire for this legally binding arrangement, and meetings – with the couple's permission – with their families. Jay's family remained adamantly against him marrying. Jay and Daisy married and moved into a double flat in the supported living complex.

Reflective questions
- How has recognition of Jay and Daisy's rights under Article 8 affected their choices about their family life?
- How can you put these insights into practice with adults at risk?

Our thoughts are that the following areas should be considered in similar circumstances:
- Jay and Daisy's understanding of marriage and relationships can be explored in a manner that recognises their right to form relationships and the mental capacity of each adult to make this decision.
- Care planning should include consideration of education regarding sexuality and positive relationships.

Article 14: protection from discrimination in the exercise of these rights

This article gives citizens the right to not be discriminated against in accessing the other rights offered within the ECHR and HRA. This ensures equality of access to rights by all, echoing the universality of access to rights that Baroness Hale referred to in the *Cheshire West* (2014) judgement when considering the rights of disabled people to have the same expectations of what amounts to a deprivation of liberty as all citizens.

Lastly, we will consider the Equality Act 2010, an important piece of legislation used to support Human Rights in the UK.

 ESSENTIAL INFORMATION: LEGISLATION

The Equality Act 2010 applies to England, Wales and Scotland. Northern Ireland did not implement the Equality Act, so previous laws on discrimination apply.

It is against the law to discriminate against anyone because of:

- age;
- gender reassignment (e.g. the person's gender identity);
- being married or in a civil partnership;
- being pregnant or on maternity leave;
- disability;
- race, including colour, nationality, ethnic or national origin;
- religion or belief;
- sex; or
- sexual orientation.

You are protected from discrimination:

- at work;
- in education;
- as a consumer;
- when using public services;
- when buying or renting property; or
- as a member or guest of a private club or association.

You are also protected from discrimination if:

- you are associated with someone who has a protected characteristic, for example a family member or friend; or
- you have complained about discrimination or supported someone else's claim (HM Government, 2018).

The Equality Act contains the concept of the 'reasonable adjustments' that public sector organisations have to make in changes in their approach or provision to ensure that services are accessible to disabled people as well as everybody else. Reasonable adjustments can mean alterations to buildings by providing lifts, wide doors, ramps and tactile signage. It also means changes in how we work with people; for example, making reasonable adjustments in how we engage and maintain engagement with an adult who is disabled by changes in their mental health as a result of trauma. Making 'reasonable adjustments' may mean changes to policies, procedures and staff training to ensure that services work equally well for all.

What should be included in the definition of 'disability' within the act has been subject to controversy (Flacks, 2012). Addiction to or dependency on alcohol or drugs is specifically excluded from the scope of the Equality Act, unless the addiction was originally the result of medically prescribed drugs or other medical treatment (Government Equalities Office, 2013). However, people who are substance dependent will often be considered under the Equality Act as a result of the consequences of their dependency.

> For example, a person who is addicted to a substance such as alcohol may also have depression, or a physical impairment such as liver damage, arising from the alcohol addiction. While this person would not meet the definition simply on the basis of having an addiction, he or she may still meet the definition as a result of the effects of the depression or the liver damage. (Government Equalities Office, 2013, para A14)

Discrimination, anti-discriminatory practice and identity

Discrimination and oppression are prevalent throughout the lives of adults at risk of harm and abuse. Social work has long acknowledged the impact of oppression and its responsibility to work to counter this. Burke and Harrison (2016) note that 'working with people who experience discrimination and oppression, who are excluded and at the margins of society, places a moral duty on the social work profession and those who work within it to move from a position of noticing and witnessing to one of engaging in political and social action' (p 41).

Discrimination will be a factor in many forms of abuse which exploit or harm people on the basis of their invisibility and/or vulnerability arising from a protected characteristic. However, discriminatory abuse is recorded as a factor in less than 1 per cent of all completed adult safeguarding enquiries (NHS Digital, 2023). This has not varied since data collection began. Discriminatory abuse features in only 2 per cent of SARs undertaken between 2019 and 2023 in England (Preston-Shoot et al, 2024a). Recorded disability hate crimes in England have risen from 1,838 in 2013 to 13,777 in 2023 (House of Commons Library, 2024). Some of this increase can be attributed to better awareness, reporting and recording, but these crimes are not reflected in data relating to adult safeguarding activity.

Why should this be? A literature review (Mason et al, 2022) identified confusion about the definition of 'discriminatory abuse'. On an individual level discriminatory abuse may exist alongside other forms of abuse and is not recognised. Davies (2019) points out that carers, families and friends of people with protected characteristics can also be affected by discriminatory abuse. Practitioners may fail to ask if the adult has a protected characteristic and for reasons of stigma or feared prejudice, the adult may not disclose their protected characteristic. For similar reasons the adult may not disclose the discriminatory nature of the abuse. Taking a person-centred approach means understanding the adult's life story and the impact of their experiences on them. We need to develop a trusting relationship while being aware of assumptions we might make about the adult. Salford Safeguarding Adults Board (2023) picks up the invisibility and lack of consideration of protected characteristics in SAR Stanley.

> Stanley and Matthew were a gay couple who entered into a civil partnership when it became legal for them to do so. There is no suggestion that either Matthew or Stanley were discriminated against or treated insensitively because of their sexuality. It should be borne in mind that gay men of the age of Stanley and Matthew are likely to have experienced adversity in their earlier lives. Whilst attitudes to sexuality have been transformed over the years, it shouldn't be assumed that because Stanley and Matthew were an 'out' gay couple living peacefully together in Salford in the 2020s that perceptions and attitudes to their sexuality would not be of relevance. It is of interest that the professional completing the Specialist Health Needs Assessment recorded 'no issues' under the heading of sexuality. Absolutely no criticism is intended for this response but research into older LGBT people's experiences has indicates that they can be an 'invisible' and 'marginalised' population in later life and that their life stories and relationships are frequently overlooked by care providers and staff and managers employed in care homes. (p 40)

There has been increasing recognition of the experiences and rights of transgender people to be recognised for who they are, and the inadequacy of health and social care services to acknowledge this (Bachman and Gooch, 2018a, 2018b). The interaction of discrimination on the grounds of gender identity can intensify the experiences of discrimination on the grounds of disability and multiply the intensity and severity of abuse and its psychological impact on the adult's mental health and well-being. Home Office (2023) data on transphobic hate crime noted an increase of 11 per cent from the previous year (2022), the highest number since hate crime began to be reported in 2012. Other forms of hate crime had slightly reduced in the same period. While reflecting on the impact of more awareness in the police, the Home Office also notes that 'Transgender issues have been heavily discussed by politicians, the media and on social media over the last year, which may have led to an increase in these offences.' (Home Office, 2023, Section 2.1) What can we do as safeguarding practitioners to promote the rights of those we work with during this extraordinary UK focus on transgender people? We may need to supplement our person-centred approaches and professionally curious empathy with reflection on how our own biases and assumptions may affect our practice and how we can support human rights, including Article 8 rights. Do take advantage of learning and training opportunities, especially from those with lived experience.

We must also consider the intersectionality of discrimination; many of the adults we work with will have more than one protected characteristic, so what does this mean for their everyday experiences, their opportunities and their experience of oppression and/or abuse? We need to understand structural discrimination within service organisations and society.

Mason et al (2022) emphasises the importance of this approach in effective adult safeguarding practice.

> Discriminatory abuse is about power dynamics, further disempowering the person who society has marginalised. Therefore, recognising and naming discrimination is important for the person to know that they have been heard and their experience of discrimination has been recognised. Safeguarding practice with discriminatory abuse should therefore act to support those who experience discrimination using an understanding of what this prejudice entails and how it can impact on people. (p 123)

Taking an anti-discriminatory approach means being aware of, and taking steps to, address the power imbalances within society as well as between the adult and the practitioner. This can include using advocacy, acknowledging power and inequality and valuing the voices of marginalised people and communities; for example, through collaboration with people with lived experience.

The structural discrimination experienced by specific groups can be identified and challenged by focused efforts via campaigns, research and national reports.

'Death by *Indifference*' (MENCAP, 2012) highlighted the impact of discriminatory treatment of people with learning disabilities in NHS services. Subsequent research and annual reports since 2015 from the Learning from Deaths Review (LeDeR) programme provided evidence and recommendations reducing health inequalities. Now renamed 'Learning From Lives and Deaths – People With a Learning Disability and Autistic People', LeDeR aims to:

- improve care for people with a learning disability and autistic people;
- reduce health inequalities for people with a learning disability and autistic people; and
- prevent people with a learning disability and autistic people from early deaths.

Forty-two per cent of the deaths reported to LeDeR between January 2022 and December 2022 (White et al, 2023) were deemed 'avoidable'. This was a reduction from 2021 data, which found 50 per cent of adult deaths were avoidable. This compares to 22 per cent for the general population. The findings and recommendations of the LeDeR reports are considered by NHS England. The most commonly reported problems are with organisational systems and processes.

Making Every Adult Matter (MEAM) is a coalition of national charities. Since its inception in 2009, MEAM has worked with over 50 local areas to design and deliver better coordinated services for people experiencing multiple disadvantages. People facing multiple disadvantages may have long-term experiences of poverty, deprivation, trauma, abuse and neglect. Many also face racism, sexism, homophobia and transphobia.

> These structural inequalities intersect in different ways, manifesting in a combination of experiences including homelessness, substance misuse, domestic violence, contact with the criminal justice system and mental ill health. Multiple disadvantage is a systemic, not an individual issue. People facing multiple disadvantage live in every area of the country. They are often failed by services and systems that focus on singular issues. This makes it harder for individuals to address their problems, lead fulfilling lives and contribute fully to their communities. (MEAM, 2024)

Well-being under the Care Act 2014 and human rights

The Care Act 2014 is underpinned by a set of principles, the most important for adult safeguarding being the overarching principle of well-being (Care Act 2014, Section 1) and the six principles of adult safeguarding. In Table 2.1, we map the well-being principle against the relevant ECHR and CRPD human rights.

Applying the six adult safeguarding principles of the Care Act 2014

The six adult safeguarding principles (DH, 2011) were issued as a statement of government policy prior to the creation of the Care Act 2014 as a statement of intent about adult safeguarding practice. The principles should inform all aspects of adult safeguarding work, from operational practice by individual practitioners through to strategic and policy decisions made by organisations and Safeguarding Adults Boards (SABs). The principles are not set in stone, they can be changed to reflect their application to any situation. In addition, they can be used as a source of reflection. Ask yourself, 'How did I apply the principle of empowerment in this piece of work, what will I do again, what do I need to develop?' Any of the principles can be used in this way.

Here we explore the meaning of each principle and present an account of how these principles can be used in practice through Freda Johnson's story.

Empowerment

Empowerment means people being supported and encouraged to make their own decisions and give informed consent: *'I am asked what I want as the outcome from the safeguarding process and this directly informs what happens.'*

Table 2.1: Care Act 2014 well-being principle mapped to the European Convention on Human Rights and Convention on the Rights of Persons with Disabilities

Well-being principle *Care Act 2014*	Human right *ECHR or CRPD as stated*
Personal dignity (including treatment of the individual with respect)	**Article 3 ECHR** The right not to be tortured or treated in an inhuman or degrading way.
	Article 8 ECHR Right to respect for family and private life.
Physical and mental health and emotional well-being	**Article 2 ECHR** Right to life.
	The right to life also includes the positive duty of state organisations to support health.
Protection from abuse and neglect	**Article 2 ECHR** Right to life is an **absolute** right. Absolute rights are rights that can never be interfered with by the state. The state has a positive duty to protect Article 2 rights by taking action to protect people at risk of abuse and neglect.
	Article 3 ECHR Right not to be subjected to torture or inhuman or degrading treatment – also an absolute right.
	Article 16 CRPD Freedom from exploitation, violence and abuse; also includes the right to 'appropriate measures to promote the physical, cognitive and psychological recovery, rehabilitation and social reintegration of persons with disabilities who become victims of any form of exploitation, violence or abuse, including through the provision of protection services. Such recovery and reintegration shall take place in an environment that fosters the health, welfare, self-respect, dignity and autonomy of the person and takes into account gender- and age-specific needs.'
Control by the individual over their day-to-day life (including over care and support provided and the way they are provided)	**Article 19 CRPD** Living independently and being included in the community
	Article 20 CRPD Personal mobility
Participation in work, education, training or recreation	**Protocol 1 Article 2 ECHR**
Social and economic well-being	**Article 14 ECHR**
	Rights under the **Equalities Act 2010** regarding employment
	Article 20 CRPD Personal mobility
Domestic, family and personal domains	**Article 8 ECHR** Right to respect for family and private life
	Article 12 ECHR Right to marry and found a family
	Article 23 CRPD Respect for home and the family
	Rights under the **Equalities Act 2010** regarding the protected characteristic of pregnancy and maternity
Suitability of the individual's living accommodation	**Protocol 1 Article 1 ECHR** Protection of property
	Article 19 CRPD Living independently and being included in the community
The individual's contribution to society	**Article 19 CRPD** Living independently and being included in the community
	Article 21 CRPD Freedom of expression and opinion, and access to information in accessible formats

The empowerment principle in practice is typified by the Making Safeguarding Personal (MSP) approach. We can support adults who have been marginalised and/or harmed, and are unable to protect themselves, by:

- exploring with them what will improve their quality of life;
- using this understanding to support them to make decisions; and
- making sure the adult's decisions, views and wishes inform what we do.

Empowering practice can have a huge impact in a variety of areas, from increased self-esteem to a reduction in the chances of the adult being harmed again.

FREDA'S STORY I

Freda Johnson lives in a care home with five other people who have physical and learning disabilities. One of the other people living there, Josh, is beginning to show the symptoms of dementia. He shouts at Freda and hit her yesterday. Freda initially appears resigned to tolerating his behaviour; they lived together in a large hospital for people with learning difficulties some years ago and she is fond of him. Yesterday she said that the care home was 'getting like the old hospital'; she isn't happy with the situation. As part of a Section 42 enquiry, Freda meets with her key care worker and social worker; she talks about how she feels and is asked what she wants to happen regarding Josh's behaviour towards her and what thoughts she has about how her current life could be improved.

Prevention

Prevention means it is better to take action before harm occurs: *'I receive clear and simple information about what I can do to protect myself and how others can support me to do this. I know how to recognise the signs of abuse, and what I can do to seek help.'*

Prevention begins with good commissioning of services and good healthcare and social work; if the adult is using services that are of good quality and meet their assessed needs, a large amount of harm will be prevented. However, life is not risk-free or harm-free and so building prevention into everything that we do, including giving clear information and promoting awareness, will enable us to support the adult's human rights and well-being.

FREDA'S STORY II

The staff involved make sure that Freda understands that although Josh does not always have control over his behaviour at the moment, they know that she is being harmed by the situation and she should not have to tolerate this. They take the opportunity to talk about any other experiences of harm that Freda has encountered in her life, emphasising that she should not have had to experience any of this. The first thing that Freda asks for is a plan about how to reduce the risk that Josh will shout at her again, or hit her, and to know when, how and who to ask for help if she is concerned about Josh or anyone else who might harm her. After some discussion with Freda, the staff also start thinking about how to promote general 'staying safe' awareness throughout the home.

Proportionality

Proportionality means the least intrusive response appropriate to the risk presented: *'I am sure that the professionals will work in my interest and they will only get involved as much as is necessary.'*

Proportional responses are essential to maintaining the adult's autonomy and promoting their Article 8 rights to privacy, and will be informed through dialogue with the adult. Practitioners should establish what is important to the adult and what the key changes are that the adult wants to achieve. Prescribed procedural approaches can get in the way of proportionate approaches; a flexible response which takes account of the adult's preferences regarding timescale and communication may be less intrusive and more appropriate.

FREDA'S STORY III

Freda's social worker is in contact with Josh's social worker who is reviewing how Josh's needs may have changed and the level of support he requires. Part of this work will involve a compatibility risk assessment to understand how changes in Josh's behaviour affect others in the home. Freda only needs to know that Josh will get help with his behaviour; her focus must be on how she can be supported to be and feel safer. Freda's social worker has written up her outcomes and the safeguarding plan made with her and has agreed to return the following week to review whether Freda feels, and is, safe from harm.

Protection

Protection means support and representation for those in greatest need: *'I get help and support to report abuse and neglect. I get help so that I am able to take part in the safeguarding process to the extent to which I want.'*

Protection from abuse and neglect is a fundamental aspect of the 'well-being' principle (DHSC, 2014, 1.11–1.17) and of the human rights enjoyed by all.

FREDA'S STORY IV

Freda doesn't expect Josh to be moved away from the home; she is fond of him and concerned about how he is coping. But she does want to know that her experience is taken seriously and that she will be protected. After a full discussion with Freda and her key care worker, the social worker agrees an interim safeguarding plan with both. Freda has been supported to devise a slightly different daily routine that she is more comfortable with and is now aware that her well-being is valued by all staff who will support her throughout the day.

Partnership

Partnership means local solutions through services working with their communities. Communities have a part to play in preventing, detecting and reporting neglect and abuse: *'I know that staff treat any personal and sensitive information in confidence, only sharing what is helpful and necessary. I am confident that professionals will work together and with me to get the best result for me.'*

The reference to communities in the government adult safeguarding policy (DH, 2011) reflects both: (i) governmental aspiration of wider community involvement in society, a 'Big Society' that trusts in the people for ideas and innovations (Conservative Party, 2010); and (ii) the localist approach to the implementation of adult safeguarding policies and legislation. However, the follow-up statement references professionals working together. Both approaches are key factors in adult safeguarding work; the mechanisms of adult safeguarding bring together the agencies who can help the adult. The community the adult lives in is also of relevance: what strengths and resources exist in what the adult considers as 'community'?

FREDA'S STORY V

Freda understands that information about Josh will not be shared with her, or information about her shared with Josh. The professionals working with Josh will get the anonymised information needed for a compatibility risk assessment. Freda agrees to this as she understands the explanation that some work needs to be done to understand how the people in the care home, with all their different strengths and challenges, can live together with the best quality of life for all.

Accountability

In our safeguarding practice we are accountable to the adult for our actions and decisions as part of our general professional accountability. If we are coordinating practitioners from other organisations as part of a safeguarding enquiry, we must ask that they also demonstrate their accountability to the adult at the centre of the enquiry. *'I understand the role of everyone involved in my life and so do they.'*

Safeguarding plans and discussions are key to ensuring that the people involved in a piece of safeguarding work are clear about their role and are held to account by the local authority to complete the actions they have agreed to undertake within the agreed time scale. The adult at the heart of this work must also be informed and supported if necessary, to understand the roles of all and the way in which they are being held to account on their behalf.

FREDA'S STORY VI

Freda understands the role of her social worker and the staff at the home, including the role of the manager. She has a copy of the safeguarding plan, which has been written simply, in clear language, and includes how staff are supporting her and what she can do to ask for further help if needed before her social worker returns to review the plan next week.

Making Safeguarding Personal in practice

The MSP development project was initiated in 2009 partially in response to feedback from people who had experienced safeguarding services and from safeguarding practitioners who had found that the focus of safeguarding work was on process and procedure, not on the experience and outcomes of the adults at the heart of adult safeguarding practice. People who were either being abused or were at risk of abuse wanted to be part of their own safeguarding, and not have safeguarding 'done to them'. Practitioners and SAB members wanted to know what difference they were making to the lives of the people they worked with, but local and national indicators and data only measured the processes used; for example, how many alerts (concerns) had been received and how many of the defined timescales had been met.

Tools and resources to support the development of MSP continue to be developed and added to a dedicated Local Government Association (LGA) website (LGA, 2022). The MSP approach is referenced in statutory guidance (DHSC, 2014, 14.207) which emphasises the importance of practitioners having confidence in using an MSP approach to adult safeguarding.

MSP seeks to achieve:

• a personalised approach that enables safeguarding to be done with, not to, people;

- practice that focuses on achieving meaningful improvement to people's circumstances rather than just on 'investigation' and 'conclusion';
- an approach that utilises social work skills rather than just 'putting people through a process'; and
- an approach that enables practitioners, families, teams and SABs to know what difference has been made. (ADASS, 2017)

MSP in practice is a relationship-based and anti-discriminatory practice approach to adult safeguarding, ensuring that the adult's right to self-determination is respected and observed while exploring well-being, strengths, risk and mitigation with the person and their networks, aiming to improve the quality of the adult's life as well as planning to prevent further harm. Trauma-aware or informed, professionally curious and strengths-based approaches support personalised approaches to safeguarding. We will explore these further in Part II of this book. Using an MSP approach does not mean 'walking away' because the adult does not want any support (LGA, 2019b). There are so many reasons why an adult may initially feel that they cannot tolerate change or 'interference' in their lives, which we will also explore in Part II.

Using the MSP-based approach is refreshing and satisfying: we are using the full range of social work skills and working with individuals and their families face to face, supporting them to engage in problem solving and to achieve the outcomes they hope for whenever possible. Instead of a decision that abuse is 'substantiated' or not at the end of the adult safeguarding process, the focus is on whether the adult's outcomes were achieved, whether their 'well-being', or quality of life, is any better as well as whether their safety has increased and the possibility of further harm been reduced. People who do not have the capacity to make decisions about their own well-being or safety are also included within the MSP approach by involving the adult as much as possible using observation, conversations and the perceptions of those around them, together with known current and previous wishes, and crucially by using 'best interests' (Mental Capacity Act, 2005) processes.

A practitioner's enthusiasm for MSP approaches can be frustrated if there is no organisational sign-up to the approach as it is challenging to use when workloads are predicated on a defined workflow system. Once used, the MSP approach can change a practitioner's approach to other social work activities, which may have been previously bound by procedural imperatives; for example, care and support assessment or reviews.

What does an MSP approach to practice involve?

Fundamental to the MSP approach is the focus on what the adult hopes will be achieved by the adult safeguarding process and what will be a meaningful improvement in their lives (the 'outcomes'). This is an important part of any initial or subsequent discussion with the adult. Lawson (2017, p 22) describes this as '(having conversations) to understand what supports well-being in their lives; seeking to support well-being alongside safety'. Once the adult becomes more aware of the facts and has time to explore the impact of risk on their lives and what support may be available, they may change the outcome that they want. For this reason, it is important to revisit outcomes during the process of enquiry. Whether and how the adult's outcomes are being met should be discussed when safeguarding plans are reviewed or ended.

It may not be possible to achieve the adult's initial outcome request as it may be unreasonable or impractical; in these situations, explaining what is possible and renegotiating from a position of respect and honesty is important.

REFLECTIVE ACTIVITY

Case examples: Harriet George and Arthur Evans

Harriet George is upset and angry about the behaviour of the care worker who shouted at her during her last stay at the respite centre. She would like the care home closed down.

Reflective question

- How would you respond to Harriet's initial thoughts on her preferred outcome?

Our thoughts are that we must be clear with Harriet what is and isn't practical, and she may need time to discuss what happened to her in more depth. Are there more concerns about the care home that Harriet hasn't talked about yet? What other outcome would feel satisfactory to her? What restorative approaches might feel comfortable to her; possibly an apology in person or via letter from the care home manager?

* * *

Arthur Evans was shouted at by a domiciliary care worker and badly frightened. He has asked that 'no one mentions this again and no action should be taken'. Arthur does not like to be a bother and wonders if he did something that upset the worker.

Reflective question

- How would you respond to Arthur's initial thoughts on his preferred outcome?

Our thoughts are that we will need to explain our obligation to take the matter further as the care worker works with others at whom they may also shout.

Arthur may feel that he does want to be involved as this will help others, or he may want assurances that he does not have to see that worker again. Arthur may want to know more about what to expect from a care worker or anyone employed to provide a service to him, his rights and who to talk to in the future if he is ever concerned again.

In order to make sure people have enough information and understanding about what is involved and what their rights and options are, we must provide the right support for each individual. For some this may be accessible written information and good verbal explanations; others, who may have no one else to support them and have 'substantial difficulty' (Care Act 2014, Section 68(3)) in understanding and being involved, must have an independent advocate.

Information and advice must be tailored to the adult and their situation, so that they can understand their situation and the risks involved and weigh up the options they find acceptable and think workable to manage risk. This may involve continuing to live in a situation of risk or engage in relationships that are risky, but this decision will be understood by both adult and practitioner and other agencies involved, with the adult having an opportunity to think through acceptable strategies to minimise risk. ECHR Article 8 rights (the right to respect for private and family life) are upheld while the impact of family relationships is considered with the adult involved. Practitioners must develop skills and confidence in a range of responses to enable people to achieve safety, resolution, recovery and access to justice.

MSP approaches are also essential to observe in multi-agency working. MSP is not just about having a conversation with the person but about the approach taken by all organisations involved in a Section 42 enquiry.

▶ KEY MESSAGES

- **Human rights, as both a legal framework and a values-driven approach, are essential to person-centred adult safeguarding practice.**

- **Your practice as a professional and as a representative of an organisation with duties and responsibilities as a public body can have a significant influence on how the adult's rights are respected within adult safeguarding.**

- **You should be aware of the potential for discrimination to affect the quality and nature of support that an adult receives and act to address this in how care and support is provided on an individual and organisational basis.**

- **Using the Making Safeguarding Personal approach is an essential tool in anti-discriminatory safeguarding practice as it will ensure that the views of the** adult are central to safeguarding enquiry and planning. MSP is used throughout all Section 42 enquiries, whether 'conversation-based' or, at the other end of complexity, coordinated multi-agency enquiries.

KNOWLEDGE REVIEW

- WHICH articles of the ECHR and HRA are relevant to adult safeguarding practice and why?

- HOW can adult safeguarding practice address discrimination and recognise the intersectional nature of discriminatory abuse?

- HOW do the six principles of adult safeguarding run through all practice? Try applying one, two or all of the six principles in reflecting on a piece of work you have undertaken. What will you do again? What would you improve on?

FURTHER READING

- Find out more about Discriminatory Abuse on the LGA dedicated web page, www.local.gov.uk/publications/discriminatory-abuse-briefing-practi tioners [Accessed 12 July 2024].

- For more information on applying the MCA and, at the time of writing, DoLS, read Hubbard, R. and Stone, K. (2022) *The Best Interests Assessor Practice Handbook*, Second Edition, Bristol: Policy Press.

- For training events, regular updates and summaries of the Liberty Protection Safeguards, sign up to the email alerts from Edge Training at: www.edgetrain ing.org.uk [Accessed 12 July 2024].

- A wealth of resources on Making Safeguarding Personal for practitioners and Safeguarding Adults Boards can be found on the Local Government Association *Making Safeguarding Personal* website at: www.local.gov.uk/our-support/partn ers-care-and-health/care-and-health-improvement/safeguarding-resources/ making-safeguarding-personal [Accessed 12 July 2024].

- Putting the six principles into practice is explored and well illustrated in Lawson, J. (2017) 'The "Making Safeguarding Personal Approach" to Practice' (pp 26–9) together with 'Top Tips for Making Safeguarding Personal' (pp 30–1), both in Cooper, A. and White, E. (eds) *Safeguarding Adults Under the Care Act 2014: Understanding Good Practice*, London: Jessica Kingsley.

3

Adult safeguarding legislation

Chapter aim

In this chapter we will explore the legal context for adult safeguarding practice, including the central role played in England by the Care Act 2014 in providing a framework for adult safeguarding practice. Other key legal frameworks will also be considered. Finally, we will explore how practitioners can develop 'legal literacy'.

This chapter includes:

- The framework for adult safeguarding within the Care Act 2014

- Other legislative frameworks for adult safeguarding practice

- Developing legal literacy

We will cover the interaction between the Mental Capacity Act 2005 and adult safeguarding in Chapter 4.

The framework for adult safeguarding within the Care Act 2014

The Care Act 2014 was implemented in April 2015 accompanied by statutory guidance (DHSC, 2014). It is worth looking at what the actual legislation says about each of the sections relating to adult safeguarding before looking in more depth at the accompanying statutory guidance so that we can be clear about our own, and others', legal duties. Further guidance, or 'suggested' guidance as it cannot replace statutory guidance, was issued via the Local Government Association (LGA, 2019a, 2020) to clarify the existing statutory guidance. Five years of experience revealed a lack of clarity in the statutory guidance. This initial lack of clarity led to some dramatic differences between local authorities in how practice under the Section 42 duty was recorded, with some local authorities claiming to undertake enquiries for 100 per cent of the concerns received, while others undertook enquiries for under 10 per cent of concerns (NHS Digital, 2018). The suggested guidance has clarified the distinction between Section 42(1) (the decision-making criteria for use of the Section 42 duty) and Section 42(2) (the duty to enquire), as well as the components of each section. The differences between local authorities in data reporting continue, although there are signs of a narrowing in difference (NHS Digital, 2023). Some of the remaining inconsistencies may be connected to differences in front door arrangements or recording systems.

 ESSENTIAL INFORMATION: LEGISLATION

Section 42(1) of the Care Act 2014. Who does the duty to enquire apply to?

(1) This section applies where a local authority has **reasonable cause to suspect** that an adult in its area (whether or not ordinarily resident there):
  (a) has **needs for care and support** (whether or not the authority is meeting any of those needs);
  (b) **is experiencing, or is at risk of, abuse or neglect**; and
  (c) **as a result of those needs is unable to protect themselves** against the abuse or neglect or the risk of it.

While all children under the age of 18 can be protected via children's legislation, only specific groups of adults are protected under the Care Act 2014 in England, and in similar legislation in Wales and Scotland and policy in Northern Ireland. Who the duty to enquire applies to is often subject to misunderstanding and controversy. The guidance issued with the Care Act 2014 is statutory; therefore, it must be acted on by a local authority unless a legally sound reason for not doing so can be demonstrated. We will focus on the legal definition of an enquiry under Section 42(2) in Chapter 9 but in this chapter we will look at who the duty to enquire applies to and the other sections of the Care Act that apply to adult safeguarding.

To whom the duty to enquire applies

A local authority need only decide that there is 'reasonable cause to suspect' that the three criteria set out in Section 42(1) are met; an enquiry under Section 42(2) will help to establish the facts with more certainty. An enquiry can also clarify whether the third criteria is met: is the adult 'unable to protect themselves'?

The three criteria for use of the Section 42(2) duty are outlined below.

1: (the adult) 'has needs for care and support (whether or not the local authority is meeting any of those needs)'

The statutory guidance specifies that the local authority duty only applies to those 'in need of care and support' but does not define 'care and support', only saying that whether the local authority is meeting these care and support needs is not relevant. Government updates on the Care Act have included this definition: '"care and support" is the term used to describe the help some adults need to live as well as possible with any illness or disability they may have' (DH, 2015b, para 1). Some local authorities use the criteria in the The Care and Support (Eligibility Criteria) Regulations 2014: 'the adult's needs arise from or are related to a physical or mental impairment or illness'. Some English local authorities have added the Skills for Care (2014) glossary definition of 'care and support' to their policies to clarify to which adults the Section 42 duty applies.

 ESSENTIAL INFORMATION

Skills for Care, 'care and support' definition

Care and support is:

> the mixture of practical, financial and emotional support for adults who need extra help to manage their lives and be independent – including older people, people with a disability or long-term illness, people with mental health problems, and carers. Care and support includes assessment of people's needs, provision of services and the allocation of funds to enable a person to purchase their own care and support. It could include care homes, home care, personal assistants, day services, or the provision of aids and adaptations. (Skills for Care, 2014)

Reflective questions

- Who do you encounter in the course of your practice who will meet this definition?
- Who might not? What actions outside of the Section 42 criteria may be needed where the person does not meet this criteria?

Our thoughts are that the kinds of wider universal support services that those not eligible for care and support under the Care Act can access (including voluntary sector agencies, GPs and so on) can also offer points of contact for safeguarding information, monitoring and concern raising.

We can see that these English definitions of care and support do not mention people whose needs are related to substance dependence. In the eligibility criteria used in Wales, the following is included: 'the *need arises from the adult's physical or mental ill-health, age, disability, **dependence on alcohol or drugs**, or other similar circumstances*'. The LGA (2020) suggested guidance added 'someone who misuses substances or alcohol to the extent that it affects their ability to manage day-to-day living' (p 19) to the list of care and support needs, but this late addition may not have had a wide impact on considerations of who has a care and support need. The wording of the English regulations is thought to have contributed to people who are dependent on alcohol or drugs sometimes being excluded from consideration for the statutory safeguarding duty (Preston-Shoot and Ward, 2021).

2: 'is experiencing, or is at risk of, abuse or neglect'

It is vital to remember that harm may not yet have occurred, but that there are indicators of a strong risk of harm in the future. This risk must be explored and preventative measures taken. For example, a woman with physical and learning disabilities is cared for by her sister who drinks heavily to the point of unconsciousness. No harm has come to her while her sister has been affected by alcohol but a Section 42 enquiry as to what her views are about any risks and how these might be planned for should be considered.

Indicators of the risk of harm need to be explored thoroughly as merely living a life involves a degree of risk of harm. The impact of harm on the adult's well-being, and their perspective on risk, are important considerations to explore.

We must also remember that the English statutory guidance specifies that 'Local authorities should not limit their view of what constitutes abuse or neglect, as they can take many forms and the circumstances of the individual case should always be considered' (DHSC, 2014, 14.16–14.17). As we will see in Chapter 5, new types of abuse have emerged since the original statutory guidance was issued.

3: 'as a result of those care and support needs, is unable to protect himself or herself from either the risk of, or the experience of abuse or neglect'

This third criteria is not defined in English statutory guidance, which contributes to inconsistency in response across local authorities. The suggested guidance advocates this third criteria being less important when thinking of making a referral about a safeguarding concern (LGA, 2020), but something that can be teased out at the Section 42(1) decision-making stage or in a subsequent enquiry via discussion with the adult themselves and the referrer.

The Welsh statutory guidance (para 84) gives a little more explanation, that a person's care and support needs 'may affect how far they are able to make and exercise informed choices free from pressure or duress' and advises 'fine professional judgements are required where an individual is experiencing, or is at risk of, abuse, and they have needs for care and support. Consideration must be given to capacity, the likelihood of duress, and to the nature and effect of the needs' (Welsh Government, 2018, para 84).

In 2022, Scotland revised the code of practice for the Adult Support and Protection Act (Scotland) 2007, adding extensive guidance on their 'unable to safeguard their own well-being, property, rights and other interests' criteria (Scottish Government, 2022). The guidance is produced in its entirety below as it offers a detailed perspective on the concept of 'unable to protect'.

 ESSENTIAL INFORMATION: LEGISLATION

Statutory guidance: Adult Support and Protection (Scotland) Act 2007: code of practice. Published 2021

'Unable' is not further defined in the Act but is defined in the Oxford English Dictionary as 'lacking the skill, means or opportunity to do something'. A **distinction may therefore be drawn** between an adult who lacks these skills and is therefore unable to safeguard themselves, and one who is deemed to have the skill, means or opportunity to keep themselves safe, but who may still then place themselves in unsafe situations.

This distinction requires careful consideration. All adults who have capacity have the right to make their own choices about their lives and these choices should be respected if they are made freely. However, for many people the effects of trauma and adverse childhood experiences can introduce levels of complexity into the circumstances within which adults are taking decisions, and which decisions they find themselves taking. In this context it is reasonable to envisage situations in which these experiences and the cumulative impact of them through life may very well have rendered some people effectively unable to safeguard themselves to the extent that some will repeatedly take decisions that place them at risk.

It is therefore important as part of the assessment to understand the person's decision-making processes. This should include an understanding of any factors that may have impacted upon them with the effect of impinging on, or detracting from, their ability to make free and informed decisions to safeguard themselves. This could therefore mean that in these circumstances they should be regarded as unable to safeguard themselves.

Similar considerations apply to coercive control or undue pressure. In such situations the control exercised over a vulnerable person may also effectively render them unable to take decisions that would protect them from harm.

Other circumstances can impact on the extent to which a person is meaningfully able to safeguard themselves. Refusing to give a random stranger money is very far removed from the situation where it is the person's grandson who is making such a request and when the adult is dependent on the grandson for support and may feel fearful of refusing the request.

It is also important to bear in mind that an inability to safeguard oneself is not the same as an adult lacking mental capacity. For example, a person may have relevant mental capacity, but also have physical limitations that restrict their ability to implement actions to safeguard themselves. (Scottish Government, 2022, Chapter 2)

The inclusion in the Care Act 2014 of *self-neglect* was welcomed by some with relief as responses to people who were self-neglecting were inconsistent, lacking a framework or confident partnership working between organisations. The definition of self-neglect within the initial Care and Support Statutory Guidance was broad and led to confusion about when to refer and when Section 42 enquiries were needed; for example, self-neglect 'covers a wide range of behaviour neglecting to care for one's personal hygiene, health or surroundings and includes behaviour such as hoarding' (DHSC, 2014, 14.17). To try to resolve the confusion, an additional sentence was added to subsequent versions of the statutory guidance:

> It should be noted that self-neglect may not prompt a Section 42 enquiry. An assessment should be made on a case-by-case basis. A decision on whether a response is required under safeguarding will depend on the adult's ability to protect themselves by controlling their own behaviour. There may come a point when they are no longer able to do this, without external support. (DHSC, 2014, 14.17)

The use of the phrase 'adult's ability to protect themselves by controlling their own behaviour' could lead to value judgements being made about the adult's ability or will to 'control their own behaviour'.

What if a person has no care needs, but does need support? A family or friend carer may also have 'support needs' and may well be unable to protect themselves from harm because they are caring for a person with care and support needs. The statutory guidance does allow a local authority to choose to undertake a safeguarding enquiry for people where there is no Section 42 duty to enquire, if the local authority believes it is proportionate to do so and will improve the person's well-being and support prevention of further harm. This is called a 'non-statutory' enquiry, and sometimes an 'other' enquiry.

Once a decision is made under Section 42(1) that an enquiry is needed, the Section 42(2) duty is activated. We will explore the components of a Section 42(2) enquiry further in Chapters 8 and 9.

ESSENTIAL INFORMATION: LEGISLATION

Section 42(2)

The local authority must make (or cause to be made) whatever enquiries it thinks necessary to enable it to decide whether any action should be taken in the adult's case (whether under this Part or otherwise) and, if so, what and by whom.

(3) 'Abuse' includes financial abuse; and for that purpose, 'financial abuse' includes:
   (a) having money or other property stolen;
   (b) being defrauded;
   (c) being put under pressure in relation to money or other property; and
   (d) having money or other property misused.

There is a detailed account of the term 'financial abuse'. This may be because there was concern that financial abuse was not being taken seriously as a safeguarding matter (see Chapter 5, Definitions).

 ESSENTIAL INFORMATION: LEGISLATION

The nature of a statutory duty

The Care Act 2014 introduced a number of new statutory duties for local authorities that are useful in safeguarding adults. These specific duties are as follows.

Section 1: The local authority has an overriding duty to promote individual well-being, which also covers the protection from abuse or neglect;

Section 10: The local authority has a duty to carry out an assessment, known as a 'carer's assessment', where it appears that a carer may have needs for support at that time, or in the future. The assessment must include the carer's ability and willingness to provide care and support, both now and in the future; the impact of caring on the carer's well-being; and the outcomes that the carer wishes to achieve in day-to-day life.

Section 11: The local authority is under a specific duty to undertake a Section 9 assessment (when an adult is refusing) and must carry out a needs assessment) if:

(a) the adult lacks capacity to refuse the assessment and the authority is satisfied that carrying out the assessment would be in the adult's best interests, or (b) the adult is experiencing, or is at risk of, abuse or neglect.

Section 19: A local authority may meet an adult's needs for care and support which appear to it to be urgent (regardless of whether the adult is ordinarily resident in its area) without having yet carried out a needs assessment or a financial assessment, or determined eligible needs for local authority support.

Section 42: If the criteria for the Section 42 duty are met, the local authority must make, or cause others to make, whatever enquiries it deems necessary to determine what actions (if any) are necessary to safeguard the adult. The local authority cannot delegate its duty under Section 42 and when it causes an enquiry to be made by an external partner, it must satisfy itself that the enquiry has been concluded effectively and determine if it needs to undertake any further enquiries under Section 42.

Section 68: Places a duty on the local authority to provide an advocate to support an adult who would experience significant difficulties participating in a Section 42 enquiry, or a Safeguarding Adults Review under Section 44. The local authority is not under a duty to provide an advocate if they believe there is an appropriate independent person to support the adult.

A duty must be undertaken: For example, while adults should be asked to consent to information sharing, the local authority can progress a s42 enquiry without their consent. The Care and Support Statutory Guidance (DHSC, 2014, 14.95) gives examples of where the local authority may choose to progress without consent, but the vital point to remember is that the adult's consent is not necessary for the enquiry to progress. The adult should contribute to the enquiry and even if they do not wish to do so, must be kept as fully informed as they wish. An enquiry cannot be ended simply because the adult has not consented.

REFLECTIVE ACTIVITY

Case study: Mrs Kaur, a family carer

Mrs Kaur hoped that she and her husband could stay together at home for the rest of their lives. He has lately been quick to anger over small frustrations. These are many as he was visually impaired after a stroke and now finds it hard to navigate life after a second stroke damaged his cognition. Mrs Kaur has to continually watch and prompt him now, and, at times, also takes care of his personal needs. **Mr Singh** hit his wife yesterday, something that has never happened before in their relationship, which has always been one of mutual respect and affection. Mrs Kaur is distraught: how can she continue to care for her husband when she feels afraid of him? She wants to leave the house but worries about what would happen to her husband with no one to care for him. She confides in her GP who asks for her consent to contact adult safeguarding services.

Reflective questions

- What harm are both Mrs Kaur and Mr Singh at risk of?
- Is the GP's response the most helpful one in this situation? What alternatives may offer a more person-centred approach?

Our thoughts are that Mrs Kaur may experience further physical assaults from her husband. She may have to leave the house in an emergency situation; Mr Singh will then be unsupported. The GP could explore with Mrs Kaur during her appointment what support she has in her networks that may help, and what options are available, explaining a referral to adult safeguarding, an assessment of Mr Singh's care and support needs and a carer's assessment for Mrs Kaur herself. Mrs Kaur may want an opportunity to think through a safety plan to protect herself immediately and, should the situation escalate, have ready contacts for the emergency duty team and police.

It is useful to compare legislation in England with the legislation and policies in the three other UK nations.

ESSENTIAL INFORMATION: LEGISLATION

Law and policy in adult safeguarding in Scotland, Wales and Northern Ireland

The earliest piece of legislation designed to protect adults is the **Adult Support and Protection (Scotland) Act 2007**. Section 4 of the Act specifies that councils have a duty to make inquiries about a person's well-being, property or financial affairs if they know or believe:

(a) that the person is an adult at risk, and

(b) that it might need to intervene (by performing functions under this Part or otherwise) in order to protect the person's well-being, property or financial affairs.

There are powers within the Act to support intervention in situations where access to an adult at risk is prevented or to use in the protection of an adult at risk. These are generally referred to as 'protection orders' and are authorised by the local sheriff.

- Assessment orders: allow professionals to enter premises and either interview an adult at risk on site or take them to another place for the purpose of conducting a private interview.
- Removal orders: enable professionals to take the adult at risk to a place of safety for up to seven days (the duration is set in the order).
- Banning orders: exclude a third party from a specified place (usually the home of the adult at risk), for up to six months.
- Temporary banning orders: can be granted, pending the determination of an application for a banning.

The Act enshrines the adult's right to participate as fully as possible (Section 2) and for advocacy to be considered (Section 6) to support participation.

The **Social Services and Well-being (Wales) Act 2014** (SSWWA) was implemented in April 2016. This adult social care legal framework for Wales has much in common with the Care Act 2014 in England. SSWWA has a similar definition to the Care Act 2014 as to whom the duty to enquire applies, and names this group of people as 'adults at risk' (Section 126). In Wales, practitioners authorised by the local authority are able to apply to magistrates for an 'adult protection and support order'. This order enables a practitioner to enter premises where there is reasonable belief that there is an adult at risk; a 'constable' must accompany the worker. The purpose of the order is to gain access to the person in order to assess whether they meet the criteria of 'an adult at risk' and to make a decision as to whether an enquiry, or some other action, if any, should be taken. The magistrate authorising the order must be assured that exercising the power of entry conferred by the order will not result in the person being at greater risk of abuse or neglect.

In **Northern Ireland,** the Adult Safeguarding Prevention and Protection in Partnership (2015) Policy gives a detailed description of situations when an adult may be at increased risk of exposure to harm, and differentiates between 'adults at risk' and 'adults in need of protection':

An '**Adult at risk of harm**' is a person aged 18 or over, whose exposure to harm through abuse, exploitation or neglect *may* be increased by their:

(a) personal characteristics;

AND/OR

(b) life circumstances.

Personal characteristics may include, but are not limited to, age, disability, special educational needs, illness, mental or physical frailty or impairment of, or disturbance in, the functioning of the mind or brain. Life circumstances may include, but are not limited to, isolation, socio-economic factors and environmental living conditions.

An '**Adult in need of protection**' is a person aged 18 or over, whose exposure to harm through abuse, exploitation or neglect *may* be increased by their:

(a) personal characteristics;

AND/OR

(b) life circumstances;

AND

(c) who is unable to protect their own well-being, property, assets, rights or other interests;

AND

(d) where the action or inaction of another person or persons is causing, or is likely to cause, him/her to be harmed.

In order to meet the definition of an 'adult in need of protection' *either* (a) or (b) must be present, *in addition to both* elements (c) *and* (d) (Northern Ireland Department of Health, 2015, pp 10–11).

In summary, each piece of legislation or policy in the UK defines a specific group of adults in need of protection, usually associated with the adult being unable to protect themselves because of illness or disability. Practitioners should be familiar with the adult safeguarding legal framework for the nation where they practice.

Scotland and Wales have powers to allow a practitioner to apply for a power of entry order and, in the case of Scotland, removal of the adult at risk or banning of the source of harm from the premises. While the Care Act 2014 gave local authorities the duty to enquire, it contains no powers to intervene in support of that duty. Stevens et al (2017) explore some of the reasons for this, noting that professional submissions to the Department of Health (DH) (2012) in the pre-Care Act consultation were in favour of introducing such powers. However, in its response to the consultation results, the DH (2013) emphasised that only 18 per cent of members of the public were in favour, compared with 72 per cent of social care and 90 per cent of health professionals. Manthorpe et al (2016) have succinctly analysed the debates within both Houses of Parliament, identifying themes regarding concerns about the overuse of state intervention in private life and a belief that powers of entry via the police already existed. Ultimately, the Care Act was passed with no statutory powers of access for practitioners. The analysis of English Safeguarding Adults Reviews (SARs) 2019–2023 (Preston-Shoot et al, 2024a–c) noted concerns about denied and/or difficult access, and the absence of a power of entry. There remains a gap in adult safeguarding law in England, while Wales and Scotland have shown how providing for a power of entry can be balanced with considerations of human rights. 'The question to answer is not the frequency with which such a power might be used but rather whether there are cases where the absence of such a provision hinders practitioners in their duty of care to ensure that an individual is not the subject of abuse/neglect' (Preston-Shoot et al, 2024c, p 12).

The analysis calls on the DHSC to consider recommending legislation for an adult safeguarding power of entry along the lines of the provision available in Wales and Scotland.

REFLECTIVE ACTIVITY

Powers of access

- When could you have used a statutory power of access in your practice?
- What were the consequences of not having a power of access at that time?
- What other measures were available to you to gain access to the adult at risk?

Our thoughts are that other legal measures should be explored such as Section 135 of the MHA, and the MCA, which may offer other routes to lawfully entering the property of an adult who may be at risk for the purpose of risk assessment and safeguarding. Any such approaches must be carefully planned and risk assessed.

Other relevant sections of the Care Act 2014

The duty to cooperate

Section 6 of the Care Act 2014 sets out the duties that local authorities have to cooperate 'with each of its relevant partners' and that 'each relevant partner must co-operate with the authority' (6.1) regarding adults with needs for care and support and their carers. These relevant partners include providers of care and support, medical services, hospitals and providers of social housing. These are essential underpinning relationships for safeguarding prevention work and for organisational safeguarding enquiries. Cooperation at a strategic level with providers of care, support and housing, health services including the NHS, and the police – for example at Safeguarding Adults Board (SAB) level – are also essential for prevention, addressing organisational issues and SARs; for example, to publicise and apply lessons learned.

Safeguarding Adults Board

Section 43 stipulates that each local authority must establish a SAB for its area and that the objective of a SAB is to 'help and protect adults in its area in cases of the kind described in Section 42(1)' (Care Act 2014, Section 43.2). A clear understanding of who the Section 42 duty applies to is important in enabling the SAB to focus on the parameters of its role and responsibility. The role of the SAB is to coordinate and ensure the effectiveness of what each of its members does. Some agencies must be members of the SAB. These 'statutory partners' are:

- the local authority that set the SAB up;
- the integrated care boards in the local authority's area; and
- the chief officer of police in the local authority's area.

Other agencies *may* be invited to be SAB members, according to local need, and include the organisations listed here together with any organisation the SAB deems necessary to carry out its duties. You can find the full list in the Care and Support Statutory Guidance (DHSC, 2014, 14.146–7). These can include representatives of providers of health and social care services, housing and housing support providers, local Healthwatch and members of user, advocacy and carer groups. SABs must be linked with other partnerships to maximise their impact and minimise duplication of work. Other partnerships include community safety partnerships, Safeguarding Children Partnership Board, health and well-being boards, and quality surveillance groups.

A 'SAB may do anything which appears to it to be necessary or desirable for the purpose of achieving its objective' (Section 43.4). This section demonstrates an important principle behind the Care Act: the idea that the legislation serves as a framework that should be adapted to meet the needs of the local population.

REFLECTIVE ACTIVITY

Safeguarding Adults Board (SAB) activity

Go to your local authority web page devoted to your local Safeguarding Adults Board. You should find the strategic adult safeguarding plan for your area and the annual report there. The SAB is legally obliged to publish these documents. You may also find:

- published SARs or learning briefings relating to the SARs the SAB has commissioned; and
- policies, procedures and protocols agreed by the SAB for local use.

By publishing these documents, all SABs aim to meet the adult safeguarding principle of 'accountability and transparency'.

Reflection

Consider the strategic adult safeguarding plan for your area.

- What impact does or should the plan have on your adult safeguarding practice?

Safeguarding Adults Reviews

Section 44 covers the duty of the SAB to 'arrange for there to be a review of a case involving an adult in its area with needs for care and support (whether or not the local authority has been meeting any of those needs)' (Section 44.1) if the following conditions are met:

- there is reasonable cause for concern about how the SAB, members of it or other persons with relevant functions worked together to safeguard the adult, and the adult has died, and the SAB knows or suspects that the death resulted from abuse or neglect (whether or not it knew about or suspected abuse or neglect before the adult died); or
- the adult is still alive, and the SAB knows or suspects that the adult has experienced serious abuse or neglect.
- SARs which are commissioned under these criteria are 'mandatory' SARs.

The law emphasises that the purpose of a SAR is learning, and that each member of the SAB must cooperate in and contribute to carrying out the SAR and applying the lessons learned to future cases. In addition, 'A SAB may arrange for there to be a review of any other case involving an adult in its area with needs for care and support (whether or not the local authority has been meeting any of those needs)'. These are known as 'discretionary' SARs. Whether a SAR is mandatory or discretionary it is commissioned under s44 of the Care Act 2014.

Supply of information

Lastly, **Section 45** covers the supply of information to the SAB. Organisations and individuals must comply with requests for information made by the SAB for the purpose of the SAB exercising its functions. This section is particularly important in ensuring that all organisations supply information to SARs and to enable the SAB to carry out its duties to ensure the effectiveness of adult safeguarding arrangements in the local area.

Legislation that underpins adult safeguarding practice is still relatively new in England and interpretation of the provisions of the Care Act is evolving, particularly regarding the duty to enquire and to whom the duty applies.

Other legislative frameworks for adult safeguarding practice

In this section we will provide a brief overview of some of the other pieces of legislation that support adult safeguarding, including:

- powers of entry;
- domestic abuse offences, including coercive control, forced marriage and female genital mutilation;
- hate crime;
- organisational abuse;
- offences relating to physical, sexual, psychological and financial abuse and neglect; and
- modern slavery.

We will include enough detail for you to connect the harm identified with the possibility of a criminal offence, which will prompt you to discuss the matter with police colleagues.

Powers of entry

There are a few legal means of gaining access to people's homes that are relevant to safeguarding. To breach an adult's human right to a private life under Article 8 of the European Convention on Human Rights, there must be significant grounds on the basis of their health and welfare. The following legal measures may be available depending on the circumstances.

Police

The police only have powers of entry in very specific circumstances, and you should not automatically assume that police colleagues can enter a private property when there are concerns. The police may enter a property without a warrant only in the following circumstances under Section 17 of the Police and Criminal Evidence Act (PACE) 1984:

- arresting a person for an indictable offence; for example, where it is believed that a serious crime has been committed;
- arresting a person for an offence under Section 4 of the Public Order Act 1986; for example, where it is considered that someone may be causing threatening behaviour, cause fear or provoke violence; and/or
- saving life or limb or preventing serious damage to property.

Officers may use reasonable force in the exercise of these powers, if necessary (PACE Section 117). 'Saving life or limb' means that there is a concern that a person is at imminent risk of death or serious bodily injury, not just a concern about a person's welfare. Officers can also enter without a warrant if there is a real and imminent risk of a breach of the peace; for example, when there is imminent violence or threat of violence. This is a measure that exists in common law (that is, not in legislation) and can only be used in an emergency.

Approved Mental Health Professional (AMHP)

AMHPs have powers of entry and inspection under Section 115 of the Mental Health Act (MHA) 1983 (2007). Under Section 115, an AMHP may 'enter and inspect any premises (other than a hospital) in which a mentally disordered patient is living, if he [sic] has reasonable cause to believe that the patient is not under proper care' (MHA 1983, Section 115(1)). The AMHP cannot force entry to a premises under this section or remove the person, and they cannot override the property owner's refusal to give permission to enter, although a co-owner can give permission to prevent a trespass occurring.

Under Sections 135(1) and (2) of the MHA 1983, AMHPs have the power to apply to a justice of the peace at a magistrates' court for a warrant to enter a person's property for the purpose of conducting, or removing them to a place of safety to conduct an MHA assessment. The AMHP will need to evidence that the appropriate criteria are evident, which are usually associated with high levels of risk to the person as a result of their mental health, and that all other options for conducting the assessment have been unsuccessful, before the justice of the peace can grant the warrant. This may be relevant to accessing an adult at risk to safeguard them from harm but the criteria for Sections 135(1) or (2) MHA must be met in order for this to be a legal option, not just that there is concern about the person's welfare in a safeguarding sense. It is worth noting that for a Section 135(2) warrant, a non-AMHP (as long as they are authorised to do so) can apply for a warrant to retake a person who is liable to be detained or absconded from hospital. For more information see Stone et al (2020).

SCIE (2018) have produced a useful guide on using the law to gain access to an adult at risk, including consideration of the Mental Capacity Act (MCA) 2005 and the MHA 1983 (2007), as well as the Police and Criminal Evidence Act 1984, the inherent jurisdiction of the High Court and the common law powers of the police to prevent or deal with a breach of the peace. There is a link to the SCIE guide (updated in 2024) in the Further Reading section at the end of this chapter.

Domestic abuse offences including coercive control, forced marriage and female genital mutilation

The Domestic Abuse Act 2021 created a statutory definition of domestic abuse (Section1).

 ESSENTIAL INFORMATION: LEGISLATION

The Domestic Abuse Act 2021

Behaviour is domestic abuse if both parties are aged 16 and over and are 'personally connected' to each other, and the behaviour is abusive.

Two people are 'personally connected' to each other if any of the following applies.

(a) they are, or have been, married to each other;

(b) they are, or have been, civil partners of each other;

(c) they have agreed to marry one another (whether or not the agreement has been terminated);

(d) they have entered into a civil partnership agreement (whether or not the agreement has been terminated);

(e) they are, or have been, in an intimate personal relationship with each other;

(f) they each have, or there has been a time when they each have had, a parental relationship in relation to the same child; or

(g) they are relatives. Relatives can be a child, step-child, sibling, grandparent, cousin or indeed relatives of in-laws. The parties do not need to live on the same premises.

Behaviour is 'abusive' if it consists of any of the following.

(a) physical or sexual abuse;

(b) violent or threatening behaviour;

(c) controlling or coercive behaviour;

(d) economic abuse; or

(e) psychological, emotional or other abuse.

It does not matter whether the behaviour consists of a single incident or a course of conduct.

'Economic abuse' means any behaviour that has a substantial adverse effect on the ability to (a) acquire, use or maintain money or other property, or (b) obtain goods or services.

The abusive behaviour may be directed towards another person – for example, a child – or a pet as part of a pattern of coercive control.

For further information, do read the statutory guidance accompanying the legislation (Home Office, 2022).

The Act also introduced Domestic Abuse Protection Orders (DAPOs) and Domestic Abuse Protection Notices (DAPNs). In addition to imposing prohibitions such as excluding a perpetrator from a specified area, the DAPO will be able to impose electronic monitoring requirements, and requirements such as attendance on perpetrator behaviour change programmes. At the time of writing, these approaches are being piloted.

The Domestic Abuse Act extended the provisions of Section 76 of the Serious Crime Act 2015, which created the offence of controlling or coercive behaviour in 'an intimate or family relationship'. There is no longer a requirement that the parties live together; the offence applies to partners, ex-partners or family members. It will therefore apply in contexts where controlling or coercive behaviour by an intimate partner takes place post-separation or is perpetrated by a family member who does not live with the victim. An offence of coercive control could be committed if a person with a personal connection to another (for example, as a family member or through an intimate personal relationship) repeatedly or continuously engages in controlling or coercive behaviour that the person is aware will have a serious effect on the other person. 'Serious effect' can include fear of violence (on at least two occasions) or causing alarm or distress that has a substantial adverse effect on the other person's day-to-day activities. 'Substantial adverse effect' could include:

- stopping or changing the way the affected person socialises;
- physical or mental health deterioration;
- change in routine at home, including mealtimes or household chores;
- attendance record at school;

- putting measures in place at home to safeguard themselves or their children; or
- changes to work patterns, employment status or routes to work.

Make sure that your records are detailed regarding instances of coercive control of an adult at risk, as these will form useful evidence if an offence is prosecuted in the future.

Forced marriage

Forcing someone to marry against their will is a criminal offence under the Anti-social Behaviour Crime and Policing Act 2014 (BCP). This offence applies to an individual who intentionally forces another person to enter into marriage, believing the person does not consent, or an individual who deceives someone into going abroad for the specific purpose of forcing them to marry; an offence is committed whether or not the forced marriage goes ahead. A person is considered to have committed an offence under Section 121 of the BCP 2014 if they:

- use violence, threats or any other form of coercion for the purpose of causing another person to enter into a marriage; and
- believe, or ought reasonably to believe, that the conduct may cause the other person to enter into marriage without free and full consent.

People subject to forced marriage that lack capacity to consent to marriage within the definition used within the MCA 2005 are referred to under Section 121(2) of BCP 2014. Section 121(3) of the Act refers to circumstances where a person deceives another person to leave the UK and intends them to be subject to forced marriage. For example, in the case of *XCC v AA* (2012) the Court of Protection (England and Wales) ruled under inherent jurisdiction that an arranged marriage in Bangladesh between a British citizen with severe learning difficulties (DD) and her cousin was a forced marriage because DD lacked capacity to consent to the marriage, which was compounded by DD having been taken from the country to conduct the marriage. The judgement also clarified that any sexual relationship within that marriage would be a criminal offence because DD lacked capacity to consent and that social services should be informed in these circumstances.

Female genital mutilation

The Female Genital Mutilation (FGM) Act came into force on 3 March 2004 and was amended by Sections 70–5 of the Serious Crime Act 2015. These provisions introduced FGM Protection Orders and a mandatory duty for front-line professionals to report FGM in under-18s. Criminal offences under the Act include offences of FGM as well as assisting a female to mutilate her own genitalia and assisting a non-UK person to mutilate a female's genitalia overseas. Failing to protect a female aged under 16 from the risk of FGM is also an offence.

Hate crime

Hate crime encompasses a wide range of criminal offences, including offences against the person, theft, fraud, sexual assault and so on. Hate crime relates to the sentencing tariff used in court; if the offence can be shown to be motivated by hostility or prejudice based on the victim's disability or other characteristics then Sections 145 and 146 of the Criminal Justice Act 2003 may be used to impose a general duty on criminal courts to treat any offence more seriously (an aggravating factor) when sentencing. The court must consider if hostility during the offence from the perpetrator towards the victim related to their (or presumptions about their):

- religious belief and ethnicity;
- sexual orientation;
- disability; or
- transgender identity.

Organisational abuse

Key pieces of criminal legislation related to the abuse of adults at risk within organisational contexts, such as care homes, care and support agencies, and hospitals include:

- Ill treatment or wilful neglect of adults who lack capacity (Section 44 of the MCA): this offence could have been committed if a person has the care of (is paid to care for the person, for instance) a person who lacks, or can be reasonably believed to lack mental capacity, or if they have a lasting or enduring power of attorney for the person or are a court-appointed deputy for the person and they ill-treat or wilfully neglect the person.
  - 'Ill treatment' is considered as a deliberate act, where the perpetrator recognised that they were ill-treating a person or behaved recklessly.
  - The 'wilful' element of the neglect offence requires that the perpetrator acted deliberately or recklessly.
- Ill treatment or wilful neglect of adults who are receiving treatment for mental disorder (Section 127 of the MHA): this offence could have been committed where a person employed by a mental health organisation (such as a hospital or care home) ill-treats or wilfully neglects a person in their care whether as an inpatient, outpatient, under guardianship or another caring role.

These MCA and MHA offences apply to individuals being cared for by people employed by organisations. Organisations with responsibilities to care for adults at risk can be considered to have committed offences under the Criminal Justice and Courts Act 2015. Offences under Sections 20–5 comprise two criminal offences of ill treatment or wilful neglect that apply both to individual workers and provider organisations who are working with adults, whether those adults have mental capacity or not. The creation of these offences was a part of the government's response to the public enquiry into the events at Mid-Staffordshire NHS Foundation Trust, which identified routine neglect of patients between 2005 and 2009 (Francis, 2013):

- Section 20(1) concerns 'an individual who has the care of another individual by virtue of being a care worker to ill-treat or wilfully to neglect that individual'. The individual concerned must be in paid employment as a care or health worker or in receipt of a benefit such as a carer's allowance to support their caring role.
- Section 21(1) concerns an organisation where:
  - an individual who has the care of another individual by virtue of being part of the care provider's arrangements ill-treats or wilfully neglects that individual;
  - the care provider's activities are managed or organised in a way that amounts to a gross breach of a relevant duty of care owed by the care provider to the individual who is ill-treated or neglected; and
  - in the absence of the breach, the ill treatment or wilful neglect would not have occurred or would have been less likely to occur.
- 'Care provider' in this context includes both health and social care providers; for example, hospitals, care homes, domiciliary care agencies and so on.

Corporate manslaughter charges may be relevant under the Corporate Manslaughter and Corporate Homicide Act 2007, which can apply when the way in which an organisation's activities are managed or organised causes or is a significant element in the breach of a relevant duty of care that has caused death. There may also be relevant offences under the Health and Safety at Work Act 1974 and subsequent regulations which cover topics such as manual handling, use of bed rails, control of substances hazardous to health (COSHH), reporting injuries, diseases and dangerous occurrences (RIDDOR) and falls. The Care Quality Commission (CQC) has the lead role in the investigation of breaches of health and safety legislation in health and care settings.

Offences relating to physical, sexual, psychological, financial abuse and neglect

Physical abuse

Common assault is considered under Section 39 of the Criminal Justice Act 1988, while assault occasioning Actual Bodily Harm (ABH), or unlawful wounding/inflicting Gross Bodily Harm (GBH) are covered by the Offences Against the Person Act 1861. False imprisonment may be charged under Section 44 of the MCA, Section 127 of the MHA or under Sections 20–5 of the Criminal Justice and Courts Act 2015 as described earlier.

Sexual abuse

Sexual abuse can be considered as an offence under the Sexual Offences Act 2003, which includes:

- **Rape**: Section 1(1) defines rape as when a person (A) 'intentionally penetrates the vagina, anus or mouth of another person (B) with his penis'.
- **Assault by penetration**: Section 2(1) defines this offence as when: (a) a person (A) intentionally penetrates the vagina or anus of another person (B) with a part of his (*sic*) body or anything else, and (b) the penetration is sexual, and (c) B does not consent to the penetration, and (d) A does not reasonably believe that B consents.
- **Sexual assault**: Section 3(1) defines this offence as when a person (A) commits an offence if: (a) he intentionally touches another person (B), (b) the touching is sexual, (c) B does not consent to the touching, and (d) A does not reasonably believe that B consents.
- **Causing a person to engage in sexual activity without consent**: Section 4 defines this offence as when a person (A): (a) intentionally causes another person (B) to engage in an activity, (b) the activity is sexual, (c) B does not consent to engaging in the activity, and (d) A does not reasonably believe that B consents, based on what efforts that A has made to establish consent.

Mental disorder and sexual offences

The Sexual Offences Act 2003 (Sections 30–3, 34–7 and 38–44) considers the situation of people defined as having a mental disorder. The legislation draws a distinction between:

- persons who have a mental disorder impeding choice, persons whose mental functioning is so impaired at the time of the sexual activity that they are unable to make any decision about their involvement in that activity; that is, that they are 'unable to refuse';
- those who have the capacity to consent to sexual activity but who have a mental disorder that makes them vulnerable to inducement, threat or deception; and
- those who have the capacity to consent to sexual activity but who have a mental disorder and are in a position of dependency on the carer.

In all these offences, mental disorder is defined as set out in Section 1 of the MHA, as 'any disorder or disability of the mind'. As well as including serious mental illness, this definition ensures the protection of those with a lifelong learning disability and persons who develop dementia in later life. Medical evidence will usually be required to prove that a person has a mental disorder.

Psychological abuse

Offences which relate to psychological abuse may include those covered by the Section 76 of the Serious Crime Act 2015 offence of controlling or coercive behaviour in an intimate or family relationship; Section 44 of the MCA; Section 127 of the MHA; or Sections 20–5 of the Criminal Justice and Courts Act 2015 all referred to earlier. The Malicious Communications Act 1988 created the offence of sending or delivering letters or other articles for the purpose of causing distress or anxiety. It was updated in 2001 to include electronic communications.

Financial abuse

Criminal legislation regarding finances can generally be divided between two offences: theft and fraud.

The Theft Act 1968 covers the offence of dishonestly appropriating property belonging to another with the intention of permanently depriving the other of it (Section 1). It is important to note that 'it is immaterial whether the appropriation is made with a view to gain, or is made for the thief's own benefit' (Section 1(2)) but that the act may not be dishonest if the perpetrator has the belief that they would have the owner's consent if they knew of the 'appropriation and the circumstances of it' (Section 2(1)(b)).

The Fraud Act 2006 covers three ways of committing a fraud: fraud by false representation (Section 2), fraud by failing to disclose information (Section 3) and fraud by abuse of position (Section 4). Section 4 (fraud by abuse of position) offences can be pertinent to the behaviour of trustees, attorneys and carers. The offence is committed when a person occupies a position in which they were expected to safeguard, or not to act against, the financial interests of another person and they have abused that position, 'dishonestly' intending by that abuse to make a gain or cause a loss.

Neglect

Criminal offences relating to neglect will include Section 44 of the MCA, Section 127 of the MHA or Sections 20–5 of the Criminal Justice and Courts Act 2015 as referred to earlier. There may also be relevant offences under the Health and Safety at Work Act 1974 and subsequent regulations that cover topics such as manual handling, bed rails, COSHH, RIDDOR and falls as well as, in tragic cases, the Corporate Manslaughter and Corporate Homicide Act 2007.

Discriminatory abuse offences have been covered under 'Hate crime', earlier in this chapter.

Offences relating to modern slavery or human trafficking

These offences can be addressed under various pieces of legislation, including offences against the person laws and the Sexual Offences Act 2003. The Modern Slavery Act 2015 consolidated and updated criminal legislation on human trafficking, slavery, forced labour, cannabis farming, organ harvesting, forced begging and domestic servitude. The two key offences under the Act relate to 'slavery, servitude and forced or compulsory labour' and 'human trafficking'.

In determining whether a person is being held in slavery or servitude or required to perform forced or compulsory labour, regard may be had to all the circumstances, including the person's personal circumstances (such as the person being a child, the person's family relationships, and any mental or physical illness) that may make the person more vulnerable than other persons. The Act makes provision for the police or immigration services to apply to a magistrates' court for prevention orders (Section 15) and for protection for people compelled to commit crimes while in slavery (Section 45).

Developing legal literacy

Adult safeguarding practitioners need to be well acquainted with the law and policy that sets out their duties, responsibilities and powers (and lack of them) in order to offer effective protections to adults at risk of harm and abuse. The term commonly used for this is 'legal literacy'.

Defining legal literacy

Legal literacy means that you understand how the law guides your practice, you can apply the law consistently in a range of circumstances and you can demonstrate how the law influences the decisions you make.

Legal literacy in adult safeguarding includes being able to:

- understand your legal duties in order to undertake these as part of everyday practice;
- recognise when a legal solution is needed;
- know how to practise using the law so that the adult's rights are upheld;
- know how to find information about the law;
- know when to get legal advice; and
- recognise when colleagues or organisations are acting outside of the law and challenge or remedy this.

Legal literacy and the implementation of the Mental Capacity Act 2005

The MCA gives clarity about how decisions are made, who can make them, and how the rights of people who do not have the capacity to make specific decisions can be protected. The government hoped that the legislation would 'over time bring about a quiet revolution in public attitudes and practice' (Lammy, 2004). In 2014 the House of Lords Select Committee on the Mental Capacity Act reported that no such quiet revolution had taken place, the empowering ethos of the Act had not been widely implemented and practice was poor across all professional groups.

Williams et al (2012) researched the best-interest decision-making practice of 400 practitioners from the health, social care and legal professions following implementation of the MCA and identified that good practice correlated with 'strong leadership' in the organisation and ready access to sources of advice about specific cases. Bishop (2012) observed the difficulties practitioners had in taking cases to the Court of Protection when the local authorities involved were concerned that enacting this legal duty was too costly. The development of a culture of legal literacy in an organisation needs to be promoted by the informed actions of its leaders.

Practitioners can think through implementing the principles of the MCA in specific cases if they have ready access to advice. In many local authorities, access to legal advice is tightly managed and direct advice from a solicitor is hard to arrange. Dedicated Deprivation of Liberty Safeguards (DoLS) teams are an excellent source of advice and guidance, but these teams have been overwhelmed with the volume of work following the *Cheshire West* judgement of 2014. Some (Braye and Preston-Shoot, 2017; Preston-Shoot, 2017) have argued that the MCA is complex and hard to enact. We believe that attention must be paid to an organisational culture that promotes legal literacy in order to effectively implement the MCA. It is not that the legislation is too complex, but that practitioners often misunderstand how to use it.

How is legal literacy developing in use of the Care Act 2014?

The Care and Support Statutory Guidance for the Care Act 2014 is regularly updated online, so reference must always be made to the most up-to-date version. See the Further Reading section at the end of this chapter for the link to the statutory guidance.

There are significant challenges in ensuring that adult safeguarding practice is grounded in legislation. Human rights legislation is enshrined within the MCA but not within the Care Act; in addition, new criminal legislation has been implemented since the Care Act but is not always widely understood or used. Case law can be complex to understand and apply to practice. How can the individual practitioner continue to attend to the development of their legal literacy?

REFLECTIVE ACTIVITY

Developing your legal literacy top tips

Do:

- Ask experts about case law, and if you do not understand the explanation, ask them to simplify it. It can help to think about a case together: how would the law apply to the case?

- Keep your knowledge updated. Go to training and seminars. Subscribe to an update service (see the Further Reading section for recommendations). Read short articles in trade journals and discuss with your colleagues. Use your learning as soon as you can in practice and reflect on how this worked with others or via your reflective journal.
- Practise applying legal knowledge to practice. Have a regular discussion slot with colleagues, work through case studies or presentations of practice, ask an experienced colleague to tell you what they did in a particular case from a legal perspective.
- Find out where you can get legal advice: specialist in-house teams can be a great source. How can you access a solicitor for more expert advice? How do you find out more about criminal law? Find out where to get advice now rather than in a crisis so you are clear about arrangements.

Do not:

- Assume that using the law will not help and will make you more anxious. If you think that you are struggling do raise this with your manager, make a plan together to build your knowledge and confidence.
- Get overwhelmed. Break down what the law requires you to do and identify one or two changes you will make to your practice now. You will feel more in control of your practice.

Understanding how to use the law

How to use legal duties and powers is an important element of legal literacy. We have described here and in Chapter 2 how the misapplication of legislation can result in breaches of the adult's human rights, resulting in them coming to further harm. An overly legalistic approach can be unhelpful without planning, careful relationship building and a consideration of the dynamics of the networks around the adult. At best, the practitioner's efforts will be ineffective and at worst, the situation for the adult will deteriorate.

REFLECTIVE ACTIVITY

Case study: The Malins

For the last month, social worker George has been concerned that **Mrs Malin** is unable to cope with caring for her husband any longer. The district nurse has referred **Mr Malin** for an assessment of his care and support needs. Mrs Malin is frail and tired, but she will not accept any care in the house. Mr Malin has dementia and is spending most of the day in bed, he is incontinent and although he can stand and walk, he isn't responding to Mrs Malin's prompts anymore. The Malins' son and daughter-in-law live around the corner. Mrs Malin says that they help to care for her and her husband, but George is not convinced of this; it may be wishful thinking on her part, or she may be finding it hard to face what is happening in her life.

Mrs Malin telephones George and is very upset. Mr Malin has hit her and she cannot cope any longer; she wants him to go into a home. George goes straight round to the house. He talks to Mrs Malin about the options, he explains that as Mr Malin has dementia he will need to assess his capacity to make a decision about where to live, and if he does not have capacity then George can arrange for him to be admitted to a care home 'in his best interests'. Mrs Malin looks bewildered by this and says she will get her son to come round. Mr Malin junior arrives, Mrs Malin explains that Mr Malin has hit her, and that George has come to take him into a home. Mr Malin junior looks very shocked. He orders George to leave the house and raises his arm in a way that George feels threatened by. George leaves but is very worried about the couple. He calls the police and asks for their assistance in getting back into the house. The police arrive and are invited into the house. After 30 minutes the officers emerge, telling George that the family do not to wish to see him but that there does not seem to be any imminent risk to either Mrs Malin or her husband.

Reflective question

- Using your knowledge of the law and creating relationships, how could you manage this situation differently?

Our thoughts are that we think that George is reacting to the crisis that Mrs Malin now finds herself in. George has powers under legislation, such as the MCA and DoLS, but they must be used to support Mr Malin's well-being and if needed, in his best interests, and not to facilitate a reactive intervention.

* * *

A cup of tea with Mrs Malin while George carries out a calm assessment of the situation is needed. Mr Malin is usually in bed; has this changed? When did he hit Mrs Malin? What was happening at the time? Is Mrs Malin injured or very distressed? How likely is it that Mr Malin will hit Mrs Malin again? What does Mrs Malin think the risk is to her of further assault? Is Mr Malin all right, physically and emotionally? Is there a reason to assume he does not have mental capacity today regarding this situation? He may be ill or have a urinary infection. He may be upset about hitting his wife. Talking over what happened may help Mr and Mrs Malin think about options now and later. Do the couple want their son and daughter-in-law to come over to contribute to thinking about what next or would they prefer to wait for a family meeting when feelings are calmer?

* * *

This is a list you can add to. George needs to calm the situation and keep himself safe while engaging everyone in thinking about how to resolve the current crisis together. Diffusing the situation without police intervention would have been ideal but in these circumstances social work skills in reducing tension and building relationships are crucial to rebuild the relationships needed to safeguard both Mr and Mrs Malin.

(▶) KEY MESSAGES

- While an organisational culture of legal literacy can be supported by strong leadership, individual practitioners must pay attention to the development of their own legal literacy.

- Knowledge of your legal powers and duties is essential to positive adult safeguarding practice but you must balance this with attention to careful planning around risks, relationship building with the adult, their family and other key elements of their network and a consideration of the dynamics of the networks around the adult.

- You need to know how the criminal law applies to different types of harm, but you do not need to be an expert in criminal law; you must work with the police and other organisations who can bring prosecutions under legislation.

KNOWLEDGE REVIEW

- WHAT is meant by the term legal literacy and what can you do to develop and maintain yours?

- WHAT are the key legal frameworks for adult safeguarding in your part of the UK?

- HOW confident are you that you can use them effectively and in the spirit of the law?

FURTHER READING

- The most up-to-date version of the Care Act 2014's Care and Support Statutory Guidance, including Section 14 on adult safeguarding, is to be found at: www.gov.uk/government/publications/care-act-statutory-guidance/care-and-support-statutory-guidance [Accessed 12 July 2024].

- Social Care Institute for Excellence (SCIE, 2018) 'Gaining Access to an Adult Suspected to Be at Risk of Neglect or Abuse: A Guide for Social Workers and Their Managers in England'. Updated 2024. Available from: www.scie.org.uk/safeguarding/adults/practice/gaining-access/ [Accessed 12 July 2024].

  This gives a useful overview of what legal powers may be considered in situations when a social worker in England cannot get access to speak with or see an adult who is at risk of harm.

- The Home Office (2022) Domestic Abuse Statutory Guidance is a comprehensive guide to the legislation, including the use of Protective Orders. Available from https://assets.publishing.service.gov.uk/media/62c6df068fa8f54e855dfe31/Domestic_Abuse_Act_2021_Statutory_Guidance.pdf [Accessed 10 April 2024].

4

Mental capacity and adult safeguarding

Chapter aim

In this chapter we will explore how the Mental Capacity Act (MCA) 2005 is used in the course of safeguarding adults' activity. In this context we consider assessments of capacity and making best-interest decisions. We ask what is meant by 'executive dysfunction' and what is the relevance of this to mental capacity? We will explore the Court of Protection and consider recent case law.

This chapter includes:

• Why assess the adult's mental capacity?

• Assessing capacity and making best-interest decisions in adult safeguarding

• What does executive functioning or dysfunction mean?

• The Court of Protection

• What gets in the way of practitioners and partner organisations using the MCA?

Why assess the adult's mental capacity?

The Mental Capacity Act 2005 (MCA) exists to protect the rights of people aged 16 and over who do not have the mental capacity at a specific time to make a specific decision. These specific decisions can be life-changing: where to live, whether to marry, whether to have medical treatment for a serious health condition. Other decisions are less impactful but still determine the everyday fabric of the adult's life. The MCA is a valuable piece of legislation. Some of us practised before the MCA, when it was difficult to protect people who lacked capacity to make decisions about their own safety or well-being without infringing on their rights. Decisions were often made about people and did not involve them or consider their historical or current wishes. Decisions were usually made by using the common law doctrine of necessity, by asking ourselves 'Is it necessary to take action?' These decisions were subjective and predicated on what a professional or family member thought was necessary, not on what the adult wished for or what was in their best interests.

What happens to adults if we do not use the legal framework provided by the MCA?

We return to Stephen who we met in Chapter 2.

REFLECTIVE ACTIVITY

Learning from Safeguarding Adults Reviews: Solihull SAB, SAR Stephen (2020)

You may remember that **Stephen** was a long-term patient in a neurological centre when he was diagnosed with terminal cancer. His discharge was arranged as it was thought he would enjoy a better quality of life in his own accommodation and near his family. Stephen had complex needs that needed the skilled support of a multi-disciplinary team. He was disabled after sustaining head injuries, he also experienced epilepsy and diabetes, and had been diagnosed with Korsakoff's syndrome. Stephen had been assessed as lacking capacity to make decisions about his own care and treatment and while in the neurological centre, decisions were made in Stephen's best interests.

After his cancer diagnosis, Stephen did not understand why he was in an acute hospital or that he needed chemotherapy, but his mental capacity was not assessed and no plans to support him in his best interests were made.

Once back in the community, Stephen was not free to leave his new flat and was 'under continuous supervision, monitoring and control' from carers at all times. No application was made to the Court of Protection to authorise his deprivation in a community setting. Stephen no longer received any specialist input. Primary health teams made no assessment of Stephen's mental capacity, which may have led to a perception of Stephen actively 'refusing' or being non-compliant and contributed to an absence of planning to manage his engagement with the service.

Without an understanding of Stephen's mental capacity, professionals were at risk of misinterpreting his understanding, motivations or intentions. Health staff found it very difficult to meet simple needs (ear care/gluing a wound/ weighing him) as well as complex needs (chemotherapy).

An application to the Court of Protection regarding deprivation in the community would have prompted more thought about the restrictions of the accommodation on Stephen, whether these could be reduced and if they were in his best interests. His rights would have been taken into consideration and the limits to his restriction understood.

Stephen died after choking when alone. His carers were advised to withdraw when he was challenging, and in the latter weeks of his life were spending hours every day standing outside of his flat. No consideration was given to what support the care provider needed to work with a man with such complex needs.

Using the provisions of the MCA 2005 would have resulted in careful assessment and planning to support Stephen through his treatment and to consider whether a return to the community was indeed in his best interests. In the light of understanding that there would be a deprivation of liberty in the community, Stephen's support plan and the impact of the restrictions on him would have been carefully considered. His voice would have been heard via a mental capacity assessment and subsequent best interests decision making, he would have had an Independent Mental Capacity Advocate (IMCA) to ensure that his rights were met. An application would have been made to the Court of Protection (COP) for authorisation of the restrictions on Stephen. In order to make an application, Stephen's care plan, and the care plan drawn up by the care provider, would have been submitted together with the evidence of how the best-interest decision was arrived at, with a clear statement of the options considered and why no lesser restrictions had been possible.

While the rights of non-capacitated adults are protected by the MCA 2005, we can also see from Stephen's story that using the MCA makes decision making and planning easier for practitioners. Everyone involved with Stephen did their best to support him, but without a legal framework these efforts could only be partial and inconsistent.

ESSENTIAL INFORMATION: LEGISLATION

Mental Capacity Act 2005

The five principles of the Act:

1. A person must be assumed to have capacity unless it is established that they lack capacity.

2. A person is not to be treated as unable to make a decision unless all practicable steps to help them to do so have been taken without success.
3. A person is not to be treated as unable to make a decision merely because they make an unwise decision.
4. An act done, or decision made, under this Act for or on behalf of a person who lacks capacity must be done, or made, in their best interests.
5. Before the act is done, or the decision is made, regard must be had to whether the purpose for which it is needed can be as effectively achieved in a way that is less restrictive of the person's rights and freedom of action.

The two-stage test of mental capacity:

1. **Diagnostic test**: does the person have an impairment of the mind or brain, or is there some sort of disturbance affecting the way their mind or brain works? (It doesn't matter whether the impairment or disturbance is temporary or permanent.)
2. **Functional test**: if so, does that impairment or disturbance mean that the person is unable to make the decision in question at the time it needs to be made?

The four capacity assessment questions:

A person is unable to make a decision if they cannot:

1. understand relevant information about the decision to be made;
2. retain that information in their mind long enough to decide;
3. use or weigh that information as part of the decision-making process; or
4. communicate their decision (by talking, using sign language or any other means).

The assessment of mental capacity also requires that there is a connection between the two stages of the test for mental capacity (the diagnostic and functional elements: a connection labelled the 'causative nexus' (*PC v City of York Council*, 2013)). If there is no evident connection between the adult's mental impairment and their inability to make the decision in question (for example, there is no mental impairment evident or the person's decision-making ability is affected by something else) then the MCA cannot be used as a legal framework to safeguard their decision making or to act lawfully in their best interests.

Summarised from the MCA Code of
Practice (2007) in Hubbard and Stone (2022)
pp 7, 41, 45, 65.

The 'two-stage' test is set out so that the diagnostic test comes first. In practice this is sometimes unhelpful. An adult may be diagnosed as having dementia, but that does not mean they have lost their mental capacity. We can be concerned about an adult's mental capacity but may not know if they have an impairment of the mind or brain. We may need to assess capacity in order to protect their rights while urgently seeking a diagnosis.

Assessing capacity and making best-interest decisions in adult safeguarding

We have to be aware of the possibility that we will need to assess an adult's capacity to make a specific decision at a specific time as part of any of the duties under the Care Act 2014. Some commentators (Pritchard-Jones, 2019) question whether there should have been a statutory requirement to assess capacity where there is reasonable suspicion about an adults capacity to make decisions about their own safety and well-being. The Care and Support (DHSC, 2014) statutory guidance does emphasise this in relation to adult safeguarding, although it is not in the Care Act legislation:

> where the adult may lack capacity to make decisions about arrangements for enquiries or managing any abusive situation, then their capacity must always be assessed and any decision made in their best interests. ... In order to make sound decisions, the adult's emotional, physical, intellectual and mental capacity in relation to self-determination and consent and any intimidation, misuse of authority or undue influence will have to be assessed. (DHSC, 2014, 14.108–14.109)

Mental capacity must be a consideration at several points during an adult safeguarding process: are there any indications that the adult may lack capacity for any of the following?

- Give consent to a concern being referred to the local authority.
- Give consent for information gathering as part of Section 42(1).
- Participate in their own safeguarding: will they need an advocate or representative?
- Decide on preferred outcomes.
- Participate in risk assessment and making safeguarding plans: can they understand the relevant information and use or weigh the information to make a decision?

We may also need to consider whether an adult is able to act on the decisions they have made. Too much weight can be placed on what the adult is saying rather than what they are doing or able to do. Social workers are prone to place an emphasis on verbal evidence. It can be more telling to ask the adult to demonstrate what they can do: 'Show me what you can do as well as tell me.' In SAR Martin (Lambeth Safeguarding Adults Board, 2019) Martin said that he could get up from the mattress on which he was lying and would get out of his flat to buy food and see his GP. The attending GP and paramedics thought that these verbal statements demonstrated his capacity to understand the information about the risks that could occur should he not be conveyed to hospital, but they did not ask him to show them how he would get up from the mattress. A demonstration of Martin's extreme weakness and inability to walk would have opened up further discussion and assessment, both of how Martin was using information to make a decision as well as professional curiosity about his rationale for the decision he had made.

The second principle of the MCA tells us that people must not be treated as incapable of making a decision unless all practicable steps have been tried to help them. This sets the expectation that every effort must be made to encourage, assist and support the adult to make the decision for themselves. It can help to have in mind that you are 'supporting this person to make a decision' rather than 'assessing this person's capacity to make this decision'. When decisions must be made on behalf of the adult because they have been assessed as lacking capacity at that time, you must take account of their past and present wishes and feelings, as well as considering whether it is possible to decide or act in a way that would interfere less with the adult's rights and freedoms of action. This should involve a consideration of whether there is a need to decide or act at all (MCA Principle 5).

Baker (2017, p 128) notes three questions that often arise when exploring the adult at risk's views of the safeguarding concern:

- Can and should this individual make their own decisions in this situation or be protected from harm?
- Do they understand the concerns? Do they understand the likely and foreseeable consequences?
- Whose risk is it to take?

The Mental Capacity Act 2005 Code of Practice (Department for Constitutional Affairs 2007) cautions us that we should be concerned if the adult:

> repeatedly makes unwise decisions that put them at significant risk of harm or exploitation, or makes a particular unwise decision that is obviously irrational or out of character. These things do not necessarily mean that somebody lacks capacity. But there might be a need for further investigation, taking into account the person's past decisions and choices. For example, have they developed a medical condition or disorder that is affecting their capacity to make particular decisions? Are they easily influenced by undue pressure? Or do they need more information to help them understand the consequences of

the decision they are making? (Department of Constitutional Affairs, 2007, para 2.11)

A self-determining adult may well make decisions that we or others would not make. These 'unwise' decisions do not mean that they lack capacity. However, if those decisions are repeated and put them at risk of abuse, we must look again. There may be capacity issues or something else may be happening. We would add to the Code of Practice list the need to consider the impacts of trauma, very poor physical health including malnutrition or hypothermia, or the influence of substance dependence. Case law (*London Borough of Croydon v CD* [2019] EWHC 2943 (Fam)) has demonstrated that a chronic dependent drinker can be viewed as lacking capacity with regard to decisions about their care.

Planning to assess mental capacity

Preparation is essential prior to undertaking an assessment of an adult's mental capacity. We need to plan how we will support the adult's decision making and we must be clear about the decision for which we are assessing capacity. We need to determine what the information relevant to the decision is.

Since the implementation of the MCA, case law judgements have refined guidance on how to conduct mental capacity assessments, particularly on what information is relevant or irrelevant to making certain key decisions (Ruck Keene et al, 2024). From the *CC v KK and STCC* (2012) judgement, the term 'salient points' has become commonly used to describe the key information that a person could reasonably be expected to understand about a decision.

 ESSENTIAL INFORMATION: PRACTICE GUIDANCE

Assessing the mental capacity of an adult who is neglecting their own needs

Martha Stroud is 50 years old and lives alone. She had an accident at work five years ago which resulted in a severe head injury. Martha was unconscious for twelve hours after the accident. She has great difficulties in moving, is often in pain and feels tired. Martha now rarely gets out of bed and when she does she is at risk of falls as her muscles have wasted. Carers come in twice a day to support her to wash, eat and dress but sometimes Martha sends them away or swears at them. Martha's care provider has made a safeguarding concern referral as Martha has become incontinent but does not always agree to wash or change her clothes. The situation will deteriorate unless Martha decides to accept support; she has developed pressure areas in the past. Her carers are concerned about her capacity to make those decisions; she is struggling to remember what she had agreed to only two hours previously. You visit Martha to find out her views on the situation, but when you ask her about whether she thinks she needs more support, she explains that she can manage without her carers. Martha describes how she washes herself and tells you that she enjoys cooking her dinner. She agrees that she has fallen when getting out of bed but cannot remember the last time this happened. Martha may be feeling embarrassed about her incontinence, she may lack capacity to make a decision about how her needs could be met, or something else could be going on.

- For which decision will you assess Martha's capacity?

Once you have decided on which decision you will assess, be clear about what information is relevant to the decision (the salient points). It is vitally important that everyone involved in the assessment process agrees on the information the person needs to be able to understand, retain, use and weigh. If this is not agreed, there is likely to be unnecessary dispute and challenge.

Why is the decision important? What are the consequences for Martha of making or not making this decision?

What are the risks? What is the level of risk to Martha?

- How will you support Martha to make a decision? Is there a good time of day to undertake the assessment? Is there anyone she would, or would not, like to be there to support her? Do you need to present the information in a particular way that she can grasp and that also minimises any feeling of shame about her incontinence? If Martha had difficulty in communicating a decision, it would be helpful to ask someone who knows her and understands her communication preference, including a speech and language therapist or advocate, to assist.
- Plan the discussion to include the relevant information, why the decision needs to be made, the risks from the current situation and the pros, cons and consequences of deciding one way or another.
- What are the expectations about Martha retaining the information? Can she retain information long enough to make the decision? Can she recall the information during the discussion, or do you have to give her the information again?
- What are your expectations about Martha using and weighing the information? Can she tell you why she has made the decision, can she show she has used the relevant information to do so?

Perhaps you have decided that Martha's decision is whether she needs care and support. In the context of decisions relating to care, each decision will be specific instead of general, and will have to be revisited should circumstances or the question posed to the person under assessment change.

39 Essex Chambers (2024) have set out relevant information derived from case law in categories of potential decisions. Each person's situation is specific, and so the information set out in case law must always be tailored to the person's actual situation.

The following constitute relevant information to an assessment of whether a person has capacity to decide their own care:

(a) with what areas the person under assessment needs support;

(b) what sort of support they need;

(c) who will provide such support;

(d) what would happen without support, or if support was refused; and

(e) that carers may not always treat the person being cared for properly, and the possibility and mechanics of making a complaint if they are not happy.

The following are not relevant to any assessment of capacity as to care:

(a) how care is funded;

(b) how overarching arrangements for monitoring and appointing care staff work;

(c) why having a support worker is important to access the community;

(d) the importance of structure and routine in a person's day;

(e) the importance of regular access to the local community to build and maintain confidence in daily life and independence and to avoid a deterioration in anxiety;

(f) the importance of developing relationships with others outside of close family to build and maintain confidence in daily life and independence and to avoid a deterioration in anxiety, to avoid a dependency upon close family members and to develop the person's own interests and opportunities for a social life with peers; and

(g) the opportunities that may be available to engage in training, education, volunteering or employment.

What does executive functioning or dysfunction mean?

Martha may be experiencing difficulties with executive brain function. This can happen to people with a brain injury – frontal lobe damage – or a neurodegenerative disease such as Huntington's Disease, dementia, substance dependence, neurodiversity or mental health conditions including schizophrenia and obsessive-compulsive disorder. Executive functioning involves the mental functions of insight, attention, planning, initiation, organisation, problem solving, inhibition, control of behaviours and emotions, evaluation, judgement and decision-making skills. Executive dysfunction is a clinical diagnosis and is useful in guiding us as to what activities we need to undertake in order to assess capacity. Beware of using the terms 'decisional' and 'executive' capacity, these terms are not mentioned in the MCA or the MCA Code of Practice and can confuse the issue.

Cognitive impairments associated with executive dysfunction can be subtle and hard to evidence. The adult might have good insight or awareness into the decision being assessed but cannot organise themselves to act on their decision. If the adult can discuss issues fluently, we might wrongly presume that the person has capacity when in reality they cannot 'walk the walk'.

Preston-Shoot and Ward (2021) note impulse-related difficulties with executive function for people who are substance dependent and may have frontal lobe damage,

> Undertaking mental capacity assessments with dependent drinkers poses a very specific challenge. Approximately 50% of dependent drinkers have frontal lobe damage as a result of brain injury. In the general population the figure is only 8.5%. The frontal lobe is the behavioural centre of the brain which has a key role in impulse control. Many patients with frontal lobe damage are wrongly considered to have capacity, because in a 'simple' assessment process they know the correct things to say and do. But when they need to act upon their knowledge in the complex settings of the real world they are driven by impulse and, therefore, can no longer weigh up options. (p 24)

Assessing the impact of executive dysfunction on mental capacity means that as well as an interview-style assessment, we must undertake observations of the adult's decision-making, often over a period of time. NICE (2018a) suggest that, where executive functioning could be impacting on decision making, 'structured assessments of capacity for individuals in this group (for example, by way of interview) may therefore need to be supplemented by real-world observation of the person's functioning and decision-making ability in order to provide the assessor with a complete picture of an individual's decision-making ability' (para 1.4.19).

Executive dysfunction does not necessarily mean that an adult lacks mental capacity: many adults with executive dysfunction are still able to make a wide range of capacitous decisions, especially when they have all practicable support to do so.

In recent case law, the judge (Hayden J) reminds us

> Executive dysfunction is ... not to be regarded as synonymous with the functional test for mental capacity. The former derives from clinical

practice, the latter is the test prescribed by MCA. Neither is 'insight'
to be viewed as equating to or synonymous with capacity. To elide
those two would be to derogate from personal autonomy, every adult
from time-to-time lacks insight into an issue or indeed into themselves.
(*Warrington Borough Council v Y & Ors* [2023] EWCOP 27, para 45)

You may conclude that an adult lacks capacity to make a decision if they cannot
understand or use/weigh the information, that they cannot implement what they
will say that they do, or (if relevant) that when needed, they are unable to bring
to mind the information needed to implement a decision. However, you can
only reach such a finding where there is clearly documented evidence of repeated
mismatch. You cannot reach this conclusion on the basis of one assessment alone.
If you conclude that the person lacks capacity to make the decision, you must
explain how the deficits that you have identified – and documented – relate to
the functional tests in the MCA. You need to be able to explain how the deficit
you have identified means (even with all practicable support) that the person
cannot understand, retain, use and weigh relevant information, or communicate
their decision.

Martha may be clear that if she remains in bed and does not wash or change
her clothing after incontinence, she will risk pressure areas developing. She may,
however, maintain that she is capable of doing these things for herself and reassure
you that this is the case. After spending time with Martha we may observe she does
not attempt to wash or clean herself after incontinence, and that when prompted
she is unable to stand for long enough to do so. We have gently challenged Martha
to account for these observations and reminded her of the impact of developing
pressure areas. Martha maintains she 'will be OK'. We must now relate these
observations and discussions to the assessment of mental capacity. Is Martha unable
to use or weigh the information she is given in order to make a decision? Has her
brain damage impaired her ability to think consequentially and ultimately, to be
able satisfactorily to understand, retain or weigh information in order to make a
decision about care needs?

Best-interest decision making

If an adult has been assessed as lacking the capacity to make a decision, a best-interest
decision must follow. This is crucial in ensuring the person's rights, maximising
their autonomy and involving those who know the adult well. Remember there
is a duty for the NHS body to instruct an independent mental capacity advocate
(IMCA) to be involved in the best-interests decision-making process where serious
medical treatment is proposed and a duty for the local authority to do so for
a long-term change in accommodation where there is no one appropriate to
consult. It is important that representatives have the adult's best interest in mind;
if they demonstrably do not, they will not be appropriate representatives. In adult
safeguarding cases, an IMCA can be instructed even where family members or

others are available to be consulted; this can be difficult given the pressure on IMCA services but is a crucial step to ensure that the adult's perspective is central, and their rights are respected. Advocacy is particularly important if there is any disagreement about what is in the adult's best interests.

Best-interests checklist

If the person has been assessed to lack capacity to make the decision at the time, the following must be considered when making the decision on the person's behalf:

*   encourage the person's participation in making the decision;
*   identify all relevant circumstances;
*   find out the person's views, past and present wishes and feelings, beliefs and values and any other factors the person themselves would have taken into account;
*   avoid discrimination on the basis of the person's age, appearance, condition or behaviour;
*   assess whether the person might regain capacity;
*   if the decision concerns life-sustaining treatment, to not be motivated in any way by a desire to bring about the person's death;
*   if it is practical and appropriate to do so, consult other people for their views about the person's best interests and to see if they have any information about the person's wishes and feelings, beliefs and values;
*   avoid restricting the person's rights by considering less restrictive options; and
*   take all of this into account when deciding by weighing up all of these factors.

(summarised from the MCA Code of Practice (2007) in Hubbard and Stone (2022, pp 7, 41, 45, 65)

As well as learning from the adult's participation, it is very useful to consult with those who know the adult. Best-interest meetings are useful in discussing options, but face-to-face or online meetings with each individual can also glean useful information about the adult's views, past and present wishes etc.

The Court of Protection

Disagreements about the adult's best interests or any other aspect of the MCA – for example, whether the adult does not have the mental capacity for a specific decision – can be referred to the COP.

The Court can make decisions about:

*   whether the adult has capacity to make a specific decision, or whether something is in their best interests;
*   disagreements that cannot be settled in any other way. For example, by using an IMCA;

- situations where a series of decisions, rather than a single decision, need to be made for the adult;
- removing an attorney under the adult's lasting power of attorney;
- removing a deputy;
- health or personal care, where there is no attorney or deputy to make decisions about this;
- whether an advance decision or lasting power of attorney is valid. Or about their meaning, if there is a disagreement; and
- whether a Deprivation of Liberty Safeguards (DoLS) authorisation has been granted lawfully.

The Court observes the principles of the MCA in all of its activities. The Court will consider how to involve the adult in the case, the adult can speak in Court or, if this is too anxiety-provoking or difficult, the judge may visit the adult. The adult can appoint a representative or a litigation friend to speak for them in court. The litigation friend can be an IMCA, a solicitor or court-appointed deputy or a family member. If no one is available, the official solicitor will act as the litigation friend of last resort. The COP must always act in the adult's best interests. Taking a disputed matter to the COP is often a relief, the Court will look closely at what the adult's best interests are while upholding the adult's rights. Court judgements must be followed.

Inherent jurisdiction

Prior to the implementation of the MCA, *inherent jurisdiction* was the only legal means of acting on behalf of mentally incapacitated adults. The legal principle of inherent jurisdiction means that 'a superior court has the jurisdiction to hear any matter that comes before it, unless a statute or rule limits that authority or grants exclusive jurisdiction to some other court or tribunal' (Szerletics, 2011).

The High Court continues to be able to consider cases where coercion, pressure or control are affecting the decision making of those who have mental capacity but are considered vulnerable for other reasons and are at significant risk from their decisions. In the case of *Southend-on-Sea v Meyers* (2019), the High Court considered whether Mr Meyers could be lawfully deprived of his liberty in a care home that he objected to remaining in and was assessed to have mental capacity to do so, in order to prevent his son acting in a way that harmed him. Mr Meyers' son lived, with his father's agreement, at his father's home where he was considered by the local authority to be causing harm to his father through abusive behaviour towards the carers commissioned by the local authority in accordance with a Care Act assessment of Mr Meyers' care and support needs. The court decided that the autonomy of Mr Meyers had been compromised; the son exerted an influence over his father that was malign in effect if not in intention. The consequence was to disable Mr Meyers from making a truly informed decision and this impacted directly on his health and survival. Mr Meyers' life required protection, an obligation of the state. Mr Meyers was not deprived of his liberty by being detained in the care home. Two orders were made: Mr Meyers could live wherever he wished, so upholding his Article 5 rights, but he could not live with his son.

What gets in the way of practitioners and partner organisations using the MCA?

Research studies show that using the MCA has magnified health and social care practitioners' focus on human rights and complemented the notion of person-centred care (Scott et al, 2020). Practitioners were concerned about the complexity of the Act and the changes that are made as a result of case law. Confidence has increased with experience and collaboration with peers while continued training has helped to embed the guidance available with the practice of assessment.

Lack of appreciation for the purpose of the MCA: Marshall and Sprung (2018) report research that found staff in one acute trust had a negative view of the MCA, viewing it as more bureaucracy, a litigation risk and yet another task to complete in a busy clinical environment. However, when the empowering and supportive aspects of the MCA for both patients and staff were discussed with them, participants looked at the MCA with a different viewpoint and appreciated its potential benefits.

The MCA is seen as 'complicated' and 'difficult' across all partner organisations. This can lead to disputes about whose role it is to carry out an assessment (Aspinwall-Roberts, 2022), or blanket presumptions of capacity (House of Lords, 2014).

> The presumption of capacity, in particular, is widely misunderstood by those involved in care. It is sometimes used to support nonintervention or poor care, leaving vulnerable adults exposed to risk of harm. In some cases this is because professionals struggle to understand how to apply the principle in practice. In other cases, the evidence suggests the principle has been deliberately misappropriated to avoid taking responsibility for a vulnerable adult. (House of Lords, 2014, para 105)

Principle 3 of the MCA, 'A person is not to be treated as unable to make a decision merely because he makes an unwise decision,' has been misunderstood and taken to have more implications than it actually has. The legislation protects the rights of those who have been assessed as lacking capacity, it does not tell us anything about the rights of those who do have capacity; it only says that we cannot judge the adult who makes an unwise decision to lack capacity. Adults are sometimes said to have 'the right to make unwise decisions' when we mean that every adult has the right to be self-determining. While respecting that right, we will still owe a duty of care to them if their decisions are likely to end in damage to their vital interests. We cannot close the case on the grounds of a 'right to make unwise decisions'.

Practitioners may also fail to use *professional curiosity* once they have assessed that an adult has capacity to make decisions about risk. What is the adult's motivation for what appears to be an unwise decision? So many factors influence decision-making ability, and we fail in our duty of care to the adult if we do not continue to engage them in a dialogue to explore these factors or make meaningful attempts to support them. An adult may be acting under duress from others or may be exploited or controlled to the degree that they cannot exercise a free choice and have lost their free will. They may be heavily influenced by traumatic past experiences and survival behaviours. They may be so dependent on substances that the need for continual use influences every decision. These are often not free choices or decisions. When risks are high impact, whether the adult has capacity or not becomes just one of the many avenues we need to explore in understanding the adult's decision-making processes.

▶ KEY MESSAGES

- Law and policy ask you to balance the adult's autonomy and self-determination with your duty of care and the adult's right to life. Attention to just one of these will distort your decision making and may leave the adult at unnecessary risk from either a lack of protection or overly restrictive intervention.

- Deciding that a person has mental capacity to make a risky decision does not mean you no longer have a safeguarding responsibility to that person. Maintaining a relationship where risk can be openly discussed and addressed remains essential to positive preventative practice.

KNOWLEDGE REVIEW

- HOW can assessment and decision making using the MCA aid clarity around the adult's risks and rights to autonomy?

- WHAT support is available to an adult within safeguarding if they may have difficulty being involved in the process?

- WHAT other legal safeguards are available where the MCA does not apply and what is their purpose?

FURTHER READING

- 39 Essex Chambers publish (and regularly revise) brief guides to carrying out mental capacity assessments and making best-interests decisions that can be accessed, along with newsletters giving updates on mental capacity case law in England and Wales, at: www.39essex.com/resources-and-training/mental-capacity-law/ [Accessed 12 July 2024].

- This practical guide to using the MCA is useful for practitioners and supports the rights and principles in the Act: Graham, M. and Cowley, J. (2015) *A Practical Guide to the Mental Capacity Act 2005: Putting the Principles of the Act into Practice*, London: Jessica Kingsley.

- For guidance on conducting capacity assessments within DoLS (which can offer good practice principles for wider assessment of mental capacity within the MCA) read pp 96–100 in Hubbard, R. and Stone, K. (2022) *The Best Interests Assessor Practice Handbook*, Bristol: Policy Press.

5

Definitions in adult safeguarding

Chapter aim

In this chapter we will explore how and why the statutory duty to undertake an enquiry under Section 42 of the Care Act 2014 only applies to a small section of the population, often referred to as 'adults at risk'. We begin with a discussion of how the legislation and accompanying guidance is applied. We will explore the challenges faced by different groups in protecting themselves and in claiming the right to protection. Over the last few years, the idea of 'transitional safeguarding' has emerged; we explore what that means, and what the consequences are if adults over 18 have no support to protect themselves.

Categories of potential harm have been detailed in Section 14 of the statutory guidance. These categories are not prescriptive and have already been expanded in local policies to include adults at risk who are harmed through forced marriage, female genital mutilation or exploitation in terrorist activities, sexual and criminal exploitation. We will examine how each type of harm is defined and how harm may be identified if it is not disclosed.

This chapter includes:

- Why definitions are useful

- Adults at risk who may be overlooked by adult safeguarding services

- Identification of harm: general themes

- Identification of harm: locations

- Identification of harm: types of abuse

Why definitions are useful

Commonly agreed definitions help to provide a coherent understanding of a subject like adult safeguarding; people from a range of settings and professional backgrounds can discuss the issue with the confidence that they share the same meanings. This supports partnership working through a common understanding, the development of effective and consistent responses to the harm described, as well as resources being more readily focused on a defined population or area.

Definitions can risk simplifying complex situations. For example, if an adult is physically assaulted, they are very likely to be psychologically damaged as well as physically hurt. In addition, if the adult has been assaulted because their assailant hates disabled people, this can also be defined as discriminatory abuse, and if the responsible agencies do nothing about their plight the adult may also be experiencing discriminatory, and potentially organisational, abuse. One label does not fit all experiences, but the clarity of defining what harms we are talking about does help to shape our response to a concern. Understanding to whom the statutory duty to enquire applies helps us to focus resources on those who are unable to protect themselves and supports the multi-agency understanding needed for effective adult safeguarding work.

Adults at risk who may be overlooked by adult safeguarding services

Although the picture is slowly changing across local areas, there are still groups of adults who are regularly excluded from the local authority duty under Section 42. There are many potential reasons for this. Local authority services have previously concentrated on people who are older, disabled or mentally unwell. Practitioners may lack confidence in working with people who are substance dependent, street homeless or being criminally or sexually exploited, and may see these groups of people as the responsibility of another organisation. There can be bias and prejudice, seeing substance use as a 'choice' and thinking that somehow the adult has responsibility for their predicament or that the person has 'a right to make an unwise decision' with which the state should not interfere. In an environment of limited resources, people who are thought to be difficult to engage or work with may be quickly directed away from the adult safeguarding duty or indeed from assessment of their care and support needs (Mason et al, 2017/18).

People who are street homeless or staying in temporary accommodation

Multiple exclusion homelessness (MEH) is extreme marginalisation that includes childhood trauma, physical and mental ill health, substance misuse and experiences of institutional care (Mason et al, 2017/18). People sleeping rough and in temporary accommodation often have multiple physical and mental health problems, and not infrequently die as a result of chronic ill health and the effects of long-term substance misuse and mental ill health. Researchers refer to the 'tri-morbidity' experienced by some homeless people:

> MEH is characterised by 'tri-morbidity' and is associated with impairments which arise from the combination of mental ill health, physical ill health and drug or alcohol misuse. It is an independent risk factor for premature mortality. (Mason et al, 2017/18, p 3)

The mean age of death for a homeless man is 45 years old and for a woman, 43 years old (ONS, 2022).

Learning from Safeguarding Adults Reviews: SAR Howard

Howard died aged 53 on 21 March 2017. He had no fixed abode at the time of his death. He was found deceased in a bus shelter on the seafront by a member of the public. The cause of death was found to be cardiac arrest, ischaemic heart disease and coronary heart atheroma, and alcoholic liver disease.

Howard had a long history of alcohol abuse. He was financially and physically abused by the people he associated with. Howard said that although they stole from him, and he felt vulnerable in their presence, he continued to mix with them to avoid feeling isolated and lonely. Howard had a heart condition for which he was prescribed medication which he found hard to manage and only took irregularly. He had alcohol-related seizures. While homeless, Howard could not manage his personal hygiene needs and he did not have access to facilities to manage his incontinence. His incontinence limited where he could stay. Howard was depressed and anxious and sometimes felt he no longer wished to live.

Homeless adults at risk may be identified in a variety of ways through contact with health, police or outreach services. It can be hard to establish a regular pattern of engagement, which can complicate enquiries and safeguarding planning. It is vitally important for practitioners to understand which organisations are involved with people who are homeless and to also adjust their own working patterns if necessary, to facilitate multi-agency working with this group. You may only be able to catch someone early in the morning before leaving their sleeping place or late at night at a regular soup kitchen. While homelessness makes people vulnerable to exploitation, the most common presenting issue is often self-neglect.

REFLECTIVE ACTIVITY

Case study: James Long

James Long was 45 years old; he was physically frail and had problems with his memory, potentially related to long-term alcohol use, head injury and poor nutrition. His previous coping strategies on the street and in hostels no longer worked to keep him safe: he had the possessions he needed for survival stolen, was too weak to sit outside for long and was increasingly disorientated. James was seen by a social worker in the hospital emergency department having been beaten up in a local car park by a group allegedly targeting homeless people for a 'laugh'.

Reflective questions

- Does the Section 42 statutory duty to enquire apply to James Long?
- What type of harm is he at risk of or actually experiencing?

Our thoughts are that we consider that the statutory duty to enquire under Section 42 is met. James's care and support needs will be assessed as part of the enquiry; he appears to have some cognitive and physical health issues that make it hard for him to protect himself and prevent further harm. James has experienced physical harm, he has been assaulted and, because his usual coping strategies are no longer working, he is at risk of self-neglect and further harm on the street. The risk of harm is imminent and the impact on his well-being is potentially severe.

People who are substance dependent

People who are substance dependent may have care and support needs as a result of their dependence that make it hard for them to protect themselves from harm. Sometimes the person is caught in a cycle; substance use may lead to the development of mental health issues, coping with the symptoms of mental ill health may lead people to use substances to mask voices or cope with intrusive thoughts, and in turn the substances themselves worsen existing mental ill health. Physically disabled people may use substances to escape chronic pain or other difficulties caused by their disability or the discriminatory social attitudes towards them. In turn, substances may increase an adult's disability, and long-term use can lead to physical damage and disability, including brain damage. The person can be more vulnerable to head injury, accidents and violence from others. Older people may use substances to cope with isolation or grief at the loss of those close to them, increasing the risk of falls, confusion, malnutrition and depression. People who began to use substances as a way of numbing the memory of historical trauma may continue to use in order to avoid the realisation of recent trauma. This may include the removal of children, the loss of family or employment, feelings of shame and hopelessness. It is important for practitioners to understand the harm the adult is experiencing, which will be masked if the addiction and the behaviour around the addiction are the only elements of the situation considered.

REFLECTIVE ACTIVITY

Case study: Nancy Wright

Neighbours complained about **Nancy Wright** who lives alone. Nancy was often heard shouting late at night and could be threatening to others in the block of flats. Neighbours believed she was a 'drug addict' and was associated with one of the dealers on the housing estate. The housing association who let the flats were considering applying for an Anti-Social Behaviour Order to tackle Nancy's behaviour. A housing officer persuaded Nancy to let him into her flat to discuss the situation. Through conversation with Nancy, he noted that she appeared to be experiencing auditory and visual hallucinations, talking to someone and shouting out in distress for them to get away from her. She was unable to hold a coherent conversation or answer questions. She wanted the housing officer to leave her alone. There was no food in the flat and Nancy had no bedclothes, the electricity was not working, and the flat was cold. There was no sign of drug paraphernalia but there were some empty alcohol bottles about. Nancy herself looked thin and smelt strongly of urine.

Reflective questions

- Does the statutory duty to enquire under Section 42 apply to Nancy Wright?
- What type of harm is she experiencing?
- What initial actions will you take?

Our thoughts are that we consider that the statutory duty to enquire under Section 42 to be met. Nancy Wright is exhibiting very concerning signs of self-neglect, which appears to be long-standing. Her current mental health, physical health and potential lack of mental capacity to make and act on decisions about her well-being are all indicators of a person in need of urgent care and support. An assessment of her physical and mental health can be arranged via her GP, while an enquiry plan is made to engage her further and develop a multi-agency approach to ensure that her well-being is maintained while an enquiry is undertaken.

Transitional safeguarding

Transitional safeguarding is 'an approach to safeguarding adolescents and young adults fluidly across developmental stages which builds on the best available evidence, learns from both children's and adult safeguarding practice and which prepares young people for their adult lives' (Holmes and Smale, 2018, p 3). An adult of 18 to

25 years old may not have care and support needs but, because of their age and life experience, can struggle to protect themselves from criminal or sexual exploitation or domestic abuse. The environmental and structural factors that increase a child's vulnerability can continue into adulthood, resulting in unmet needs and costly later interventions. The children's and adults' safeguarding systems have developed from different theories, come under different laws, and have different processes as a result. This can make the transition to adulthood harder for young people facing ongoing risk and can mean that young people entering adulthood experience a 'cliff-edge' in terms of support. While under 18, they will be seen as a 'victim' of exploitation; when over 18, there is a risk that they will be seen as complicit.

Transitional safeguarding is not to be confused with the transitional arrangements made between children and adults services for children who do have care and support needs. Some, but not all, of these adults may have been looked-after children. All care leavers may have a personal advisor from a care leavers team and a regularly reviewed pathway plan (Children and Social Work Act 2017). This will continue up to the age of 25 years if the adult wishes. Under Section 1 of the Act, local authorities and their partners have a corporate parenting duty towards a care leaver until the age of 25 years. This does not mean the adult has preferential treatment or services that they do not need, but that we work well with personal advisors and colleagues across all services to make sure that the care leaver does have access to all relevant support and services.

The transitional safeguarding approach is about partnership working and prevention. Trauma-informed approaches as described in Chapter 6 are valuable. If adults are not supported to recover from exploitation and trauma, if they are criminalised, if they become dependent on substances to cope with their experiences, their life chances and well-being will be damaged, and they will need more support from a range of health, social care and criminal justice organisations. Many areas will work with 18–25-year-olds using risk management frameworks, sometimes called 'multi-agency risk management' meetings. Using preventative and person-centred approaches while working closely with relevant partner agencies, including care leavers and children's services colleagues, can provide essential support if the person's situation does not meet the criteria for use of the Section 42 duty.

Learning from Safeguarding Adults Reviews: Richmond and Wandsworth SAB, SAR Jasmine (2020)

Jasmine was a 20-year-old woman who was known to children's services because of safeguarding concerns arising from poorly managed diabetes and emerging mental health issues. Jasmine found it difficult to maintain positive relationships in her personal life and would often refuse help from professionals. Her history shows patterns of seeking support in managing her chronic health and conditions, but not attending appointments or complying with her medical regime. She was found dead in her supported accommodation in September 2019; it is believed that this was a consequence of complications relating to her diabetes. The SAR noted that at 18 years old Jasmine was repeatedly offered an assessment in respect of her care and support needs, but refused to engage with the assessment or accept any services. She was assessed as having the capacity to take this decision, and consequently her case was closed in November 2017. However, Section 11(2) of the Care Act 2014 imposes an enduring obligation on the local authority to complete a needs assessment if there is concern that the adult might be at risk of abuse or neglect, including self-neglect. The impact of trauma on adolescent brain development, cognition and decision-making ability is understood and this should have been explicitly considered in Jasmine's mental capacity assessments. Where necessary, advice or cooperation should have been sought from other professionals working with Jasmine, to ensure that her mental capacity was explored in a nuanced way. Presentation to a multi-agency panel may have assisted practitioners to identify more effective ways to engage with Jasmine. This would also have ensured that health professionals were more alive to safeguarding issues when assessing Jasmine's risk rating to determine her priority level for services. Multi-agency networks need to be used more widely to holistically assess capacity in complex areas such as the impact of trauma on cognition.

Identification of abuse: general themes

Abuse comes in many forms: it can be something that is done to an adult, or something that should have been done but was not (an act of omission). Harm can result from an adult neglecting themselves to a life-threatening extent. Abuse can sometimes be unintentional; the actions of the carer are misguided and have resulted in harm. The emphasis of adult safeguarding is on the impact on the adult, and what can be done to resolve or reduce risk in the situation.

REFLECTIVE ACTIVITY

Case study: John and Max

John Stanley cared for his partner **Max**. Max was very frail; he could not manoeuvre himself without assistance. In helping Max to move from his bed to a chair, John pulled him and dislocated his shoulder. It is not the first time that John has unintentionally injured Max, but it is the most serious. John was distraught, and very ashamed of causing such pain; Max was upset and wished John would give in and ask for help. Both of them were exhausted.

Reflective questions

- Does the statutory duty to enquire under Section 42 apply to Max?
- What type of harm is he experiencing?
- What will help to resolve or reduce risk in this situation?

Our thoughts are that Max has been physically harmed by John. The harm was unintentional but there is a risk of further harm to Max if John does not agree to get support to care for him. Max is dependent on John to help him at the moment and because of this will not be able to protect himself from further harm. Max could be offered a care and support needs assessment while using hospital services, but if John or Max decline this, further enquiries under Section 42 will be needed. A carer's assessment for John may also give him some time to reflect on what he needs to be able to continue with his caring role.

There are ten types of abuse detailed within the Care and Support Statutory Guidance (DHSC, 2014, 14.17). In general, all UK adult safeguarding legislation and policy covers similar types of abuse, including the principle that lists of types of abuse are not 'exhaustive' and that new forms of abuse will emerge and can be included in policies and procedures. Remember that to define something means that there can be a common understanding and focus on it, but we must look further than the type of abuse; we must also understand the circumstances of the adult, the strengths and risk that exist in the situation and the impact of the abuse on them. A conversation with the adult at the heart of the concern, visiting them to see their circumstances and talking with others who know them will help you to understand the extent of the impact on the adult's well-being and what they experience or consider as harmful.

REFLECTIVE ACTIVITY

Case study: Vera Jones

Vera Jones lived in a care home; she was visited regularly by her sister who reported that Vera was regularly subjected to racist abuse from another resident. The care home believed that Vera was not affected by such abuse. Vera had Alzheimer's dementia which led to memory loss and difficulty in communicating her thoughts and feelings; it was hard for her to convey how she felt. Her sister was very concerned that the care home permitted such abuse to happen. The adult who was identified as the source of harm also had dementia and 'didn't understand' what he was saying. You visited the care home with Vera's sister and both of you noted that Vera became tense when taken into the dining area, the place where the abuse occurred. Vera kept asking to be taken back to her room, and the care staff told you that she had recently stopped eating so well and seemed more relaxed when on her own.

These signs tell you that Vera is distressed about something. It may well be the racist abuse or some other factor, but you are clear this needs to be explored and resolved.

Reflective questions

- Does the statutory duty to enquire under Section 42 apply to Vera?
- What types of abuse is she experiencing?
- What will help to resolve or reduce risk in this situation?

Our thoughts are that Vera cannot protect herself because of her care and support needs and she is being subjected to psychological and discriminatory abuse. The Section 42 duty applies. A range of options may be considered, from planning ways of reintroducing Vera to areas of the care home and arranging for the other adult not to be present, finding activities Vera might enjoy, or that the other adult enjoys, finding ways to communicate with Vera, educating the care home on challenging discrimination and supporting diversity, and on the impact of abuse on people with cognitive impairments, exploring how her sister can be her advocate and whether she wants further support to do this.

The Care and Support Statutory Guidance picks out exploitation as an overarching theme across many types of abuse (DHSC, 2014, 14.17).

What is meant by 'exploitation'?

In the context of adult safeguarding, exploitation means to use or treat an adult unfairly in order to gain an advantage. The advantage may be material – money or resources – or may be an emotional or physical advantage. The person who gains advantage, who exploits, is more powerful than the adult who has care and support needs. Understanding power, and how it is used in abuse and exploitation, is essential to skilled practice, as we also discuss in Chapters 2 and 6. Power over the adult may be derived from position (for example, that of an employee paid to care for the adult) or from emotional significance to the adult, such as that of partner or adult child, or simply because the powerful person is stronger, more capable, has more resources and has deliberately set out to exploit. Groups or gangs will seek to exploit people criminally or sexually, using the power of numbers and well-tested methods of coercion and intimidation. We will explore themes of exploitation under the types of abuse set out in the remainder of this chapter.

In each of the sections that follow, we will take an overview of the definitions of types of abuse that can happen to an adult with care and support needs. Do refer to Chapter 3 to remind yourself what criminal offences may be involved in all types of abuse: the abuse of adults at risk is frequently a crime as well as an infringement of human rights. The local procedures used in practice will contain lists of 'indicators' of abuse; we might add to these indicators using our own experience and lessons gained from learning events, Safeguarding Adults Reviews (SARs) and research. The purpose of an indicator is to alert us that the adult may be experiencing abuse. Indicators do not automatically mean the adult is being abused but that we need to look closer at what is happening. For example, the adult who cannot communicate verbally and who is unusually withdrawn and flinches when approached may be being physically harmed or may simply have a very bad toothache that they are unable to tell you about. Rather than jumping to conclusions or making assumptions, careful exploration of the context of the indicator is needed.

Identification of abuse: locations

Adults are abused in a range of locations, in their own home or community, or in an institution, which is most often a care home although hospital settings may also be a location of abuse. NHS Digital data on Section 42 enquiries in England during 2022 to 2023 shows that the adult's own home was the most recorded location of abuse (47 per cent) (NHS Digital, 2023).

Location of harm: home or community

Abuse in domestic settings can be most often typified as domestic abuse and/or violence. Do look again at Chapter 3 for the statutory definition of 'domestic abuse'.

Domestic abuse in older age

Older people are slightly more likely than those under 60 years old to experience abuse by adult family members rather than intimate partners. A total of 48 per cent of victims over 61 years old have a disability (SafeLives, 2016c). Adults aged 60 and over account for at least one in four domestic homicides in the United Kingdom, despite constituting only 18 per cent of the population (Bows, 2019). Older women are also disproportionately at risk of being killed by their (adult) children (Holt, 2017) and this dynamic accounts for half of all domestic homicides of older adults (Bows, 2019). Research undertaken with practitioners across all public services (Bows et al, 2023) highlighted mental health as a key issue where the abuser is a son or grandson, noting that:

Perpetrator vulnerabilities meant that domestic abuse may be missed, either because the victim and/or professional is focused on these issues as being the cause of abuse, or because ageist stereotypes mean the abusive son or grandson is seen as caring for the victim ... risk of missing the woman's perspective. (pp 10–11)

Child-to-parent abuse is not covered by domestic abuse legislation if the child is under 16 years old. Disabled parents can be harmed by their younger children but may not disclose this for fear that their child may be removed from them. Home Office (2015) guidance stipulates that these children must be referred to children's safeguarding services. Partnership working with children's services is important in getting help for both parent and child and must be agreed between children's and adult's services through face-to-face contact between practitioners and with the adult and child. Response to the phenomenon of children under 16 harming their parents is beginning to be researched (Bonnick, 2019) but data remains hard to gather and the invisibility of such abuse compounds the harm for both children and adults.

The definition of domestic abuse within the Care Act 2014 also encompasses *honour-based violence*, sometimes referred to as 'so-called honour-based violence', as there is no honour in abuse. Honour-based violence can be described as a collection of practices used to control behaviour within families or other social groups to protect perceived cultural and religious beliefs and/or honour. Such violence can occur when the perpetrators think that a relative has shamed the family and/or community by breaking the honour code. Concepts of coercive control can be useful in identifying honour-based violence. There is no specific criminal offence of honour-based violence; the term encompasses various offences covered by existing legislation and is dealt with under these (for example, assault, stalking and harassment, kidnap, rape, threats to kill and murder) (CPS, 2019a).

Forced marriage is not mentioned in the Care and Support Statutory Guidance (DHSC, 2014) but can be considered as domestic abuse if a person unable or unwilling to enter into marriage is forced to do so by people 'personally connected' to them. Honour-based violence may include forced marriage if this is undertaken to reinforce an honour code. In arranged marriages, both parties are free to change their mind at any point and not go through with the marriage. Forced marriage is different, and sometimes can involve coercion and violence, or may involve people who do not have the mental capacity to consent to marriage. The pressure put on people to marry against their will may be physical (for example, threats, physical violence or sexual violence) and/or emotional and psychological (making someone feel like they are bringing 'shame' on their family, for example). Financial abuse (such as taking someone's wages) may also be a factor. Adult safeguarding practitioners may well encounter adults who lack the capacity to understand what is involved in 'marriage' and will not be able to consent to marriage.

> ▶ **ESSENTIAL INFORMATION: LEGISLATION**
>
> *Case law: Capacity to understand marriage*
>
> **Southwark (The London Borough of) v KA (Capacity to Marry) [2016] EWCOP 20**
> The test for capacity to marriage is: (1) marriage is a status, not person specific; (2) the wisdom of the marriage is irrelevant; (3) P must understand the broad nature of the marriage contract; (4) P must understand the duties and responsibilities that normally attach to marriage; (5) the essence of marriage is for two people to live together and to love one another; (6) P must not lack capacity to enter into sexual relations.

In 2022, 21 per cent (62) cases of forced marriage known to the Home Office Forced Marriage Unit involved people whose mental capacity to consent to marriage was in doubt. Victims with mental capacity concerns were more likely to be male (52 per cent) and older (47 per cent of victims were known to be aged 26 and over) than in cases on average where younger women formed the majority of alleged forced marriage victims (Home Office and Foreign and Commonwealth Office, 2023).

We cannot be confident about how many unknown cases of forced marriage there are. These can involve disabled adults of any gender or at any age. There may be dilemmas for practitioners: the families who have arranged these marriages may not have used any coercion but have arranged for the adult to be married in order to obtain a carer for the adult, or financial security for them, or for a culturally relevant reason, perhaps seeing marriage as a rite of passage for all, or simply because to be married is the only option for an adult. Families may argue that mental capacity has no relevance in their culture but that their actions are intended to preserve a sound future for their child. However, the experiences of an adult who has been forced to marry can include abandonment once their spouse realises their disability; financial and sexual exploitation; prosecution of the spouse who will be committing a criminal offence in having a sexual relationship with an adult who cannot consent to this. The spouse may experience violence or coercion if trying to leave the marriage. Practitioners cannot be complicit in forced marriage and must take careful and skilled action to either prevent the marriage or solve the consequences of the marriage.

Indicators that a forced marriage may be planned for an adult can include the adult talking about marriage, jewellery or wedding clothes; they may appear happy about being married or anxious; a family member may raise concerns that a relative is being forced into marriage or may inform a professional that their relative is to be married or ask the practitioner to sign a visa immigration or passport application; the adult may be removed from services or leave the country without explanation or warning.

Forced marriage is a criminal offence under the Anti-Social Behaviour Crime and Policing Act 2014. See Chapter 3 for more detail on this offence and on Forced Marriage Protection Orders.

In some circumstances forced marriage can also be referred to as 'predatory marriage'. This is more commonly associated with older people who may have dementia or cognitive issues and are being groomed or coerced into marriage by a younger person with the aim of inheriting wealth.

Female genital mutilation (FGM) is not mentioned within the Care and Support Statutory Guidance but is important to recognise as a form of domestic abuse. FGM is a term for procedures which involve partial or total removal of the external female genitalia for non-medical reasons. FGM is usually carried out on girls between the ages of 1 and 15, but younger babies, older girls and women can be victims too. In some areas the practice is carried out just before marriage or after the birth of the first baby. The health risks to adult women who have undergone FGM are severe and include high risk of infections, damage to other organs and difficulty in urinating, multiple problems relating to both penetrative and non-penetrative sex or giving birth. Women may experience post-traumatic stress disorder, anxiety and depression. They may need further surgery to open the vagina for sex and childbirth.

There is no requirement for mandatory referral of an adult women who has had FGM to adult social services or the police. Each woman's situation must be carefully assessed at the woman's pace, and a safeguarding adult referral made for any woman who is also an adult at risk. An adult woman who has had FGM may also be an indicator that others in the family, including children, may be a risk of FGM. There is a mandatory requirement to make a child protection referral for under-18-year-olds who are at risk of, or have had, FGM.

What might indicate domestic abuse?

Indicators of domestic abuse will include all of the indicators of other forms of abuse described here. These will include unexplained injuries or implausible explanations for those injuries, sexual assault, financial difficulties, depression, anxiety, self-neglect and/or low self-esteem. The presence of a third party or parties who are overly intrusive in conversation, or who control whom the adult sees or speaks to should also raise concern. Coercive behaviour can include isolating the adult from sources of support, including health and social care agencies. The adult being abused may express shame and be quick to blame themselves for any abuse, particularly if the abuse is being perpetrated by their (adult) child or has been going on for some years.

Remember: domestic abuse can happen to anyone, no matter their age, sexual orientation or gender. While women remain the largest group in all data relating to domestic abuse, it is also evident that male adults at risk are also subject to domestic abuse and violence. Domestic abuse can occur in same-sex relationships and between family members, including parents and children. Only small and limited surveys of domestic abuse perpetrated against transgender people are currently available in the UK. A survey of 60 transgender people carried out in Scotland (Roch et al, 2010) found that 80 per cent of respondents had experienced some form of abuse by an ex or current partner. The majority of perpetrators were male (81 per cent). Some abusers used the trans identity of the person against them, as a deliberate tactic of abuse (SafeLives 2021).

Disability hate crime and mate crime

Disability hate crime or *mate crime* are useful concepts to use in recognising abuse in a community setting.

Mate crime is defined as the befriending of people who are perceived to be vulnerable, for the purposes of taking advantage of, exploiting and/or abusing them. The term 'mate crime' is contentious, and the Crown Prosecution Service uses the term 'disability hate crime' (CPS, 2022a) believing that the term 'mate crime' is confusing for people with learning disabilities.

Landman (2014) has argued that the definition of hate crime (see Chapter 3) has led to a perception that hate crimes are perpetrated on the street by strangers and are bullying in nature (for example, name-calling, throwing objects, spitting). However, the Crown Prosecution Service current advice is that disability hate crime perpetrators:

> are often partners, family members, friends, carers, acquaintances, or neighbours. Offending by persons with whom the disabled person is in a relationship may be complicated by emotional, physical and financial dependency and the need to believe a relationship is trusting and genuine, however dysfunctional. Where perpetrators are partners or live with the disabled person and are either members of the same family or have previously been partners, the offence of controlling or coercive behaviour may apply. (CPS, 2022b)

Some campaigners (Landman, 2014) emphasise the incidence of mate crime committed against people who have learning disabilities or autism, but the phenomenon can be observed in other groups; in particular, people with mental health issues and/or substance misuse or simply any adult at risk who may be perceived as being vulnerable to exploitation by so-called friends. McCarthy (2017) describes how domestic abuse, hate crime and mate crime are connected, for example, in 'cuckooing', a crime in which drug dealers take over an adult's home in order to use it as a base for drug dealing. The home of an adult can also be taken over by 'friends' who are homeless or wishing to hide. Control over the adult is maintained via physical and verbal threats and humiliations regarding disability or frailty.

Indicators of 'mate crime' or exploitation by friends/acquaintances and disability hate crime include the source of harm presenting as the adult's carer or caring friend. The source of harm isolates the adult by alleging that other friends or paid carers are not trustworthy. They involve the adult in activities where alcohol or drugs are used and exert control through withholding/using alcohol or drugs and playing on any guilt or shame the adult feels. The source of harm exploits the adult, initially in minor ways, which then increase in severity. These can include financial or sexual exploitation; making the adult commit minor criminal offences such as shoplifting; and using or selling the adult's medication. Control over the adult is maintained by public accusations of the adult being a paedophile or another untrue and socially despised identity (CPS 2022), by threats and intimidation, or public and private displays of power over the adult. There can be increasingly cruel and humiliating treatment of the adult, often related to the nature of their disability; for example, blindfolding someone who is deaf or destroying mobility aids. The adult's accommodation may be taken over by the source of harm and their associates, to have somewhere to live, and/or use to take or sell drugs, hide stolen goods and encourage under-age drinking or sexual activities. Other adults at the same property may also be at risk; for example, adults in sheltered housing or supported accommodation. Individuals, couples and groups can perpetrate crimes against adults, and can encourage each other by filming cruel treatment and sharing with each other or on social networking sites.

Adults can be wary of reporting crimes committed by friends, through fear of these so-called friends, or being afraid of statutory agencies, especially the police. Sin (2013) notes that some disabled people may experience regular unkind and discriminatory behaviour from others, finding such behaviour so endemic to their lives that it becomes internalised and normalised. Other adults may have such low self-esteem after experiences of institutionalisation and marginalisation through the life course that such acts of unkindness do not appear to be abusive to them, but an expected part of their lives.

REFLECTIVE ACTIVITY

Learning from Safeguarding Adults Reviews: Devon and Torbay Safeguarding Adults Partnership, SAR Stephen Fogg

Stephen was a 60-year-old man who lived alone in a property left to him in trust after his father died in June 2017. Stephen had a learning disability. Stephen had significant and recent bereavements. Stephen could be overfriendly with people. He wanted to please people, to be liked. He invited people he had not met before back to his bungalow and gave his address and personal details to strangers. He was extremely lonely and either because of his feelings of isolation, and/or his struggle to use and weigh the information given to him by his support workers about risks, he placed himself in risky situations. Stephen appears to have had a long history of alcohol use that impacted on his daily life. Stephen had not had support to reduce his drinking or to deal with the experiences or emotions that might be leading to increased use. Stephen did not have a great deal of money to spare. When Stephen was very intoxicated with alcohol, it was because others had supplied it.

Stephen thought that he had found new friends in a group of men who he met in his village shop. These men stole from him and intimidated him. He found it difficult to keep away from them. Stephen was murdered by a man and woman he had met at the village shop. They are described in press reports as being under the influence of both alcohol and heroin when they murdered him.

Location of abuse: institutional settings, including care homes and hospitals

Abuse that occurs in an institution (for example, a care home, hospital, day care or supported living) or harm that is caused by a member of an organisation providing a service to an adult can be described using any of the types of abuse listed here.

When the institution or service itself is so dysfunctional that there are risks to all living in the setting or using the service, this is defined as *organisational abuse*. The statutory guidance defines organisational abuse as:

> Including neglect and poor care practice within an institution or specific care setting such as a hospital or care home, for example, or in relation to care provided in one's own home. This may range from one-off incidents to ongoing ill-treatment. It can be through neglect or poor professional practice as a result of the structure, policies, processes and practices within an organisation. (Section 14.17)

The statutory guidance definition can confuse: is organisational abuse about poor practice, or a one-off incident involving individuals who live in a care setting, or is it about the organisation itself? The key phrase is that harm has occurred 'as a result of the structure, policies, processes and practices within an organisation'. Harm has occurred because of a feature of how the organisation is operating, not because of the action of one member of staff. The case study may help to clarify the difference.

REFLECTIVE ACTIVITY

Case study: Mr Greene

Mr Greene has been assaulted by a member of staff at Blueskies care home. She shouted at him when he threw his meal onto the table, and she rubbed his face into the food. The care home manager immediately suspended the staff member, called the police and reported the matter to adult safeguarding. The member of staff has a recently updated Disclosure and Barring Service check, is a long-standing member of staff but has recently been exhibiting some out of character frustration with other staff, but until the incident with Mr Greene, no concerns have been reported about conduct towards the people who live at Blueskies. Mr Greene is reported to be upset and frightened. The manager has taken measures to reassure him and is requesting a review of his support needs and an advocate to support him during the police investigation.

Reflective question

- Is this 'organisational abuse' or physical and psychological abuse perpetrated by a person with power over Mr Greene?

Our thoughts are that the care home manager is responding appropriately to the incident and is focused on Mr Greene's current and future well-being.

If the indicators of organisational abuse were present, we might see a different scenario:

Mr Greene's mother reports that he has been assaulted by a member of staff at Blueskies care home; the assault happened in the last week. Mr Greene says that the staff member shouted at him when he threw his meal onto the table and rubbed his face into the food. When you contact the Blueskies manager, she confirms that this happened but said that Mr Greene did not seem unduly upset. The incident has been recorded as 'Mr Greene was challenging at mealtime yesterday and told off by X.' The staff member is long-standing and nothing like this has happened before; the staff member cannot be suspended from duty as the home is already short-staffed. The manager cannot see any purpose in investigating further and is horrified by the thought that this is viewed as an assault against Mr Greene.

Reflective question

- What concerns do you have about how the care home manager is responding to Mr Greene being harmed?

Our thoughts are that, at best, the care home manager has minimised any impact on Mr Greene. She has not put his needs at the centre of her concerns but is preoccupied with the running of the home. We might be concerned that the home does not take a person-centred approach to the care of the adults living there.

Indicators of organisational abuse are explored in research (Marsland and White, 2015) identifying six areas of concern about the practice of organisations working with older people. This was preceded by research into early indicators of concern in organisations working with people who have learning disabilities. These areas have been considered and developed by adult safeguarding practitioners over the years and form a simple framework that can be used for a variety of purposes, including risk assessment. We will revisit this framework and how to use it in risk assessment in Chapter 7.

 ESSENTIAL INFORMATION: PRACTICE GUIDANCE

Early indicators of concern in organisations

Examples are given under each heading.

1. *Concerns about management and leadership*
   - Managers are not leading the service; they do not make decisions and do not appear to be able to change the culture or working practices.
   - The service/home is reactive to crises but has no structured plan on how to improve matters.
   - Managers appear unaware of serious problems in the service.
   - The manager has left and there are no practical interim arrangements.

2. *Concerns about staff skills, knowledge and practice*
   - Staff appear to lack the information, skills and knowledge to support the needs of the people using the service.
   - Members of staff are controlling of residents/service users.
   - Members of staff use negative or judgemental language when talking about residents.

3. *Concerns about residents' behaviours and well-being: one or more adults using the service*
   - Have lost weight or have deteriorating physical or mental health with no documented explanation.
   - Show signs of injury or harm through lack of care or attention.
   - Moods or psychological presentation have changed, including anxiety, depression, anger, fear.

4. *Concerns about the service resisting the involvement of external people and isolating individuals*
   - Available external health or support services are not considered or referred to.

- Managers/staff do not respond to advice or guidance from practitioners and families who visit the service are dismissive or hostile towards advice.
- The service does not consider or make applications for Deprivation of Liberty authorisation.
- The service is not reporting concerns or serious incidents to adult safeguarding, regulators, families, advocates or attorneys, external practitioners or agencies.

5. *Concerns about the way services are planned and delivered*
   - There is a lack of clarity about the purpose and nature of the service.
   - The service is accepting adults whose needs they appear unable to meet.
   - Adults' needs as identified in assessments, care plans or risk assessments are not being met.

6. *Concerns about the quality of basic care and the environment*
   - The service is not providing a safe or clean environment.
   - There are a lack of activities or social opportunities for residents; the service does not support a good quality of life.
   - Equipment is not being used or is used incorrectly.

Marsland and White (2015) suggest that indicators across two or three of the themed groupings should be considered significant. Our practice experience has taught us that any indicators in the first grouping, 'concerns about management and leadership', is a significant early indicator; other indicators will follow if this indicator is present.

Identification of harm: types of abuse

The types of abuse described here may occur in any setting, including the adult's own home, hospitals, care homes and the community.

Physical abuse

Physical abuse is defined in the statutory guidance as including offences against the person (for example, assault, hitting, slapping, pushing, misuse of medication, restraint and inappropriate physical sanctions), including unlawfully depriving an adult of their liberty. Although the list of behaviours that constitute offences against the person looks straightforward, there are several factors to consider. The Care and Support Statutory Guidance does not differentiate using ideas of 'significance' or impact of harm. Using the person-centred Making Safeguarding Personal approach enables consideration of the meaning of the behaviour to the adult concerned. Is a push part of a playful interaction with another or is it part of a pattern of threats and intimidation? If the push results in no harm, but is part of a pattern of intimidation, is it physical abuse? If the playful push which the adult was enjoying results in an injury, was that abuse, or an unfortunate and one-off accident? Understanding the context of the harm helps to understand the experience of the adult.

Sexual abuse and sexual exploitation

Sexual abuse is defined in the statutory guidance (DHSC, 2014, 14.17) as including 'rape, indecent exposure, sexual harassment, inappropriate looking or touching, sexual teasing or innuendo, sexual photography, subjection to pornography or witnessing sexual acts, indecent exposure, sexual assault, sexual acts to which the adult has not consented or was pressured into consenting'.

Sexual abuse and exploitation can be perpetrated by one individual, or by an exploitative group who target individuals or a group of adults who have care and support needs; children may also be targeted as part of organised sexual exploitation.

The sexual exploitation of adults with care and support needs involves exploitative situations, contexts and relationships where adults with care and support needs receive affection or inclusion or some type of 'reward' (for example, food, accommodation, drugs, alcohol, cigarettes, gifts or money) as a result of performing sexual activities, and/or others performing sexual activities on them. Sexual exploitation can occur through the use of technology (for example, being persuaded to post sexual images or videos onto social media or being sent images by the person causing harm). In all cases, those exploiting the adult have power over them by virtue of their age, gender, intellect, physical strength and/or economic or other resources.

REFLECTIVE ACTIVITY

Learning from Safeguarding Adults Reviews: Teeswide SAB, SAR Molly (2021)

It was not disclosed until **Molly** was 23 that she had been the victim of child sexual abuse from the age of nine years and that continued until she was an older teenager. Molly started using substances at a very young age and this continued to escalate. Within the timeframe of the review, Molly's substance misuse had escalated to the injecting of heroin. It was known by those working with her that Molly had stated that she was not able to inject herself and so this was done by others; there were reports from police that Molly stated that perpetrators had taught her to inject herself. Substance misuse in the last couple of years of Molly's life was very much linked to the exploitative and abusive nature of the relationships with perpetrators. Having turned to substances in her teenage years, perpetrators would offer her drugs in exchange for sex. As time progressed, it became clear to those working with Molly that perpetrators also provided drugs in order to control and traffic Molly for sex. Molly told workers that those injecting her with heroin had started to do it when she was asleep, and this created a fear in her. There was work undertaken relating to the risks that this posed.

Following on from this it is important to note that Molly had been sexually exploited within her teenage years and this was an extension of that. Molly did not recognise all of her relationships as exploitative and felt that some of the perpetrators were her boyfriends.

There was occasional mention in reports for this review regarding Molly being engaged in sex work. The author would suggest, as would those who worked closely with Molly, that at no time was Molly engaged in 'sex work'. Those working in the sex industry indicate that there is a difference between those who choose that as a career and that there is choice and control over the decisions that a sex worker makes. It is not without its risks but is far removed from anything experienced by Molly. In exchange for sex, Molly felt that she was offered care in terms of food and a roof over her head at times. This is often described as 'survival sex'.

As time progressed, the risks escalated as those perpetrating harm were involved and known to be part of organised crime gangs and as the abuse increased, so did the substance misuse. More importantly, Molly spent more time in the accommodation of those perpetrators. The perpetrators were very powerful in terms of being able to manipulate Molly and knew the systems well and how to continue to perpetrate their crimes while evading arrest and prosecution.

Sexual exploitation can also be part of modern slavery and human trafficking.

Any sexual relationship that develops between adults where one is in a position of trust, power or authority in relation to the other (for example, support worker, social worker, therapist, nurse, doctor, other health or care worker, and so on) will constitute sexual abuse and is likely to be a criminal offence.

There can be challenges for the practitioner when receiving concerns about sexual abuse. In some situations, the adult may perceive sexual exploitation as a relationship that is valued and may wish to continue despite the harmful effect on them. Others may report an adult's consensual and much enjoyed sexual intimacy as harmful simply because of their own prejudices about age and sex, or the way in which the adult is expressing their sexuality. It is important to reflect on and understand your own values and prejudices and ensure that you are comfortable about discussing sex, sexuality and sexual orientation in your everyday adult safeguarding practice.

Psychological abuse

Psychological abuse can be seen as a single type of abuse but can also occur as part of all other types of abuse. The statutory guidance (DHSC, 2014, 14.17) defines psychological abuse as constituting 'emotional abuse, threats of harm or abandonment, deprivation of contact, humiliation, blaming, controlling, intimidation, coercion, harassment, verbal abuse, cyber bullying, isolation, unreasonable and unjustified withdrawal of services or supportive networks'.

Psychological abuse involves the use of humiliation and fear and can range in intensity from the daily coercive control exercised in the adult's own home by a family member through to regular teasing of an adult with learning disabilities by a member of staff enjoying a joke at the expense of a less powerful person. The impact of psychological abuse can be damaging and long-lasting, from loss of self-esteem to depression, self-harm and suicide. Any type of abuse can contain an element of psychological abuse or be intensified by the psychological impact of abuse. For example, if an adult is physically assaulted, they will often feel intimidated, or if financially abused, the adult may experience strong feelings of humiliation and shame.

Indicators of psychological abuse can be observed in three areas:

1. *Changes in the adult's behaviour*
   They may appear depressed and lack energy, be sad or anxious, particularly in the presence of the source of harm; the self-esteem of the adult changes, they express feelings of worthlessness; there may be changes in their sleeping patterns or continence. The adult harms themselves or their possessions. They may neglect their own needs.
2. *The adult's circumstances*
   The adult is allowed only restricted contact with the outside world. Visitors and phone calls are restricted. They might be locked in their room or in their home. There is a punitive and controlling approach to the adult's daily needs, in particular continence and personal hygiene, sometimes access to aids or equipment, or the features of life that give happiness and support identity and relationships. This can also be a feature of coercive control or organisational abuse.
3. *Observed behaviour towards the adult*
   Threats to abandon or 'put away' the adult; verbal abuse including teasing, threats and intimidation; talking about the adult as if they were a child or object; use of racist, ageist, disablist, sexist, homophobic or transphobic language. Bullying via social networking internet sites or via mobile phone communication.

Financial abuse

The statutory guidance gives more detailed guidance on situations of financial abuse than any other form of harm (DHSC, 2014, 14.24–14.32). Financial abuse can be fairly simple to identify but removing the risk of further abuse or mitigating its impact can be complex. In 2022–23, 70 per cent of adults at risk who were the subject of a Section 42 enquiry into alleged financial abuse were being abused by someone they knew: a family member, friend or neighbour (NHS Digital, 2023). The dynamics of these relationships can make it difficult for the adult to decide on criminal prosecution, even when large amounts of money have been stolen from them. There are many different forms of financial abuse, and good partnership working with banks, the police, the Department for Work and Pensions, Trading Standards and the Office of the Public Guardian (OPG) is key. The statutory guidance (DHSC, 2014, 14.24) reminds us that: 'Financial recorded abuse can occur in isolation, but as research has shown, where there are other forms of abuse, there is likely to be financial abuse occurring. Although this is not always the case, everyone should also be aware of this possibility.'

Financial abuse can take a number of forms:

Theft

Money or property taken from a person without their knowledge, and/or without their consent.

Fraud

The act of gaining a dishonest advantage, often financial, over another person. The Crown Prosecution Service (CPS, 2023) reports that fraud accounts for over 40 per cent of all crime. It is estimated that over 80 per cent of fraud reported nationally is 'cyber-enabled'.

Types of fraud include:

- **Rogue traders**: being charged over the acceptable rate for household repairs, which may not exist or be over-exaggerated.
- **Online or cyber fraud**: any type of fraud committed using the internet. Examples may include fraudulent sales of goods, romance scams, or any other type of fraud facilitated online.
- **Investment fraud**: can occur online but also involves cold calls, emails or direct approaches encouraging investment in something that is either worthless or does not exist.
- **Identity fraud**: bank accounts or shopping accounts are opened in the name of the adult at risk.
- **Fraud by abuse of position**: where a person abuses a position of responsibility in which they are expected to safeguard the financial interests of another person or organisation.

Coercion regarding wills and property

Coercion is a strong word that implies intimidation. Although this can occur, a frequent presentation is one of strong persuasion or pressure, using emotional connections and the portrayal of oneself as in need. Behaviours include being continually asked for loans that are not repaid, being asked to sign over property or give a large sum of money as a gift. Prosecution of these offences is difficult; the adult has given over money and property willingly and charges of theft and fraud are hard to prove.

The impact of financial abuse on the well-being of an adult at risk can be profound. Being unable to afford food, heating or rent damages physical health while the emotional impact can profoundly affect the adult's mental health. Davison et al (2015) summarise research on the emotional impacts on older people: 'These can include feelings of betrayal, feelings of distress, especially if a house or other assets need to be sold, embarrassment, loss of self-esteem and confidence in one's own judgement, denial, fear, self-blame, social isolation, and the loss of confidence to live independently' (p 7).

Neglect

While the types of abuse already listed are about what is done to another person, *neglect and acts of omission* are about what should have been done but was not. Adults who are neglected can be those most dependent on others to meet their care and support needs. Neglect was the most common type of abuse in Section 42 enquiries concluded during 2022–23, comprising 32 per cent of all enquiries undertaken (NHS Digital, 2023). Neglect can mean failing to ensure the adult has enough to eat and drink, is warm or comfortable and has the correct medical support for any physical needs. The impact of neglect is damaging to the well-being of all adults at risk. Neglect of basic needs can be fatal to those who are frail. Heath and Phair (2009) explain frailty as:

> a weakened state of being in which a person's reserve capacity is reduced to an extent whereby health, functioning and well-being are compromised. In the precursor stage a range of indicators can identify people who are vulnerable to frailty. Advanced frailty threatens life. Complications of frailty occur when care delivered fails to compensate for the effect of frailty and other medical conditions on the person's physical, psychological or spiritual health, resulting in harm to the person. Complications are mostly avoidable. (2009, p 126)

Heath and Phair (2011) point out the risk to frail people of neglect of their basic needs as 'immobility, insufficient fluid intake or untreated pain, even within a short time span, are potentially sufficient to trigger the domino effect resulting in death' (p 51).

Examples of the neglect of physical care and support needs include not treating pressure areas, not providing the correct diet for an adult who has diabetes and leaving an adult in soiled clothing. Other indicators include ignoring call bells, or not arranging dental or medical care. Neglect of emotional and social care and support needs creates despondency and despair. Remember that harm can sometimes be unintentional; for example, denial of an adult's emotional and social needs can be based on a mistaken idea that people who are cognitively impaired do not experience bereavement, trauma or loss in the same way as others. This is profoundly untrue but can result in no emotional support being given during times of grief or fear.

Self-neglect

Section 42 enquiries regarding self-neglect only comprise 5 to 7 per cent of those undertaken between 2019 and 2023 (NHS Digital, 2023). However, 60 per cent of Safeguarding Adults Reviews during the same period are about self-neglect. Safeguarding partnerships are engaging positively in looking at the best approaches to self-neglect; for example, developing trauma–informed approaches or tools with which to work with people who are substance dependent. Creating a trusting relationship is a key factor in working with people who self-neglect, but fast workflows and the resulting pressure on practitioners' time can make this difficult.

Braye et al (2015) offer a detailed picture of the impact of severe self-neglect, gleaned from research undertaken with practitioners working with people who are neglecting their own well-being:

> The stories featured individuals who sometimes showed an almost total lack of attention to personal hygiene, by not washing or bathing, not changing clothes and bedding, not cutting hair or nails, or incontinence and soiling. There might be no food in the adult's home and little evidence that they were eating, or the food they consumed might be mouldy, rotten or composed of leftover scraps. Combined, these factors often led to malnutrition, skin breakdown and pressure sores and dehydration, requiring hospital admission, sometimes on a repeated basis. Neglect of their own health care often made things worse. A number of people also lived in extremely dirty and sometimes infested conditions, which had often built up over many years, during which cleaning had not taken place. (2015, p 6)

Hoarding of found objects, consumer goods, animals or, in extreme situations, bodily waste, may occur in addition to self-neglect. Equally, people may also live in very sparse surroundings, with little or no possessions.

Discriminatory abuse

The definition of discriminatory abuse in the statutory guidance is short; such abuse includes 'forms of harassment, slurs or similar treatment because of race, gender and gender identity, age, disability, sexual orientation, religion' (DHSC, 2014, 14.17).

As we explored in Chapter 2, discriminatory abuse is prevalent throughout the lives of adults at risk of abuse and neglect. The indicators of discriminatory abuse may take the form of any of those listed under any of the other categories of abuse. The difference lies in that the abuse is motivated by discriminatory attitudes, feelings or behaviour towards an individual. The adult may change their behaviour and become withdrawn and isolated; they are fearful of going out or of certain places. The adult may be refused access to services or be excluded inappropriately or, because of past experience of discrimination, resist or refuse to use the services that are required to meet assessed needs. Only 0.6 per cent of Section 42 enquiries between 2022 and 2023 were about discriminatory abuse (NHS Digital, 2023). It is important to engage with the adult's experience of discrimination and explore the impact of current and historical discrimination on their sense of identity and well-being. Mason (2023) reminds us that 'harassment' and 'slurs' are the outcomes of discrimination towards an individual. We must attend to the discrimination that people with protected characteristics will experience while using services. This may involve professional stereotyping; for example, assuming a person lacks capacity because they have a diagnosis of dementia. There may be institutional bias such as racism in decision making. There may be practitioner bias, with a lack of attention to the impact of the person's sexual, cultural or gender identity on their lives. We need to understand the discrimination inherent in where a person lives, whether that is about their treatment in long-stay hospitals or in care homes, or whether that is about the experience of rough sleeping and the prejudice towards people who are homeless.

Modern slavery

The Care and Support Statutory Guidance includes modern slavery as a type of harm that adults at risk may experience (DHSC, 2014, 14.17). Kidd and Manthorpe (2017) cite examples of people with learning disabilities being used in domestic servitude and examples of homeless people used in forced labour. Craig and Clay (2017) describe the impact modern slavery has had on the people caught up in it, including physical injuries or the development of addictions as a coping strategy. They highlight the possibilities of carers being victims of domestic servitude, either bought into the family home to care for free or working in care homes.

Children and adults from vulnerable groups may be exploited by organised drug groups who use them in the supply of drugs, the movement of cash proceeds (Home Office, 2018) and who use their homes to store and supply drugs. The former practice is often known as 'county lines' and the latter practice as 'cuckooing'. Both are forms of modern slavery. The National Crime Agency (2017) reports that 74 per cent of 100 UK police forces noted exploitation of vulnerable people within the modern slavery definition; 37 per cent of these forces reported exploitation of people with mental health issues and 12 per cent reported exploitation of people with physical health issues. Modern slavery offences can be addressed under various pieces of legislation, including the Sexual Offences Act 2003. The Modern Slavery Act 2015 consolidated and updated criminal legislation on human trafficking, slavery, forced labour, cannabis farming, organ harvesting, forced begging and domestic servitude. Public authorities, including local and health authorities, have a duty to cooperate with the Independent Anti-Slavery Commissioner.

Terrorist activity

Prevent is the government policy designed to prevent people being drawn into terrorist activity. The Care and Support Statutory Guidance does not reference the Prevent duty contained in the Counterterrorism and Security Act 2015, but many Safeguarding Adults Boards (SABs) include the Prevent duty in their overarching policies and procedures. The Act requires specified authorities, including local authorities, to have 'due regard to the need to prevent people from being drawn into terrorism' (Section 26(1)). Other authorities include educational provisions, the health sector, police and prisons. Most SABs will have policies that include adults at risk and exploitation into terrorism. The Prevent Strategy (Home Office, 2011) is the governmental initiative that aims to work with vulnerable individuals who may be at risk of being exploited by radical groups and/or being drawn into terror-related activity.

Indicators that an individual may be being groomed into extremism can be:

- they may possess or search for extremist literature online;
- they may express feelings of anger, grievance, injustice;
- using language that supports 'us and them' thinking;
- they have a new group of friends who have an extremist ideology;
- becoming withdrawn and stopping participating in their usual activities; and
- they may go missing from their care, home or school setting.

▶ KEY MESSAGES

- Shared definitions support multi-agency working, but risk simplifying complex and unique situations.

- Exploring the adult's situation with them or those close to them can help us decide whether the statutory duty to enquire has been met.

- Harm may be unintentional: the emphasis of adult safeguarding must be on the impact of the abuse on the adult and what can be done to resolve or reduce risk in the situation.

KNOWLEDGE REVIEW

- WHAT does 'exploitation' mean in adult safeguarding?

- WHAT are the two useful concepts to help you understand the dynamics of harm in domestic or community settings?

- HOW does organisational abuse differ from one-off incidents of harm or neglect in an institution?

- WHAT is 'transitional safeguarding'?

 FURTHER READING

There are plenty of good practice guides to help you extend your knowledge and skills in working in particular situations of abuse. Do develop your own library. Here are some resources to start you off. Do always check who you can ask for advice in your organisation and with contacts in your local safeguarding adults team. Some situations can be unusual but there may be a practitioner who has developed their practice in a particular area, such as forced marriage. The local authority adult safeguarding team or similar may be able to point you in the right direction.

- Alcohol Change UK (Preston-Shoot and Ward, 2021) 'How to Use Legal Powers to Safeguard Highly Vulnerable Dependent Drinkers' is a valuable resource on the needs of this group and the legislation that can be used to make a difference to lives. Available from https://alcoholchange.org.uk/publication/how-to-use-legal-powers-to-safeguard-highly-vulnerable-dependent-drinkers [Accessed 12 July 2024].

- If you want to read about some of the SARs on alcohol dependence, the Alcohol Change UK's report 'Learning from Tragedies' analyses 11 SARs concerning people where alcohol misuse was a significant issue. These people were often highly vulnerable, dependent drinkers; the reviews highlight their vulnerability and social exclusion. Available from https://alcoholchange.org.uk/publication/learning-from-tragedies-an-analysis-of-alcohol-related-safeguarding-adult-reviews-published-in-2017 [Accessed 12 July 2024].

- Lessons from SARs on homelessness are reviewed in Preston-Shoot, M. and Taylor, G. (2022) 'Learning from Safeguarding Adults Reviews and Fatality Reviews' in Cooper, A. and Preston-Shoot, M. *Adult Safeguarding and Homelessness*, Jessica Kingsley: London.

- The Local Government Association has produced the guidance, 'Adult Safeguarding and Homelessness. A Briefing on Positive Practice Guidance' Available from www.local.gov.uk/sites/default/files/documents/25.158%20Briefing%20on%20Adult%20Safeguarding%20and%20Homelessness_03_1.pdf [Accessed 12 July 2024].

- A wealth of resources on coercive control can be found at Research in Practice for Adults (RiPfA) at: https://coercivecontrol.ripfa.org.uk/ [Accessed 12 July 2024].

- SafeLives have a range of resources to use with people experiencing domestic abuse who may also have care and support needs: www.safelives.org.uk/knowle dge-hub/spotlights/spotlight-2-disabled-people-and-domestic-abuse [Accessed 12 July 2024].

- The My Marriage My Choice website has helpful practice guidelines on working with families and adults where there are concerns about forced or predatory marriage. These include a detailed guide on assessing mental capacity and advice on approaches to be taken to avoid the risk of the adult being removed from the country. Visit http://mymarriagemychoice.co.uk/ [Accessed 12 July 2024].

- A wide range of resources on transitional safeguarding can be found on the Local Government Association website at www.local.gov.uk/our-support/partners-care-and-health/safeguarding-resources/transitional-safeguarding-resources [Accessed 12 July 2024].

- There are a number of toolkits to help with financial abuse work, including cyber-scamming and fraud, on the Bournemouth University website at https://nccdsw.co.uk/clusters/research/financial-scamming-and-fraud [Accessed 12 July 2024].

Part II
Good adult safeguarding practice

6

Relationships, values and ethics

Chapter aim

Adult safeguarding practice demands that you are able to build a working relationship with an adult at risk and those who are close to them including, at times, the person who has caused harm. In this chapter we outline the competencies that practitioners need to build relationships and work with confidence in adult safeguarding. We will explore the ethical and communication challenges of working with people experiencing harm, abuse and discrimination as well as working alongside other professionals.

This chapter includes:

- Definitions and descriptions of relationship-based adult safeguarding

- Using professional curiosity in building relationships

- The importance of understanding power and oppression through the life course

- Ideas for extending relationship-building skills

- Building relationships with colleagues from other organisations

- Understanding your own values and how these interact with professional ethics

Definitions and descriptions of relationship-based adult safeguarding

Contemporary approaches in adult safeguarding such as Making Safeguarding Personal are predicated on the practitioner being able to make a relationship with the adult and the people and services around them. Building a relationship will support the adult to be involved in their own protection, by exploring their situation, identifying potential outcomes and recovering from harm.

You may need to build a relationship quickly in a crisis situation such as during a mental health crisis or when an adult needs to leave a dangerous situation. These relationships need to be effective in the short term but may not be sustained beyond the initial crisis. Relationships can take longer to develop with people who have experienced trauma, either historically or more recently, or have had experiences that make it hard for them to trust others. Trusting relationships can sustain the adult through the ups and downs of change. Whether short- or long-lived, helpful relationships have a number of important elements in common. These elements may be present after one meeting or may take several meetings to build up.

ESSENTIAL INFORMATION: PRACTICE GUIDANCE

Important elements of relationships to think about when planning to meet a person:

1. **Preparation:** what do I need to know before I contact or meet this person? Are there records of previous contacts, and/or anything the referrer says I should note? If meeting the person, is the meeting place safe for them and me, is it accessible, comfortable? When is the best time of day to meet with them?

2. **Engagement:** how will I communicate with the person? Do I need any help to do this? How will I explain clearly and in plain language who I am and why I am contacting or meeting with them? How will I encourage the person to talk with me, to begin to trust me and engage with the possibility of change?

3. **Listening:** what is the person's perspective? What is their story about the situation they are in? What are they afraid or worried about? What are their hopes? Listening and responding continues throughout the relationship.

4. **Collaboration:** sharing mutual understanding of problems and options. What has the person tried previously, what worked and didn't, what is an acceptable option and what is not? Who is helpful or has been helpful in the past?

5. **Working together:** clarity about what needs to happen and what can happen now and who will do this. How will we know what has helped?

6. **Creating a shared plan:** by planning the next steps together with clarity about who does what and when.

Being able to communicate with an adult is fundamental to being able to create a relationship with them. Practitioners often struggle to convey the reason for contact without using bewildering professional jargon. For example, how do you describe adult safeguarding? Do you use this term or another such as safeguarding adults or adult protection? Do you try to explain what they mean in everyday language?

REFLECTIVE ACTIVITY

'I have received a concern regarding financial abuse in which your son was named as the alleged source of harm. I am from the Blankshire adult safeguarding team. Following information gathering, we have determined that we have a duty to undertake a Section 42 enquiry and I need to meet with you to discuss your desired outcomes.'

- Try to rephrase this sentence in everyday English.
- Think about the jargon you use – is there anything you think would be important to include and explain?

People cannot be involved in their own safeguarding if they cannot understand what we are saying or doing. Using professional language or jargon is alienating and will create unhelpful barriers between you, the adult and the people supporting them. It can be empowering at times for people to understand what jargon is used so they can connect with and explain the systems they are involved with; jargon should only be used when explained and contextualised.

When a person is being abused, or has abused others, they may feel at their lowest ebb, and have low self-esteem and energy. It is important to convey respect in the way you communicate with people whose self-esteem is low; use respectful language and observe their pace of communication. Do not rush because you are busy. If you need help to communicate with a person, do plan ahead where you can. Is there someone who already knows the adult who can support you to understand what they are saying? How can you quickly access translation services? Is it possible for a colleague from Speech and Language Therapy to attend or offer guidance to you on how to communicate with a person with specific communication needs?

Using professional curiosity in building relationships

'One of the skills best tailored to engaging, building rapport and developing person-centred relationships is the exercise of professional curiosity. It is also sometimes an important gateway to identifying abuse and neglect, probing below the surface of appearances to reveal a safeguarding need' (Preston-Shoot et al, 2024b, p 17).

How can we use our professional curiosity to build relationships?

Listening to the person is key to how we build relationships. As busy practitioners we are tempted to problem solve quickly, but we must learn to take time to truly hear the person, asking prompting questions to expand the conversation. Ask yourself: when was the last time someone listened to you, without interrupting with their own solutions or experiences? If a person feels understood, trust may begin to grow.

What stops us from listening fully? We may be busy rehearsing our response to what the person is saying, or busy filtering out what we do not expect or want to hear, or thinking through what our solution to the person's predicament will be (McKay et al, 2009).

It can help to use a listening framework that can be adapted to the unique circumstance of the person.

 ESSENTIAL INFORMATION: PRACTICE GUIDANCE

Listening or conversation frameworks

To focus yourself on listening fully, you can design a framework. These will helpfully start with closed questions that can help to relax the person before moving on to open questioning. Some ideas for strengths-based and person-centred open questioning might be:

- What is most important to you at the moment?
- What is currently working well in your life?
- What isn't working so well? How does this affect you living your life?
- What have you tried to improve matters? What was hard/easy?
- Who is helping you/getting in the way?
- What could make things better?

If there was a time when life was not so difficult:

- What were you doing then/where were you living, etc. What was different? Who was there?

If you are struggling to stay focused on just listening, you could try a listening model. The Tell, Explain, Describe (TED) model can help you and the person you are with fully explore a topic. Examples of TED questions, which you can add to:

Tell me, has this happened before? Tell me, when did you first notice ... or simply, tell me more about ...

Explain to me, what happened when you ... explain to me ... has this caused other problems?

Describe to me, how did it feel when ... describe to me, how would you like things to be?

It is important to paraphrase what a person has told you at intervals in order to check your understanding of the issue and check if there is anything you have misunderstood or that they would like to add.

Each framework must end with a summary of what has been discussed to check your understanding again.

Remember that through conversations you are not only listening to the words people use but also observing their body language and what they are communicating through their emotional state. You may pick up incongruities in communication which may be explored as trust builds (for example, the persons says they are fine but looks sad) or patterns of communication (for example, the person repeats the same phrase, 'it is hopeless' or 'he doesn't mean it' or 'it has been a difficult marriage').

Many of the behaviours that support professional curiosity, including listening, using empathy, making efforts to understand uniqueness and taking a collaborative approach, are valued by adults who are experienced in working with social workers. Ingram (2013, p 994) collated over 40 years of social work research to identify the practitioner behaviours that adults who are experienced in working with social workers value:

- practitioners who understand and value their perspectives and views and who are good listeners;
- valuing personal uniqueness;
- involvement that is purposeful and supportive;
- being asked to define problems and goals, leading to a mutual understanding;
- practitioners who adopt a friendly approach, showing warmth, empathy and genuineness; and
- practitioners who demonstrate respect, honesty and reliability.

Adults identify empathy, or the ability to be sensitively aware of another's perspective, as a valued skill in the practitioners who work with them. How can you continue to develop empathy for another's experiences, feelings and situation?

 ESSENTIAL INFORMATION: PRACTICE GUIDANCE

How to develop and nurture empathy

- Be curious and ask how the person felt and thought, hearing the whole story: 'What happened next?'

- Listen without interruption or preconceptions. Allow yourself to absorb the person's experiences, feelings, values and hopes; resist any thoughts of interrupting with problem-solving ideas. This can be hard but is the way to understand the other's perspective without putting your own interpretation onto their lives.
- Try to see things from the perspective of the other person; put yourself in their shoes and focus on how that feels.
- People may be able to talk about their feelings by telling stories about their lives.
- Listening with empathy and curiosity helps to build trust, while sharing the experiences of the past is important in understanding the meaning of harm and risk to the person.
- It is important to understand the dynamics of harm in specific situations, and how a person feels about these, in order to explore the sometimes conflicting or unspeakable emotions experienced that may prevent the person or their family moving forward.

Some of the more commonly encountered emotional responses to being harmed, or to harming others, may be found in the Reflective Activity.

REFLECTIVE ACTIVITY

Consider how your approach will take account of the person's emotional response in these case studies:

Shame: a feeling caused by the person's belief that they are, or that others think they are, inferior or unworthy of attention and respect because of their thoughts, actions, lifestyle or past experiences.

- **Mrs Gill** did not tell anyone about her daughter stealing from her. She thought that if people knew, they would think she was a bad mother. She must have been a bad mother to be in this position.
- **Amanda Gill** hated herself. She could not think about how much money she had taken from her mother over the last year. She tried to keep up being a caring daughter: she did love her mum, but she knew that if anyone found out what she had done she would be seen as the nasty woman she really was.

Fear: a feeling of distress, apprehension or alarm caused by impending danger or pain, or a belief that danger or pain is likely.

- **Mr Roberts** grew up in a hospital for children with learning disabilities. He was very afraid at night when the lights were put out and no staff were around. Another child would bully him, and sometimes others joined in. One of the staff nurses on duty would make fun of him being afraid of these boys. These days Mr Roberts is still afraid at night. He now lives in a residential home and one of the night staff called him a 'cowardy custard' on one occasion, apologising afterwards. He is now terrified of going to bed. The home manager is unsure what to do or why Mr Roberts is suddenly so afraid.

- **Ms Joliffe** cares for her father. She lives with him and, since her mother died, the pair have been close companions. She has recently had to acknowledge that her father is dying; his doctor says that his cancer is now terminal. Ms Joliffe feels terrified; separated from her father, she will be lost. The fear feels overwhelming. She has stopped any professional coming into the house and hopes that if she continues to watch him carefully, he may not leave her.

Guilt: while shame is about how you think you may appear to others, guilt is about recognising that your thoughts or actions have violated your personal moral code.

- **Ms Rose** was sexually assaulted by another resident in the supported living house in which she lives. She hasn't told anyone about this as she allowed him into her room, against the agreed rule of the house that separates men and women into different corridors of flats. She also let him bring alcohol into the flat, although she doesn't drink and knows what alcohol can do. She feels that she only has herself to blame for what happened.

- **Nurse James** gave Mr Brown the wrong tablets. This happened because he was the only nurse on shift and was completely overwhelmed by all the events that day. He feels terrible and has started to worry that he will be struck off or something bad will happen to him. He is not going to say anything about what happened.

Sadness: a feeling of disadvantage, loss, despair, grief, helplessness, sorrow. At its most severe, sadness will manifest as depression.

- **Mr Smith** is neglecting himself to a dangerous extent. He might eat once a day and he does not wash or change his clothes. He has stopped taking his medication. When his father died, he felt that his heart stopped working and that he cannot keep going any more.

- **Mrs Jones** didn't mean to scold her disabled sister. Some days she just doesn't seem to be able to think straight. Since her husband died it has been hard to get out of bed in the morning and she wonders what the point is in keeping going. No one seems to care about her life, and nothing will ever change.

Anger: a hostile response to perceived provocation, hurt or threat. Anger can occur when a person feels their personal boundaries are being violated. Some people have a learned tendency to react to anger through retaliation as a way of coping. Others use anger as a protective mechanism over sadness, fear or pain.

- **Mrs Peters** gets angry and hits out at staff when they are giving her personal care. Staff are now avoiding taking care of her needs and she is being neglected.
- **Mr Michaels** hit his wife today. It's the first time in their 50-year marriage that he has ever done this. The district nurse says he is experiencing 'carer stress' but he doesn't think it's that. It's more that she isn't his wife anymore, just some woman he looks after. He feels so angry about it all.

Shame is a particularly powerful emotion that impacts on the individual, their family networks and community. Frost (2016) details some of the individual responses to being shamed, which include feelings of incompetence, inferiority, powerlessness and self-harm. People can also numb their feelings with alcohol or drugs, or take dangerous risks in response to the need to deny, hide or escape. The person may become submissive or compliant, or angry and violent.

Individuals may also belong to a social group that is labelled as inferior in some way; for example, people receiving benefits being called scroungers. Being labelled in this way leads to an internalised feeling of being ashamed. People who feel shame are less likely to ask for help. People who hoard objects often experience overwhelming shame (Barnett, 2018) to the extent that they find it difficult to discuss their behaviour or to allow others to see their accommodation. Older people experience a range of barriers to identifying and reporting domestic abuse and can struggle with a sense of shame in tolerating abuse, which may have lasted for over 40 years or from being abused by their son or daughter (SafeLives, 2016c). Shame can cause identity damage, which can be mitigated through being listened to and valued within a relationship of trust and respect. The process of telling your story and being accepted for who you are can begin to reduce the power of shame.

The importance of understanding power and oppression through the life course

How much power or agency do people have in the circumstances in which they are living? This consideration enables us to understand how people view their situation and the options for improving their well-being. Stories of oppression, and how this has affected an adult's self-esteem and identity need to be understood as part of the process of relationship making. An adult may have spent their life as a member of a marginalised group and developed mechanisms for living well with this status. All this may change if they are now in a situation of dependency on the goodwill of others.

REFLECTIVE ACTIVITY

Case study: Mr Ray

Mr Ray is 85 years old. In his early youth, expressing his love for other men was illegal and in his middle years many of his friends died in the UK AIDS crisis. Throughout much of his life he has actively campaigned against prejudice and violence, for better healthcare and for an open and respectful society. His husband visits him in the care home in which he now lives, but they have been asked not to hold hands or kiss in public areas, 'or the other old people might be offended'. Mr Ray is devastated, saying 'I know how to tackle people like these, but I am just too ill to stand up for myself and others yet again.'

Reflective question
• How can you work with Mr Ray to put a stop to this abuse?

Our thinking is that you should listen to his wisdom and experiences as a campaigner, to his expertise on standing up to prejudice and use these to inform your anti-discriminatory safeguarding practice and how you will tackle this situation.

Family relationships may also change as previous coping strategies are no longer possible. The impact of disability on a person can mean the end of previous coping strategies:

'When he got angry and shouted at me, I used to go round to my friend, but now the Parkinson's is so bad I can't get out by myself so I have to put up with it.'

Or those who were once powerful are now diminished, causing ambivalence in those caring for them:

'I used to watch my dad beat my mum up. He terrified me as a child and being near him still makes me feel afraid. He can't move or speak since the stroke. I have power over him now, and I don't let him mess me about, he has to watch himself with me.'

By listening to their experience of power and oppression, we can begin to understand the person's history, their triumphs and sadness, what strengths they had in the past and how these might be drawn on in the present, and what support they may need to make changes in their lives.

Ideas for extending relationship-building skills

Relationship-building adult safeguarding practice skills can be extended with some of the suggestions in this section. Training in using these approaches is recommended.

Using trauma-informed approaches

The evolving understanding of trauma in relation to adult safeguarding merits a book to itself. Do take up development opportunities to understand the impact of trauma on the person's mental and physical health, their life chances, neurophysiology and relationships.

Guidance in England (Office for Health Improvement and Disparities, 2022) and Scotland (NHS Education for Scotland, 2019) use a common definition of trauma derived from the American Substance Abuse and Mental Health Administration (SAMHSA, 2014): 'an event, a series of events or a set of circumstances that is experienced by an individual as physically or emotionally harmful or life threatening' (SAMHSA, 2014, p 7).

It is important to understand that it is how these events have been experienced that is significant. In England, adults' experiences might be discounted because they have not been included in the Adverse Childhood Experiences (ACEs) research (UK Parliament, 2018). As with any person-centred approach, we must understand the impact on the child or adult rather than dismiss the experience.

We must be aware that the adults we work with may have had traumatic childhood experiences and have also experienced further trauma from events in adulthood. The adult may have experienced loss, abuse or trauma in childhood. In adulthood they may be living in situations of domestic abuse, coercive control or exploitation. Some have lost custody of children, or their parents or partners have died.

Trauma is not only caused by overwhelming events but also by the response to those events by others and the context of the event, including racism, poverty, gender identity, sexual orientation and cultural contexts (ACE Hub Wales, 2022).

Why is understanding trauma important?

We need to understand the impact of traumatic experiences in order to engage and work with the adult while avoiding a 're-traumatisation' through our contact with them.

In adult life a person will often develop 'survival behaviours' to cope with traumatic experiences and the feelings they are left with. These behaviours can include addictions, hoarding objects, hostility or disengagement/avoidance of interaction with services.

These behaviours may serve to numb emotion or make the person feel safe. They may have important benefits for the person.

The person may be experiencing low self-esteem, shame or guilt as a result of their experiences.

Change can be very threatening, it may make the person feel that they are going to be overwhelmed, they will not cope, they are not 'capable' or do not 'deserve'.

 ESSENTIAL INFORMATION: PRACTICE GUIDANCE

What is a trauma-informed response?

We should assume that any adult might have a history of traumatic experiences, and that these experiences may impact on their ability to feel safe within or develop trusting relationships with us. Trauma-informed practice seeks to minimise the barriers that can prevent traumatised adults engaging with support. We need to consider:

- **Safety.** How to promote the adult's feeling of physical and emotional safety: where to meet? How is the adult welcomed? Give clear explanations at each point in any process. Make it clear you are working at a pace comfortable to the adult. Explain that you do not need to go into details about the actual traumatic events, but you do want to know about the impact on the person.
- **Trust.** You may need to continually re-establish trust. Be consistent and reliable, non-judgemental and compassionate.
- **Choice.** Be clear about options, and any boundaries to those options. Acknowledge power differences. Ask for consent.
- **Collaboration.** Encourage collaboration, the adult may not trust that they are important enough to engage with you in considering options and making decisions, so start with small steps.
- **Empowerment.** Respect the adult as an equal. You are working towards mutual problem solving, which may also involve challenging the adult's perceptions or ideas.
- **Cultural considerations.** Be aware of your own culture-based values. Develop your awareness and appreciation of other cultures. Are there barriers for the person arising from the dominant social culture, from their own cultural perspective? Or from racism, islamophobia, transphobia, homophobia, etc.

We can start with how we approach the possibility of a collaborative relationship with the adult, asking the question, 'What happened to you?' instead of 'What's wrong with you?' and, if appropriate, asking, 'How has this affected you?' and 'Who is there to support you?' (ACE Hub Wales, 2022).

It is hard to use a trauma-informed approach if your organisation is not trauma informed. For example, if the organisation will not be flexible in how it engages with people, always sending letters and expecting people to attend appointments, it will be hard to make the adjustments needed to engage with an adult who feels safer avoiding contact. Beginning to be trauma aware can help you to change your own relationship building practices. Working with people who have experienced trauma is draining and challenging. Many of us who work with people have our own childhood traumas to live with. It is important to have good and reliable supportive supervision and peer support. A trauma-informed organisation will strive to support you and the people you are working with, will collaborate with experts by experience and adjust policies and procedures to enable consistent trauma-informed responses.

Using tools from systems thinking

Every individual is part of a wider system. Even the most isolated of us have connections in the present to others in our community, including neighbours and professional services. We may also have strong connections to past systems, which can have relevance to understanding our current dilemmas. The systems around us can act as facilitators or blocks to making change. It is important to understand who is part of an adult's system when understanding current and historical relationships, assessing risk of recurrence of harm, or drawing up a safeguarding plan together.

You can use a *genogram* to explore and understand family connections. Genograms look like a family tree but have many functions. As the genogram is drawn, you can talk about the people within it, their connections to the adult, and the adult's feelings about them. Drawing genograms together can help people talk about historical abuse within a family, as well as the sources of strength available to them. There are particular symbols used within genograms. There is a link to further information on how to compose a genogram at the end of this chapter. You don't need special software, just a big piece of paper, a pen and time with the adult or their family.

An *ecomap* can be used to define who else is relevant in the system around the adult. These are useful in exploring meanings, experiences and options to address the current situation. Ecomaps depict the adult's relationships and the positive and negative factors in their life. The adult is represented by a large circle in the middle of the chart. Smaller circles around the large circle represent different relationships – friendships, services, groups – and other relevant factors in the adult's life.

These smaller circles are connected to the adult's circle by different types of line. The line provides information about the nature of the relationship. There is a link to further information on how to compose an ecomap at the end of this chapter.

As a relationship-building exercise, using these tools provides opportunity for practitioners, the adult and their family to discuss and reflect on the current situation. Systems tools are also helpful in strengths-based assessment – who can help, who might hinder – and in formulating a safeguarding plan that can utilise the people and resources the adult has in their lives.

Motivational interviewing

Motivational interviewing is a person-centred approach that supports and guides adults to explore and resolve the ambivalence they feel about making changes in their lives.

Prochaska and DiClemente (1982) developed the motivational interviewing approach while working in addiction services. Practitioners are now using the principles of motivational interviewing across many fields. You may be keen to problem solve and suggest changes in others' lives, but this tendency will reduce the chance of people making changes. People are often ambivalent about change; they may not believe change is possible or are fearful of the consequences. The practitioner trained in motivational interviewing accepts that ambivalence is to be expected, and that the desire to make change comes and goes but that we can influence this by paying attention to 'readiness' for change. Motivational interviewing is underpinned by the values of collaborative partnership with acceptance of the adult, their expertise and goals, while acknowledging their absolute worth and autonomy to make their own decisions. This approach is valuable when working with people who have experienced trauma, are self-neglecting as well as other adult safeguarding scenarios such as domestic abuse.

Building relationships with colleagues from other organisations

Relationship-building skills are also vital in creating and maintaining working relationships with colleagues from other organisations or teams, whether these are temporary or part of a regular working partnership. Invaluable starting places are valuing each other, communicating clearly and taking time to listen to the concerns, challenges and successes of a partner practitioner.

Adult safeguarding work is a cause of anxiety for practitioners in all organisations who work with adults at risk. Practitioners are concerned to do the right thing, and worried about the consequences should they miss a warning sign. One voluntary sector worker says that: 'We spend the majority of the staff meeting debating whether this is an adult safeguarding concern and if we should refer on.'

Time pressures can reduce opportunities to talk with other practitioners in partner organisations. In order to control workflows, some organisations may use overly bureaucratic approaches to communication such as asking colleagues to fill in a form and await contact. Practitioners can become resentful and dismissive if one service is perceived as offloading work, feeling that it 'refers everything and then doesn't want to know'.

Adult safeguarding approaches are reliant on the ability of multi-agency partners to work together to enable the adult concerned to get the best possible outcome. All organisations are experiencing the pressures of an increasing volume of work against diminishing resources, so how can you create partnerships around an adult at risk that are effective and efficient in time and resources?

 ESSENTIAL INFORMATION: PRACTICE GUIDANCE

Top tips for building positive relationships with colleagues in other organisations

- Make sure you clearly understand the other organisation's role, responsibilities and powers.

For example, a practitioner may record feeling stuck with a case of financial abuse and record 'the police won't do anything', meaning that the police are not bringing a prosecution against the source of harm. However, an understanding of the police role and powers may result in a fuller picture of the situation: 'The police spoke with Mrs Green who did not wish to press charges but has said that she will ring 101 if the man returns. A PCSO will look in on her next week and report back any concerns.'

The second recording reflects an understanding of the police position and the details of a plan with which Mrs Green and the practitioner can work.

- Be clear with other organisations about your role, responsibility and powers.

Other organisations can also be mistaken in what the role of an adult safeguarding practitioner involves. Be clear in your own mind and make sure you can clearly communicate your role, responsibility and what powers you do and do not have.

- Understand and appreciate the invaluable skills and knowledge of colleagues from other organisations.

Acknowledge the assistance of other colleagues. Listen and use their experience and advice. They may know the adult better than your service does, especially if they have been supporting them on a daily basis or over a long period of time.

- Reflect on the pressures other organisations are experiencing, find out about the working lives of staff in other organisations.

Use empathy. How would you feel in their position?

- Discover the best way of communicating.

You will have your preferred method of communicating, but how does this work for colleagues in other organisations? Is there any point in emailing a practitioner who is focused on clinical work in the community and never opens their email? Do they have a mobile where you can leave a message? If a vital practitioner is currently on night shift, contact them when their shift starts. The inconvenience of having a ten-minute conversation in your non-work time will be outweighed by resolving an issue that would otherwise be protracted by a lack of appreciation of others' work patterns.

- Understand the partner organisation's culture and values. What is most important to them?

Patient safety? Public protection? What do they worry about? What do they pride themselves on doing well?

- Express appreciation and always get back to colleagues who refer concerns or ask for advice.

Understanding your own values and how these interact with professional ethics

Safeguarding practitioners work to professional codes of ethics. Ethical codes are moral codes of conduct or statements of behaviours that are considered professionally correct. Any judgement made about whether a practitioner's behaviour is acceptable or unacceptable will be based on the relevant code of ethics. Ethical codes will contain statements about professional values and guiding principles. Values describe what is important to a profession, an organisation or an individual.

Ethical dilemmas occur for many reasons. Dilemmas can relate to a lack of alignment between professional ethical frameworks and values, organisational policies and your personal values. Personal values contain the guiding principles used throughout life. They guide the way we live our lives and the personal decisions we make. Personal values are derived from a variety of sources: our family, life experience, education, religion, political group, peer group or the culture of the society we live in all influence us and make us unique. You are also influenced by your professional values and must be guided by these when working. However, it is not always easy to align personal and professional values.

REFLECTIVE ACTIVITY

Case study: Mr Short

Mr Short is 83 years old, very ill and frail. He is currently on Ward 20 in the local general hospital. It is hoped he will be able to go home for his last days. Your team has received an adult safeguarding concern. The ward manager reports that Mr Short's daughter assaulted him yesterday, while his other daughter was verbally abusive to him. Security were called and the police will visit Mr Short later today to ask if he wants to discuss the matter. On further enquiry you discover that Mr Short sexually abused both daughters for many years when they were children, but neither daughter had really discussed this until now. They feel angry and outraged that their father had brought such pain to both of them. Mr Short's partner would like him to die at home, but ward staff are concerned that this may be risky for him as his daughters are now threatening his safety.

You have worked with the survivors of sexual abuse for years and have a close friend who was raped by her uncle and is still traumatised. You have thought of the men who perpetuate such crimes as less than human and not worthy of your respect. You do not wish to spend any of your energy on a man who has sexually abused his children. The BASW social work code of ethics tells you that you must 'respect, uphold and defend each person's physical, psychological, emotional and spiritual integrity and well-being. You must work towards promoting the best interests of individuals and groups in society and the avoidance of harm.' You cannot treat Mr Short as if he were exempt from this principle.

Reflective question

•   What will you do?

Our thoughts are that we have encountered similar dilemmas and are sure you have too. Adults at risk have many life experiences and will have made decisions or taken actions that we do not agree with or do not feel comfortable with. If an aspect of working with an adult is challenging to your personal values, then it is very important to seek support, either through formal supervision or mentoring to ensure that your practice meets ethical professional standards and that you are not discriminatory in your decisions and actions.

Being aware of your own values, and how these have developed, is an important exercise to undertake early in any professional career. It is also important to keep reflecting on these as your life and work experience develops.

- How do your personal values affect your approach to practice?
- What biases do you have?
- How might those biases affect your decision making?

REFLECTIVE ACTIVITY

Identifying my personal values

Reflect on the following questions:

- What are my values?
- What do I think is right or wrong?
- Fair or unfair?
- What is important or valuable to me in life?

To guide you further, you might want to think about the following areas:

- Life: what do I think is a life worth living?
- Gender: what do I think is acceptable and unacceptable behaviour between men, women and others?
- Abuse: what do I think are the root causes of the abuse of certain groups in my society?
- Family: how important is family to me? Are there behaviours that would cause me to cut off contact with my family?

There may be other areas that occur to you in the course of your work, such as your values about your culture, religion or social justice. It is important to make time to reflect on your own values by writing them down or discussing them with a peer.

Where did these values come from?

- How did you formulate these values? From your cultural background? Your family or friendship group? From your life experience? From a social, political or religious group?
- It is interesting to reflect on your values throughout your career. You may keep some strong core personal values but increasingly identify with the values of your profession.

How might my personal values affect my professional judgement?

Consider each of the personal values you have identified: how might they emerge during your work with others? What impact could they have on your attitude or on the decisions you make? Write down what the consequences may be.

For example, you may find it so intolerable that an adult child exploits their parent that you do not explore with the adult whether they want the child who has harmed them to remain in their life. Conversely, family may be so important to you that you do not fully explore their wish to report the matter to the police. You may find the control an older man has over his wife's finances so unreasonable that you start to worry that he is controlling her, rather than explore the cultural expectations of the era in which the couple were married.

Becoming aware of your personal values and how these may affect your working life does reduce the risk that these will create bias. Now you have identified your personal values, and the history of their creation, are there areas you need to further reflect on in order to relearn values that are out of step with your professional code of conduct? Listen carefully to what the people you work with are telling you about their values, find out about their culture and ask them what is important in their lives.

Dilemmas between professional ethics and values and organisational values are also common. Organisational constraints may lead to the breach of ethical codes, particularly in the areas of human dignity and well-being. It is important to recognise and discuss organisational values that challenge your professional ethics. Do raise your concerns in supervision or at staff meetings, or there may be a forum to discuss professional issues in your organisation, such as a social work board or forum, or you can approach the principal social worker in your organisation to discuss and start to find a way through. Sometimes understanding another perspective will help you find an ethical route through these dilemmas and sometimes you can engage with others to initiate changes in practice.

▶ KEY MESSAGES

- **Relationships underpin all aspects of adult safeguarding work, from working with individuals and their networks, to working with individual organisations and multi-agency partners. These relationships have common elements that can be developed through practice and reflection. Empathy is a valued and useful skill that can be developed.**

- **Listening to the stories that people tell us helps us to understand the meaning of harm and risk to the adult, the emotional impact of harm and the experience the adult has of trauma, power and oppression.**

- Ethical dilemmas occur for many reasons. Dilemmas can relate to a lack of alignment between professional ethics and your personal values, or to a conflict between the values of the organisation that employs you and your professional ethics.

KNOWLEDGE REVIEW

- WHAT are the vital components of relationship-based adult safeguarding?

- WHAT do all professional relationships have in common?

- HOW do your personal values influence your professional decision making?

- IDENTIFY the core values of the organisation in which you currently work. Are there conflicts with your professional values?

FURTHER READING

- Find out more about motivational interviewing in Rosengren, D.B. (2017) *Building Motivational Interviewing Skills: A Practitioners Handbook* (2nd edn), London: Guilford Press.

- Trauma Informed Lancashire's concise and very useful *The Little Book of Trauma Informed* is worth reading for a good overview of trauma-informed or aware approaches. Download it at: https://traumainformedlancashire.co.uk/wp-cont ent/uploads/2023/05/Little-Book-of-Trauma-Informed-A5-Final-print-2023.pdf [Accessed 12 July 2024].

- See www.genopro.com/genogram/ for a practical guide to composing genograms. Why not try it out using your own family first? You can get a practical example of an ecomap at: http://barefootsocialwork.weebly.com/uploads/3/9/7/4/39743 910/ecomap_activity.pdf [Accessed 12 July 2024].

- For further reading, and thought-provoking exercises on ethics and values, read: Beckett, C., Maynard, A. and Johnson, P. (2017) *Values and Ethics in Social Work* (3rd edn), London: Sage.

7

Assessment of risk

Chapter aim

In this chapter we will consider how assessment and management of risk is central to the adult safeguarding process. This includes how to ensure that risk assessments are informed by the adult wherever possible and that changes in the level and nature of risk result in further assessment. We will consider carrying out risk assessments in a range of situations and environments, such as where people live in their own homes or in care settings, where risks to others are present – to other adults and children in the same environment or similar circumstances – as well as risks to workers in these settings.

This chapter includes:

- Working with risk: the practitioner's perspective

- Principles of best practice in risk assessment

- Approaches to risk assessment

- Risk assessment as a part of an adult safeguarding process

- Examples of risk-assessment tools: with individuals and in organisational settings

Safeguarding means protecting an adult's right to live in safety, free from abuse and neglect. It is about people and organisations working together to prevent and stop both the risks and experience of abuse or neglect, while at the same time making sure that the adult's well-being is promoted including, where appropriate, having regard to their views, wishes, feelings and beliefs in deciding on any action (DHSC, 2014, 14.7).

Working with risk: the practitioner's perspective

Situations where there is a risk to an adult with care and support needs can promote anxiety in all involved. The adult will be experiencing the impact of being harmed, and also the worry of statutory agencies being involved in their life. Although the intention of the practitioner is to improve the quality of the adult's life, the power that practitioners are perceived to have can be stressful and alarming for the people at the centre of any adult safeguarding concern. The adult's family and friends may be anxious about risk and may well have a preference for a course of action that will completely remove risk from the life of the adult but damage their independence and well-being irrevocably. Partner organisations involved can be anxious about risk and may also have a preferred course of action. In Chapter 6 we talked about understanding partner organisation cultures and how this can help in discussing risk together. There may be expectations that risk will be completely removed from an adult's life, but a lack of understanding of the potential cost to the adult's well-being of doing so.

The adult safeguarding practitioner will be aware of all these different anxieties while having some of their own. When we talk about risk with practitioners, some feel excited and interested in the dilemmas and challenges involved, while others are concerned about getting it wrong and worry about a blame culture in their organisation or society at large:

- 'I might get it wrong and then lose all my professional confidence.'
- 'What if I get it wrong and the adult dies?'
- 'I will be on the front page of the newspaper.'
- 'It may all go wrong, and there will be a Safeguarding Adults Review.'
- 'I could lose my job, and my professional registration, at the end of the day the finger will point at me.'

Working with risk can feel risky for the practitioner; public servants are very aware of demands for public enquiries and media reports on who is to blame. Safeguarding Adults Reviews (SARs) focus on the systems that help or hinder around practitioners, rather than the performance of the practitioner themselves, but SARs still create anxiety in practitioners and are focused on learning from the failure of multi-agency systems, rather than learning from multi-agency successes.

Organisations employing adult safeguarding practitioners can also feel anxious about the impact on their reputation and their culpability if things go wrong. Organisations may use managerialist approaches to attempt to reduce the impact of risk on the organisation; for example, using tick boxes rather than professional expertise and expecting complex recording of risk assessments. The Local Government Association and Association of Directors of Adult Social Services (Lawson, 2018) urge Safeguarding Adults Boards (SABs) to lead the change in the culture around risk-taking and blame:

> The SAB and partner organisations must provide the necessary context for effective working with risk in front line practice. This includes an emphasis on the importance of, and support for, a culture of positive risk taking that helps practitioners to work in risk enabling ways, where

the adult is 'at the centre.' It includes leadership and a culture that supports front line staff in balancing sometimes conflicting principles (for example empowerment and protection).

...

Support for a learning culture and a 'no blame' culture ... should be reinforced in communications with front line staff. These should openly support staff who have made and documented transparent and defensible decisions, even where these do not go to plan. There must be clear acceptance that there is responsibility at organisational level not just with front line staff. These messages should also be communicated to stakeholders and residents. (Lawson, 2018, p 8)

Practitioners should expect support from their organisations in their day-to-day work, including ready access to peer and managerial consultation, access to legal advice as needed, and regular reflective supervision together with the time to create engagement with people and the systems around them to enable meaningful risk assessment.

The UK law courts support the view that all risk cannot, and should not, be removed from a person's life. During a case in the Court of Protection concerning contact between MM and her partner (*Local Authority X v MM and Anor*, 2007) Justice Munby made the now famous statement:

Physical health and safety can sometimes be bought at too high a price in happiness and emotional welfare. The emphasis must be on sensible risk appraisal, not striving to avoid all risk, whatever the price, but instead seeking a proper balance and being willing to tolerate manageable or acceptable risks as the price appropriately to be paid in order to achieve some other good – in particular to achieve the vital good of the elderly or vulnerable person's happiness. What good is it making someone safer if it merely makes them miserable?

Anxiety about risk is often associated with the idea that the practitioner must be an expert on such matters and if only the right approach or tool is used then the risk will be successfully identified and managed. However, this way of thinking ignores the importance of the adult's expertise in their own life. The adult brings their own assessment to the process of sharing, what the meaning of the risky situation or behaviour is to them, the impact of the risk on their well-being, what strategies they have tried, what worked and what didn't, how they want their lives to be, what options are acceptable and unacceptable to them. A practitioner must bring their understanding of the circumstances that may indicate existing or increasing risk of harm, and knowledge of options that may reduce or increase a risk in the adult's circumstances. Risk is ideally assessed mutually, as a process of gathering, sharing and considering information, thoughts and wishes.

Principles of best practice in risk assessment

Using professional curiosity

As we have seen in Chapter 6, a professionally curious approach can help to build the relationships we need to work well with an adult. There are two important principles within the approach which will support risk assessment: respectful uncertainty and safe uncertainty.

Respectful uncertainty

Respectful uncertainty means taking seriously (or 'respectfully') what you are told by adults, families and other organisations about a situation while retaining an open mind. You must analyse and compare (or triangulate) the information you have in order to try to achieve an objective and deeper understanding about what may be happening.

The phrase was first used by Lord Laming during the 2003 enquiry into the death of Victoria Climbié, an eight-year-old child murdered by her great-aunt and the great-aunt's partner.

> The concept of 'respectful uncertainty' should lie at the heart of the relationship between the social worker and the family. It does not require social workers constantly to interrogate their clients, but it does involve the critical evaluation of information that they are given. (Lord Laming, 2003, p 205)

Before you see the person, you will have looked at what your organisation already knows about them. What is different now? Is there a pattern to previous contacts? Is risk increasing (cumulative risk)?

We will be gathering information from what people say, but also how they sound, look and behave. The person may tell you they are managing well, but your observations tell you that they look tired and sound depressed, the house is freezing and there is no food evident. Further conversations are needed to go deeper into finding out what is happening to them; you cannot walk away with the optimistic belief that because they say all is well, that they are. In listening to the person you will also be picking up any patterns in what they say, how they describe their situation and any incongruities in their speech or behaviour that may need further exploration.

With their permission you may also speak with their family members and other organisations who work with them. How does any new information contribute to or contradict your initial thoughts about what is going on? What do you need to check out further? What do you need to be curious about?

We may have also looked up further information about the adult's situation. For example, what do you know about the person's cultural background? What do you need to learn before you get in touch with them: are you trying to see them during a religious holiday? Are you likely to be the wrong gender for the adult to feel comfortable with? There is much you can check out with the adult, but you need to take the time to find out some basics beforehand, particularly if you have not encountered the issue previously. What about any neurological, physical or mental health issues? Ask yourself: what do I know about autism? Multiple sclerosis? Korsakoff's syndrome? Do I know how a head injury can impact on a person's mental health? How will you find out? You may have colleagues in your own or other organisations who can tell you more, or you may need to use a reputable source of information. For example, the Huntington's Disease Association has useful information about how Huntington's disease is linked with executive dysfunction and assessing mental capacity.

In order to avoid many of the pitfalls in risk assessment, we need to retain an open mind and be prepared to change our initial assessments. Because we are anxious about risk, we may want to jump to the conclusion that all is well and little or no further enquiry is needed. This is about our insecurities, not about the person's situation or our duty as practitioners.

Using respectful uncertainty will help you to avoid making the following assumptions:

- Lifestyle choice: the idea that a person has made a free choice about how they are living. If you explore the context of this so-called choice – perhaps domestic abuse, childhood trauma, discrimination, mental or physical health struggles, poverty, exploitation, substance dependence or trauma-based 'survival behaviours' – you will begin to understand how the adult has come to be in this situation.
- Normalisation: the idea that something is 'normal' for the person or family. You need to be curious about 'what has changed?', 'why now?' and be curious about what works and what is distressing for the adult and their family.
- Thinking other professionals know best: 'professional deference'. While we respect the expertise of other professionals, we will need to challenge this if we have our own observations that this may not be accurate. Other professionals may also make assumptions about what is happening, a healthy safeguarding system must involve challenge with the adult's well-being at the heart of all debates.

Safe uncertainty

There are two aspects to this principle.

If we work from the position that we can never know 100 per cent of information about a situation, we remain curious and open-minded. Mason (1993) says that practitioners should hold 'authoritative doubt', but never get caught up in looking for the 'right' answer. Be curious as to what else might be happening; be willing to be educated by the adult, their family and networks. There can be a false sense of security if you think you are 'certain' you know what is happening and why; confusing certainty with safety makes the situation and our practice less safe.

The second aspect of safe uncertainty relates to the need to keep the basic needs of the adult as a focus while you create a relationship, seek out information and develop a deeper understanding of the situation. If someone is physically or mentally unwell, has no food or is very cold/overheated – that is, their lives are at risk – keep your focus on resolving these risks as soon as possible.

Exploring the risk with the adult

Good risk assessment is built on exploration with the adult or adults experiencing the meaning of the risk. The meaning of different types of risk is unique to each individual. Some attitudes may change through the life course as experience of life is collected. Furedi (2011) interviewed 14 older people who used care services. He reported that they did not seem interested in any right to take risks but were very concerned that their views should be taken seriously, that they should be listened to and respected.

Younger people who use care services may be keen to take risks, and to explore their own potential and limitations. In order to build life experiences, we take risks and learn from them. However, we should not rely on stereotypes, there are older people who feel most alive while risk-taking, and younger people who prefer caution.

Some people may have limited experience of decision making about risk: they have been protected from life experiences and have not been able to learn about their own attitudes and responses to risk; or they may be unused to the process of weighing up the advantages and disadvantages of potential options.

Attitudes to risk can be influenced by how the adult perceives themselves and maintains their identity, the important aspects of their lives, which can include place, family and friends, and religious or moral principles.

Decisions are often made by professionals about risk in care settings without the adults who live there being consulted or made aware that a risk assessment is being undertaken. Those making decisions may justify the lack of individual involvement on the basis that the risk assessment is about an entire population using a service, not just one individual. People are not only experts in their own lives, but in the experience of living in a particular care setting. The experience of living in a care setting can contribute to a feeling of powerlessness, so it is essential that people in all settings are able to share their assessment of their own situation, and their perception of risk to themselves and to others in the same service.

REFLECTIVE ACTIVITY

Case study: Brownstone Nursing Home

The local adult safeguarding team were enquiring into concerns about organisational abuse in **Brownstone Nursing Home** for older people.

The enquiry began with a visit to the premises by two members of the team and later the commissioning of two advocates to represent adults living at the home who had 'substantial difficulty' in participating in the adult safeguarding process. Adults were asked what their experience was of living there and whether they were concerned for themselves or any other adult at the home.

Initially adults generally said that they were all right but expressed concerns for others, particularly those on a 'dementia floor', and regarding the general conduct of the night shift which they had observed being neglectful and unkind. Adults living at Brownstone were consulted throughout the enquiry and were given updates on the progress of the subsequent action plan as often or as little as they wished.

The nursing home later commissioned independent advocates to run regular sessions in the home to facilitate the identification of good quality or poor practice and to build partnerships between the people living at the home and the staff and management there.

Reflective questions

- What might make residents of Brownstone Nursing Home wary of expressing concerns about their care?
- How could advocacy promote the involvement of residents and families in improving care at the home?

Our thoughts are that power relationships, such as relative powerlessness and fear of retribution, can impact on the ability of residents to raise concerns about the risks in the nursing home environment. Building the role of independent advocates in this setting can aid the confidence of residents and families to speak out and the organisation to be more open to scrutiny.

The role of the practitioner is to act as facilitator in conversations about risk, not to be the expert. In addition to promoting mutual risk assessment, such conversations can also have an empowering impact on the adult. The practitioner can ensure the adult is respected, given time and space to make choices and is supported to act on their decisions. A discussion about harm, rights and how to get help if needed leaves an adult informed and aware that there are avenues of advice and support available to them.

The adult's well-being must be at the centre of decisions we make with them about risk

This includes promotion of the adult's human rights. In Chapter 2, we have considered how the well-being principle (Care Act 2014, Section 1) corresponds to the promotion of human rights, giving a sharper focus to ideas about duty of care, self-determination or autonomy.

ESSENTIAL INFORMATION: PRACTICE GUIDANCE

Human rights to bear in mind during risk assessment, from the ECHR

Article 2: Right to life

- Do I have the food, drink, shelter and medical treatment I need to stay alive?

Article 3: Prohibition of inhuman and degrading treatment

- Am I being physically or sexually assaulted, verbally abused, left in soiled clothing or having my dignity regularly disregarded?
- Does my own self-neglect lead to me living in degrading circumstances?

Article 5: Right to liberty and security

- Am I unable to leave where I am currently living and are people always aware of where I am and what I am doing?
- Is there no legal framework in place to make these restrictions lawful?

Article 8: Right to respect for your private life, your family life, your home and your correspondence

- Can I enjoy my home and relationships safely?

We will sometimes work with people who do not wish to engage with the adult safeguarding process but are living in high-risk situations, such as with domestic violence or self-neglect. The practitioner must be able to weigh their duty of care towards the adult and others, with the adult's right to self-determination and right to respect for private life. Focusing on the person's human rights can help us to start unpicking these dilemmas.

REFLECTIVE ACTIVITY

Case study: Michael Downes

Michael Downes has neglected his own health needs, nutrition and hygiene for many years. He is currently living in a bedsit that is unheated and cold, there is no food and the toilet is blocked. Michael has no bedclothes and does not appear to have washed for a long time. He is thin and his hair and fingernails are long and dirty.

Neighbours have called an ambulance as they helped him home after he collapsed in the street and are worried about his physical and mental state. Michael refused to be conveyed to hospital, so the ambulance crew assess his mental capacity to make a decision about having a medical assessment. They conclude that Michael does have capacity but appears to be making a decision which will lead to harm. They are not sure about any underlying medical condition, but Michael may be experiencing the symptoms of malnutrition. The crew are very aware of their duty of care to Michael and must balance his right to life with his right to autonomy. They cannot simply leave him as he wishes them to do.

They contact his GP surgery, explaining the situation and make a direct referral over the telephone to adult safeguarding, explaining the urgency of the situation. The crew stay with Michael for the next hour until the GP and duty social worker appear. He is enjoying their company although still declining to go to hospital. Michael agrees to emergency help with food, heat and bedding as an alternative to going to hospital. He also agrees to a daily visit for the next week from a support worker who will convey him the next day to the GP surgery for further tests and discussion with the GP. The social worker will visit again to undertake an assessment of his care and support needs within the next week. She is aware that support offered to Michael must be acceptable to him, and that a proportionate focus on his survival and access to health assessment in a place that is acceptable to him is a good start. He may retreat back into himself tomorrow, but he has the necessities of life for a while longer and hopefully a positive experience of getting support.

Reflective question

•   How do you use your awareness of human rights in thinking through dilemmas about self-determination and autonomy where these may conflict with your duty of care?

Our thinking is that dignity plays a key part in human rights-based adult safeguarding practice. Through sensitivity to Michael's views and right to autonomy, a dignified and sensitive relationship can be built with Michael that is likely to offer more successful long-term and low-key intervention than removing him from his home to the hospital would have. While ensuring that Michael's basic needs are met, we can hope to begin to be curious about his situation and life story.

Clarity about the balance of the practitioner's duty of care and the adult's self-determination/autonomy is vital to all risk assessment activities

Risk assessment and management processes that involve careful consideration of the adult's perspective, capacity, abilities and strengths, and how these can be supported, will help professionals avoid overly simplistic approaches that emphasise either a purely self-determining or overly protective approach. Approaches must be balanced to ensure that adults can exercise their right to self-determination while ensuring that they also enjoy their right to a life free from harm, exploitation and mistreatment. Duty of care is described in UK tort law as 'the obligation to exercise a level of care towards an individual, as is reasonable in all circumstances, by taking into account the potential harm that may reasonably be caused to that individual or his property' (*M'Alister (or Donoghue) v Stevenson*, 1932).

If an adult is unable to protect themselves from a risk that may cause their death or serious injury, we have a duty of care towards them and must respond to prevent a profound loss of human rights. Braye et al (2011) explore how practitioners approach concerns about adults who self-neglect but can make capacitated decisions about their own well-being. The principle of beneficence – the idea of kindly concern about another's welfare and the wish to promote another's well-being – acts as a counterpoint to any tendency to accept a capacitated adult's initial refusal of help. Respect for an adult's autonomy and self-determination does not, and should not, mean disengaging from continued involvement with them.

We can use professional curiosity as an approach to consider what factors may influence the adult's decision, including all contextual and cultural issues. When working with people who are in situations that threaten their human rights, but refuse or are ambivalent about help, remember:

- Relationship: to allow the adult's story to unfold and to develop an understanding of their context and perspective. Options to promote well-being may emerge from these understandings.
- Start with solutions to small problems and build from there.
- Collaboration with colleagues from partner organisations can maximise choice for the adult, as can be seen in the Michael Downes case study. Work with multi-agency colleagues on the least restrictive options that can be offered.
- Continue to be determined, curious and to demonstrate kindly concern.

Use the recording and supervision methods within your organisation that support defensible decision making

Defensible decisions are decisions that can be judged as well-considered and evidenced decisions, regardless of any outcome, and are taken with the full involvement of the adult and, where appropriate, their network of support, other services and professionals.

Kemshall et al (2013, p 19) describes defensible practice as practice that 'intertwines' aspects of professionalism with procedural compliance, noting that procedure should support professional judgement, and not limit the application of skills and knowledge. Decision making must be evidenced, in order to be accountable to the adult and to your organisation, and to provide a rationale for the decision you have reached.

Recording well will provide an accurate picture of the nature of the risk and the responses made to other practitioners. Risk assessments can influence future decisions about an adult, and badly made or recorded decisions will risk unfair and unjust treatment of the adult or misunderstanding of their true situation in the future.

 ESSENTIAL INFORMATION: PRACTICE GUIDANCE

Top tips for evidencing defensible decision making

- Make sure that all reasonable steps have been taken to respond to the concern and risks described.
- Use reliable assessment methods to inform decisions.
- Thoroughly analyse and evaluate all the information available.
- Record how you have arrived at the decision. Communicate this to others and keep reviewing with the adult and evaluating the need for further decisions.
- Follow your local policies and procedures and make sure you have considered your legal responsibilities.

Approaches to risk assessment

Positive risk-taking

The word 'risk' is often seen as synonymous with danger or harm in adult safeguarding. Risk assessment can become unbalanced if we only look at the negative impact of risk on an adult's life. Positive risk-taking is a process that starts with the identification of the potential benefit as well as harm in continuing with a risky behaviour or in a situation where there are risks. An emphasis on the positive aspects of risk-taking aims to encourage and support people to take risks in order to achieve personal change or growth.

We need to understand the adult's perspective of what they will gain from taking risks, and understand what they will lose if they are prevented from doing so.

REFLECTIVE ACTIVITY

Case study: Simon Grant

Simon Grant's daughter, Jemma, was addicted to heroin. She started seeing Simon again after two years of absence. He was initially delighted and, when she said that she had moved back to the area and was looking for accommodation, he invited her to sleep on the sofa in his sheltered housing flat. Jemma moved in, but so did her partner, and after a week various friends also began to frequent Simon's flat and use drugs there.

The sheltered housing landlord supported Simon to tell his daughter to leave and she did so, but Simon was heartbroken; he wanted to stay in touch with Jemma and help her all he could. Jemma was his only family and Simon wanted her to be part of his life.

Reflective question

- It is important for Simon to have his daughter in his life. He hopes that she will fulfil his need for family and relationship. What can you do to support Simon to take this risk?

Our thoughts are that the relationship between Simon and his daughter is very important to him. A risk management plan that ignores or sidelines this key part of life is likely to fail as he is not likely to follow it. A plan that minimises the actual, not presumed, risks to Simon from his daughter and supports him to maintain contact in a considered way is likely to be more successful for him.

A *strengths-based approach* will support shared conversations about risk between practitioners and adults. A strengths-based assessment focuses on the adult's situation and identifies the factors that get in the way of living without harm and those that can help the adult to protect themselves. Strengths-based approaches underpin the idea of Making Safeguarding Personal.

Contrast these two statements:

1. Jane has a learning disability and is vulnerable to exploitation from men. She is in need of protection against exploitation.
2. Jane has a wide social circle and attends two social clubs a week. She would appreciate some support around understanding relationships as she has never had the opportunity to do this, and an opportunity to plan ahead what she will do should an abusive man try to exploit her. Jane would like to involve her two closest friends in the planning activity as they are her frequent companions when she is out enjoying her life.

In a strengths-based conversation:

- The **practitioner** brings their knowledge and understanding of the factors that can increase or reduce risk and their knowledge of options that may help.
- The **adult** brings their knowledge and understanding about their own life and well-being:
  - What does well-being mean to them? What do they think is important now in supporting their well-being and what isn't important? What kind of life do they want to lead?
  - What solutions they have tried? What worked, or didn't work? What have they concluded from this?
- What gets in the way of the adult being able to use their strengths and make changes in their lives? These factors can include being in an institution with no access to representation or advocacy, their own feelings of depression, fear or previous experiences.
- What are the formal and informal systems around them? What supports and resources are available for them to use? What helps the adult; for example, family members, friends? Are there positive risk-taking opportunities, or opportunities to develop a supportive social network?

These conversations can begin to shape a safeguarding plan that will protect the adult while enhancing their well-being.

Key areas to think about in risk assessment

Every individual and every situation is different. However, there are key areas that can be usefully explored when talking about, and thinking through, risk and the assessment of risk:

Consider *power relationships*:

- Is the adult dependent on others to provide for their basic needs, such as food, drink, heating, clothing, safety and so on? How much can they influence how they are supported?

Dependency on others can limit the adult's ability to self-protect. Needing support with basic needs can be used as a tool for exploitation and control by others; for example, threatening to withhold food or care, or using the relationship to control an adult's finances.

- Family dynamics, current and historical:
  - What is the story of relationships within the family? Has the adult at risk previously abused or been abused by family members? Is there a family history of domestic abuse? Did the adult have a particular role within the family that they can no longer fulfil, leaving others feeling frustrated or

angry? Is the adult being subject to abuse, coercion or control by another family member?

- The adult's history, including historical abuse, trauma and how the adult is affected by those experiences:
  - Has the adult experienced abuse while in an institution? Have they had any childhood or life trauma? How does this affect their self-esteem and identity now? How does it affect their ability to self-protect? Are there services they will not engage with through fear or because of previous experiences?
- Addiction:
  - Does the carer or carers, and/or the adult have an addiction to a degree that their everyday lives are affected? Substance dependence can impair the adult's ability to self-protect and leave them more vulnerable to exploitation. Carers, family members or friends who are substance dependent or addicted to gambling may find it difficult to focus on the adult's care or may exploit them in order to fund their habit.

People who say go away: risk assessment where risk is high

Despite all of the practitioner's relationship-building skills there will be occasions when risks to the adult or others are reported as being high in potential impact but it is impossible to engage the adult in any conversation about this. If other adults or children are affected, or if the person's right to life ('vital interests') or other absolute human right is reported to be at risk, we must continue to enquire and try to mitigate risk.

When working with risk where there is difficulty engaging with the adult, you should consider:

- How imminent is the risk and how severe is the potential impact on the adult or others? If the risk is imminent – the situation occurs daily and the consequences of the risk could happen soon or now – and the impact on the adult or others will be serious, you may well need to convene an urgent multi-agency strategy meeting with services who know the adult, or who can contribute to a plan to engage them.
- Work with colleagues from primary health teams, fire and rescue, police, any care providers, environmental health and, as appropriate, children's services, the adult's housing provider or third sector groups to problem solve together and find a way forward to engage and work with the adult and protect others in the situation.
- Look again at the information you have. Is there a service or person who is able to help you engage with the adult? Is there someone who can begin engagement or help you to get in through the door or facilitate a conversation?
- Try to understand the adult's beliefs, fears and previous experiences. Why are they refusing to see you? Is there something that can be done to reassure the adult? People are sometimes reacting to the last experience or practitioner they saw, so try to discover what happened and whether anything can be different now.

Ultimately, there may be adults who decline to engage with any offer of support but are still in high-risk situations. Your local authority may have a forum in which to discuss cases where it is difficult to engage the adult but risks to their well-being or that of others is high.

 ESSENTIAL INFORMATION: PRACTICE GUIDANCE

Practice example: Plymouth Creative Solutions Forum

Services and commissioners in Plymouth saw an increase in the numbers of people presenting with highly complex pictures of substance misuse, physical and psychiatric co-morbidities. In addition, the Care Act 2014 required a more integrated response to people with issues of self-neglect and who present a risk to themselves or others.

The Creative Solutions Forum developed from the need to establish a way to support individuals, staff and agencies to understand and manage risk fluidly. The aim of the Forum is to provide an additional multi-agency, multidisciplinary response, which includes commissioners who can agree bespoke packages of care, enable better risk sharing and risk management between agencies, and facilitate improved outcomes for people than could be achieved with a 'usual care' approach. The Forum members work as partners to consider creative options for people with highly complex needs and presentations that require a multi-agency response and where other single or multi-agency processes have been exhausted.

The Forum meets monthly and is chaired by a safeguarding adult's independent officer. Accountability for the individual person remains with the referring agency; however, where the level of risk or complexity demands multi-agency intervention or escalation, the Forum will identify appropriate actions, agencies or resources to reduce the level of risk. The Forum considers two or three referrals per month, ordinarily allowing one hour to discuss each referral. The agency making the referral will present a case summary for no more than 15 minutes, followed by focused consideration of risk, options and solutions for 30 minutes, and finally 15 minutes to conclude and agree actions with a review date. At the beginning of each Forum meeting, a short review/update of the previous month's referrals is made to monitor agreed outcomes. The Forum representatives or agencies agree to take responsibility for delegated actions and principally support the referring agency with managing risk. Referring agencies agree to return to a future Forum as appropriate to update on progress towards outcomes.

> The Forum has had an impact on partnership work across strategic and operational teams. Agencies no longer feel alone with high-risk situations, the existence of a safeguarding partnership is tangible and is being built on across the Plymouth safeguarding system.
>
> Plymouth SAB (2019)

Risk assessment as a part of an adult safeguarding process

Assessing risk is particularly pertinent at different intervals in any piece of adult safeguarding work. Here we give an overview of relevant questions you could ask about risk at each interval.

On receiving a concern from a third party

- Has the referrer taken any immediate action needed to protect the adult if they are reported to be at high and imminent risk of harm? If not, what immediate action needs to be taken and by whom?
- Has the harm already created an unsafe situation for the adult that needs to be addressed urgently? For example, are they in need of accommodation or urgent financial support? Why refer now? Has there been a sudden or cumulative change in the risks the referrer is aware of?
- Will the risk to the adult be increased by contact with a safeguarding adults practitioner? Is a plan needed to ensure the adult can be seen in a safe location, and how any safety risks will be minimised? Are there any risks to the visiting professional?
- Are there children who may be at risk of harm in the situation? Or other adults with care and support needs? Are there organisations, including child protection or children's services, that must be contacted?

Gathering the initial information to support a risk assessment about the concern and way forward

Remember to use the principles of respectful uncertainty and safe uncertainty. Primary information comes from talking with the adult, or adults, concerned. Information also needs to be gathered from the person referring the concern: what do they believe the risks to be, and what have they done so far to mitigate risk?

You could also talk with other services involved with the adult as proportionate to the reported concern. If risks are reported as life-threatening or others are at imminent risk of harm, other organisations can be contacted without the adult's permission. Otherwise, do wait until you have the adult's consent to contact others. There may be practitioners who have specialist knowledge of relevance to the concern; for example, tissue viability nurses, primary care nurses, and doctors, including psychiatrists.

Do look at your organisation's existing records. Have there been previous concerns about the adult? What helped or hindered? Is the situation getting worse? If the adult uses a care service, or is in a hospital or social care setting, have there been previous concerns about the provider? When were the adult's care and support needs last reviewed? What were the outcomes?

REFLECTIVE ACTIVITY

Case study: Delores Wilson

Delores Wilson lives with her daughter, Michelle. Delores is 50 years old and a wheelchair user. She has a diagnosis of secondary progressive multiple sclerosis (MS) and is also partially sighted. Delores' sister, Evelyn, has contacted the adult social care front door service as she is concerned that her sister is being kept away from her and has said that she is frightened of Michelle, who shouts at her.

An adult safeguarding practitioner follows up this conversation with Evelyn who is worried as Michelle will not let her into the flat and thinks that she is intimidating Delores. Delores has telephoned her and says she is very down at the moment as she is feeling weaker, and the symptoms of MS are progressing. Delores says that Michelle has been shouting at her and leaves her in bed on the weekends so she 'doesn't get in the way'. Evelyn does not want Michelle to know that she has contacted social services and explained that Michelle was mentally unwell 15 years ago and was sectioned and taken to hospital. If she knows that social services have been contacted, Michelle may prevent all access to Delores.

The social worker contacted Delores' GP who had a different view of Michelle. The GP explains that Michelle had always seemed supportive of Delores and has a good relationship with the GP and MS consultant.

The social worker looked up both Delores' and Michelle's records and noted that there was a concern six months ago when Delores said that Evelyn was continually asking to borrow money and she suspected was stealing from her. Part of the safeguarding plan was that Evelyn no longer saw Delores alone but only when Michelle was present. On balance the social worker decided to telephone Delores and ask if she could visit to talk about her current well-being as she had received a report from a 'concerned person' that Delores was struggling.

> ### Reflective questions
> * What different views of the nature, level and type of risk to Delores are present in this case?
> * What should you do to ensure that all alleged risks are considered?
>
> *Our thoughts* are that Delores' views of both Evelyn and Michelle are crucial to understanding the nature and level of risk in this situation. Building Delores' trust in the safeguarding practitioner is essential to ensure that she feels safe to explain her views.

When planning an enquiry

You need to consider the known risks and explore the need for an interim safeguarding plan to promote the well-being of the adult or adults involved while enquiries are undertaken. Remember the principle of safe uncertainty: are the person's basic needs met? Any planning discussion should also consider how risk will be assessed with the adult or their representative, and how to mitigate any risks caused to the adult concerned by the enquiry itself.

In our example of Delores Wilson, the social worker had a discussion with her team manager before going out to see Delores. They decided that it was important for the social worker to see Delores alone. If this proved to be challenging the social worker should work with the services already in place to find opportunities to see Delores alone. This allows the practitioner to consider other possibilities for seeing Delores alone; for example, when Michele is out or at any external venue Delores might attend. Delores can then be told about her sister's concern. The social worker will also talk with Michele about her well-being as the carer of a parent who is becoming more disabled, and find out how she is feeling about her life.

During the Section 42 enquiry

A central activity within any enquiry is establishing facts and assessing risk with the adult and the system around them. We may be able to have a full discussion with an adult, but if they have 'substantial difficulty' in being involved we need to make sure that they are supported by an advocate or representative who knows them well. If the adult does not have the mental capacity to understand information about risk, we can still follow the steps below as part of a best-interest decision-making process, ensuring that we get the fullest picture possible of the adult's previous history and wishes and current situation. Below we present a framework for gathering information about risk from individuals. It is adapted from a framework devised by White (2017).

ESSENTIAL INFORMATION: PRACTICE GUIDANCE

Making decisions about risk with individuals

Step 1 *Understanding the adult's wishes and feelings in relation to the risk identified by the concern*

Listen to what the adult says about the situation; gather information about the history of the situation and the relationships and networks around the adult. Who is important to the adult? Who do they think knows and understands what is happening? Are they isolated? Do they have someone they can count on? Gather information about their life, what is important to them, their wishes and feelings. What outcomes do they want from working with you? This approach will begin to develop a sense of shared responsibility for safety as well as trust and shared understanding.

- What has happened previously?
- What works, what didn't and what can be learned?
- What are their views on the risk, and the benefits and drawbacks of the situation?
- Explore other aspects of their well-being: what about physical, social and psychological well-being?

Speak with others who are identified as important to the adult, with their permission.

Work with the adult to write a list of wishes and needs in order of importance to them.

Step 2 *Understanding and clarifying the impact of risks on the adult*

After listing wishes and needs, set out the risks and the impact of these, including benefits and drawbacks, in written or another accessible summary form. This will provide a good basis for further discussion with the adult, their family or other representatives, and other professionals as well as providing a means of sharing information and challenging perceptions. The adult may change their view after seeing information listed like this. If there are limited benefits but serious negative impacts identified and the adult remains unable to see the risk, further exploration of what is happening to lead the adult to this conclusion is needed. Are they under duress, or counting on previous history and coping mechanisms/survival behaviours, or is there some impairment of the adult's ability to understand, retain, use and weigh information?

When listing the risks with the adult, you can apply the simple tests of likelihood and impact to understand the extent of perceived risk (see Figure 7.1). List how much the identified risks contribute to the adult's desired quality of life and well-being. Identify what strengths or positive factors are present that may mitigate risk. Consider what recovery and restorative actions are needed.

Step 3 *The safeguarding plan: enabling and responding to risk*

We will explore how Steps 1 and 2 inform safeguarding planning in Chapter 9. These key steps are:

- Use multi-agency meetings, or strategy discussions with multi-agency partners, or reflective or peer supervision to support you to consider the range of concerns, opinions, experiences, culture, perceptions, risks and legal responsibilities. These aspects can be shared with the adult while agreeing a response to risk.

Key questions to consider:

- How can safety be promoted without damaging the adult's human rights, or other benefits from the situation?
- Are there ways of supporting the adult to change the situation to reduce risk while still respecting choice and promoting the quality of life they want?
- What could go wrong; what contingencies are needed?
- Does everyone involved have a joined-up understanding of the adult's situation, what is important to them and what the risks are?

The safeguarding plan is made either during the enquiry or after it has concluded. The safeguarding plan brings all the previous steps together into an agreed plan. This will summarise the adult's wishes, views and feelings, the agreed risk assessment, enablement solutions and agreed actions to respond to residual risk and contingency planning, plus how the plan will be considered successful and reviewed.

Useful questions to think about may be:

- Does the adult feel safer? If they are concerned, who will they contact and how?
- How are the person's identified outcomes being met?
- When will you both agree that the need for the plan has ended?
- If the adult cannot tell you themselves, how will you assess the success of any plan? Who will tell you and how often?

The impact of existing risk on the adult's well-being must be considered with the adult at every review of a safeguarding plan. Risk assessments and plans are not static and can be revisited usefully throughout the course of working with the adult.

Examples of risk assessment tools: with individuals and in organisational settings

Now we present some examples of risk assessments with individuals and in organisational settings. Remember that tools are there to support your professional judgement; they must be used to focus and support your thinking rather than give you an outcome or formula that tell you what to do.

Simple risk assessment tools are usually based on the idea of likelihood or imminence and degree of harm. 'Red amber green' (also known as RAG) ratings are often used to denote the degree of likelihood or harm. An example template for simple RAG-rated risk assessment may be found in Figure 7.1:

- If the likely imminence of harm is low and the impact of the harm is low or medium, risk may be considered low or 'green' (G).
- If there is a high or medium likelihood of the harm occurring or recurring and the impact is low, the risk is medium or 'amber' (A); if the impact is medium or high then the risk is high or 'red' (R).
- If there is a high likelihood that the harm will occur or recur and the impact of the harm is medium or high then the risk rating is also high or 'red' (R).

There are more complex versions of RAG ratings, sometimes with numerical values attached. However, understanding the concept of RAG rating will help you understand how a number of agencies, in particular the police, will rate and present risk information.

Figure 7.1: Risk assessment RAG rating template

Likelihood				
	High	A	R	R
	Medium	A	R	R
	Low	G	G	A
		Low	Medium	High

Impact of harm

Risk assessment, self-neglect and hoarding

Do start with an assessment of all aspects of the adult's well-being. This may mean a care and support needs assessment under Section 9 or 11 of the Care

Act 2014. Do involve colleagues with other specialisms – for example GPs, substance misuse services, mental health, learning disability – while making sure that all assessment activities take account of the person's own pace and engagement preference.

Do explore:

- The adult's story, including the background to the self-neglect or hoarding: when did it start, was there a trigger event? Is there a benefit for the person in maintaining the behaviour? Are there survival behaviours?
- The adult's hopes, fears and goals.
- The relevant factors: the adult's mental capacity, mental ill health, physical health, disability, autism or other neurodivergence, substance dependence, age and frailty, social isolation and support, acceptance of care and support, the degree of insight the person has into their difficulties.
- The type and level of self-neglect/hoarding. What is being neglected? What is the potential impact of the self-neglect?
- What is the likely impact on other people, including any children?
- Is there a cumulative risk to the adult and others?
- Is there any suspicion of abuse: could self-neglect be an indicator of domestic abuse, criminal or sexual exploitation? Is the person also being neglected by someone responsible for their care?
- What are the relevant legal frameworks: is the person at risk of eviction? Are there pressing environmental concerns or public health concerns, or anti-social behaviour? Are there debt issues that may lead to prosecution, other criminal convictions, or child protection concerns?
- Is there anyone obstructing or preventing work with the person, including family members or other people at the property?

Some supplementary questions to think about for adults who hoard (adapted from Barnett, 2018):

- What do they hoard?
- Are they **saving** items (hoarding) or allowing clutter to **accumulate?** (accumulation may be indicative of physical or mental health issues, impairment of executive functioning, substance dependence etc.)
- What level of distress (on a scale of 0–10) do they feel when losing/throwing away/recycling an object?
- What is most difficult to remove?
- How did they feel when they obtained the items?
- How do they feel about the clutter? Use a clutter scale: how much do they think there is? In this way, you can understand the amount of insight an adult has, and perhaps the amount of shame they feel.
- When did the hoarding begin? If recent: what happened? If in the past: how do they think it started?

- Can they use their kitchen/toilet/bathroom/bedroom? Is it now difficult to eat, store food, sleep, keep clean? Are essential repairs needed to heating, lighting etc. that cannot take place? Is there mould or damp?
- Is there a risk of fire?
- Do they lose objects or important paperwork in the house?
- Do they have problems sorting things out and finding places for things? Are they able to physically or mentally manage these things?
- Has anyone helped them lately? How do they feel about people coming into the house and seeing the clutter?

Specific risk assessment tools are used by agencies working with people who are experiencing domestic abuse

The tools available through SafeLives are widely used by multi-agency partnerships. The domestic abuse, stalking and 'honour'-based violence (DASH) risk checklist is a tried and tested way to understand risk between intimates in domestic settings. SafeLives have produced some additional guidance about older people and disabled people (2016a, 2016b) to accompany the more generic DASH assessments. Older or frail people may not always score as high risk on DASH (Bows et al, 2023) and professional judgement will be needed to adjust the DASH checklist to account for a serious risk of injury when an older or frail person is pushed over, something that can be as serious as using a weapon. 'High' or 'medium' risk from harm from domestic abuse can also present differently for older or disabled adults; there may be no weapon involved but the threat of or actual disconnection or removal of medical equipment or medicines can be life-threatening. Some areas have developed a specific DASH risk assessment for older people to account for these differences (Cambridgeshire and Peterborough, 2021).

The DASH risk assessment is used to ascertain whether a referral should be made to a Multi-Agency Risk Assessment Conference (known as MARAC), where different organisations will work together to make a plan to address further harm to the adult. As well as MARACs to address domestic abuse, you may also have specific MARACs in your area that focus on sexual exploitation.

Multi-Agency Public Protection Arrangements (known as MAPPA) are risk-assessment meetings to support multi-agency working with people who present a significant risk to the public. Through this mechanism, various organisations, led by the police, probation and prison service, can assess, plan and work together to manage the risks posed by violent and sexual offenders. The police, probation and prison service are 'responsible bodies' for the MAPPA process. Local authorities are one of the 'duty to cooperate' bodies; that is, they must cooperate with the MAPPA arrangements to manage the risk posed by an offender (MoJ, 2018). It is worth considering a MAPPA referral for individuals who are controlling and exploiting vulnerable groups, including adults at risk. MAPPA enables organisations to share information and cooperate to manage the risk posed by such individuals.

Do find out who the MAPPA coordinator is in your area who can discuss potential referrals with you.

Risk assessments in organisations

We first explored Marsland's work in Chapter 5. The six themes within the research (Marsland et al, 2015) are useful in identifying areas of risk for the people who live in or use a service. The researchers suggest that concerns spread across a range of the thematic groups can indicate an increased risk of abuse, harm and neglect; however, our practice experience is that a concern about management and leadership alone can indicate the possibility of a failing service where people may be harmed – if not imminently then at some point in the future – unless remedial action is taken.

The six thematic areas are:

- concerns about management and leadership;
- concerns about staff skills, knowledge and practice;
- concerns about residents' behaviours and well-being;
- concerns about the service resisting the involvement of external people and isolating residents;
- concerns about the way services are planned and delivered; and
- concerns about the quality of basic care and the environment.

An example of how the themes can be used in assessing risk to adults using a residential service is presented in the Reflective Activity.

REFLECTIVE ACTIVITY

Blueskies Care Home: initial risk assessment

Evidence has been gathered via a contract compliance visit, complaints from residents and relatives and the accounts given by Blueskies staff. In setting out the information in this way, we can see individual and group risk, and identify what risk-mitigating actions need to be taken.

Using Table 7.1 can enable you to spot individual as well as group risk. You can also easily see where actions need to be taken.

- What actions can be taken to try to stabilise the situation while further improvements are made? *Our thoughts* are that an urgent discussion is needed with the provider regarding the need for the manager to be present and urgent attention to the need to improve staffing to manage the morning shift and address staff and resident morale. We must also identify all who live at Blueskies who require time-specific medication, have a low Waterlow score (an indication of high risk of pressure areas), who require lifting, who must have specific daily health support or who are distressed. We need to prioritise these individuals for a health and social care review of their needs with a view as to how to further mitigate risk, including distress.

There also needs to be a discussion with the provider and commissioners and potentially no new admissions until the home is adequately staffed.

Table 7.1: Example, Blueskies Care Home – Risk themes in organisations against the six thematic areas (Marsland, 2015)

Theme	Evidence	Who is affected
Concerns about management and leadership	The responsible manager is covering two other services.	All who live at Blueskies.
	No plans have been made regarding low levels of staffing on the morning shift.	
Concerns about staff skills, knowledge and practice	Staff are cutting corners to try to get people up and washed in the mornings.	All who live at Blueskies, and particularly people who need assistance to move (60% of current residents).
	Residents report that their dignity and that of others is being compromised.	
	There are two complaints of staff being rough and short-tempered and one incident when correct manual handling procedures were not used.	
Concerns about residents' behaviours and well-being	People are being left in soiled beds for two hours into the morning shift.	All who live at Blueskies and particularly those who rely on time-specific medication (such as Mrs X who has diabetes, Mr G and Ms P who have Parkinson's). People who need assistance to move.
	One observation of a person crying.	
	One incident when medication was missed.	
	One injury reported through poor lifting practice.	
Concerns about the service resisting the involvement of external people and isolating residents	No reports made to adult safeguarding or CQC regarding these incidents.	All who live at Blueskies and particularly Miss V and Mr T who have new physio post-cerebrovascular accident plans.
	People left in their rooms for long periods.	
	Advice of physiotherapists sought but not acted on.	

(continued)

Table 7.1: Example, Blueskies Care Home – Risk themes in organisations against the six thematic areas (Marsland, 2015) (continued)

Theme	Evidence	Who is affected
Concerns about the way services are planned and delivered	Insufficient staff on morning rota. No plans to recruit or use agency staff. Home is still admitting people who are not mobile or have dementia and cannot self-care.	All who live at Blueskies and particularly newly admitted people, whom staff do not have time to get to know.
Concerns about the quality of basic care and the environment	Staff cannot support people in the morning so that people are left at risk of not getting meds on time; no one to assist with eating; injuries through poor lifting practice; loss of dignity and resultant distress; increased risk of pressure area and other injury through being left in soiled bedding. Emotional harm as some staff are short-tempered and poorly led.	All who live at Blueskies and particularly all those already mentioned plus people with existing pressure areas or low Waterlow scores.

▶ KEY MESSAGES

- An adult is the expert about their own life, about the risks they personally face and the risks in the service they are using or living in.

- Practitioners bring expertise about indicators, resources and options and can facilitate discussions about risk.

- Using a professional curiosity approach will enable a deeper and objective assessment of risk.

- Risk assessment tools are not a substitute for professional judgement.

- Remember that decision making about risk must be well-evidenced and defensible.

KNOWLEDGE REVIEW

- WHAT are the two important principles of professional curiosity?

- WHAT do we mean by strengths-based assessment?

- HOW can you assess the risk of harm in organisations?

📖 FURTHER READING

- It is worth reading Emily White's chapter to help you reflect further on how strengths-based approaches inform a Making Safeguarding Personal approach to risk assessment: White, E. (2017) 'Assessing and Responding to Risk', in A. Cooper and E. White (eds) *Safeguarding Adults Under the Care Act: Understanding Good Practice*, London: Jessica Kingsley, pp 110–27.

- There are some good adult safeguarding resources on professional curiosity around, try South Gloucestershire SAB (2023) at https://sites.southglos.gov. uk/safeguarding/wp-content/uploads/sites/221/2015/05/Professional-Curios ity-Guidance-2023.pdf or Leeds SAB (2020) https://leedssafeguardingadu lts.org.uk/learning-and-development/professional-curiosity-for-practitioners [Accessed 12 July 2024]. Have a look at your local SAB website to see if there is a professional curiosity guide there.

- It is important to have training on how to safely use the SafeLives DASH checklist, but in the meantime find out more at: https://safelives.org.uk/sites/default/files/ resources/Dash%20risk%20checklist%20quick%20start%20guidance%20FI NAL.pdf [Accessed 12 July 2024].

8

Decision making in adult safeguarding

Chapter aim

In this chapter we will discuss decision making in adult safeguarding, when decisions are made and who makes them. Barriers and supports to effective decision making are reviewed. We will look at how some of the organisations who are involved in adult safeguarding make decisions and what factors and information are used to do this.

This chapter includes:

- Making a referral about a concern

- Decision making about the Section 42 duty

- Concerns that do not meet the criteria for the Section 42 duty

- What if there is disagreement about the decision?

- Quality and adult safeguarding

- Decisions about advocacy

- Who should undertake the enquiry?

- Decisions about what happens as a result of an enquiry

- Decisions made by other organisations

Making a referral about a concern

A set of decisions have to be made before making a referral to the local authority about a concern. The vast majority of referrals are made by other services rather than the adult or their family and friends (NHS Digital, 2023). A self-referral has the advantage of the adult consenting to and wanting help to protect themselves. In order to decide to refer themselves, the adult must know that adult safeguarding exists and how to get in touch, and have the means to do so, such as access to a telephone or the internet. The adult must be able to quickly and simply contact an adult safeguarding service and have trust that the social workers or contact centre workers they are talking to will listen to them and help rather than make their situation worse. Adults at risk need to know that adult safeguarding is the right service for them to speak with.

REFLECTIVE ACTIVITY

Self-referrals

How easy is it for adults at risk in your area to self-refer for help from adult safeguarding? What can be done to increase their awareness and access to contact with the adult safeguarding service?

Here are some ideas:

- Accessible leaflets and other materials which highlight the 'right number' to ring.
- Local awareness raising events: some local authorities and Safeguarding Adults Boards support and promote Adult Abuse Awareness Week or World Elder Abuse Day every year.
- Mini awareness events in groups or one-to-one with service users and carers linked into provided services.
- Support from other professionals and providers to self-refer, rather than making a referral on the adult's behalf. In this way the adult will be involved in their own safeguarding from the initial point. Or, if this does not increase risk to the adult, the professional could consider contacting adult safeguarding services while still with the adult; in this way the adult can inform how the concern is expressed and give information for themselves.

Another service may be referring because the adult has disclosed harm to them, or they have witnessed abuse or indicators of potential harm. The referrer should make an assessment of risk with the adult in order to decide what steps are needed to address any immediate safety issues. The emergency services may need to be called if there is a threat of or actual violence or injury.

The adult may need support if they wish to call the police. In considering this decision with the adult, it is important to appreciate the implications of not doing so for any future prosecution. Although the adult and those supporting them must strive to retain evidence of harm where there is a likelihood of the need for an investigation of a crime, the police are best at advising how and taking action to do so. If, for example, a sexual assault has occurred, the adult will want to wash at some point and may be unsure initially whether they want to speak to the police. Forensic evidence will be lost unless it has been secured via a specialist sexual assault forensic service. Sexual assault referral centres (SARCs) offer the opportunity for evidence to be secured and allow the adult to think through the decision about whether to speak to the police at their own pace. SARCs can provide support and advice as well as the facilities to report the assault to the police. The Survivors Trust (2023) offers further details on SARCs across the UK.

ESSENTIAL INFORMATION: PRACTICE GUIDANCE

Consent to make a referral

If the adult is unable or unwilling to make the adult safeguarding referral themselves, it is important that the referrer asks for the adult's consent to make a referral. If the adult lacks the capacity to consent to a referral, the referrer must be sure that they are making the referral in the adult's best interests. It is very helpful if the referrer can give information about the adult's mental capacity with regard to adult safeguarding. For example, can the adult make a decision about whether a referral should be made or not? Are they able to engage in discussions about their own safety, including an understanding of the potential for longer-term harm as well as immediate effects? If an enquiry is subsequently initiated, it will be the responsibility of the organisation making the enquiry to assess the adult's capacity to make the relevant decisions as they will be the decision maker at that point, but an early indication that there may be a need for support with decision making is very useful, so that early contact with an advocate can be considered.

To give meaningful consent to a referral, the adult needs to have enough information to understand what making a referral to adult safeguarding entails, and what is likely to happen next. That means that the referrer must also have a good understanding about what a referral entails and what the response is likely to be, and to be able to explain this in a way that is honest and supportive.

It may not be safe to see the adult to ask for their consent before referral, in which case the referral must go ahead with the safety concern information highlighted so that the local authority is aware of the risk. Remember, if children are present and at risk of harm, then a referral must be made to child protection services.

If the adult decides not to consent to a referral, one can still be made in the circumstances detailed here. It is important that the adult knows a referral has been made and, although their lack of consent has been overridden, that they can still be involved or kept informed as much or little as they wish. Referrals can be made without the consent of the adult if there is a public interest (when others are also at risk) or a vital interest (when the adult may die or be injured). Reasons for making a referral without the consent of the adult can be:

- there are other adults at risk from the same source of harm;
- the adult is subject to duress or coercion to prevent them consenting to a referral;
- there is a high risk to the health and safety of the adult at risk (their 'vital interests' or ECHR Article 2 right to life is endangered);
- the adult does not have the mental capacity to decide to consent or not to a referral and a decision has been made that a safeguarding referral should be made in their best interests; and
- a serious crime has been committed or it is believed is about to be committed. A 'serious crime' can be defined as in Schedule 1 of the Serious Crime Act 2007, which lists a number of serious offences that:
  - involve the use of violence, including the use of weapons and firearms;
  - are sexual assaults;
  - result in substantial financial gain;
  - cause substantial financial loss to the victim; and
  - are conducted by a large number of persons 'in pursuit of a common purpose' such as gang intimidation, sexual exploitation or modern slavery.

What should I do if the adult refuses to consent to an adult safeguarding referral?

It is important to consider what prevented consent being obtained. Does the referrer need to return to the adult to obtain their consent? In situations where there appears to be an imminent risk of harm to the adult's vital interests, this may not be appropriate. In other situations, as already noted, it will be important for the referrer to explain to the adult that they want to refer to adult safeguarding, explain their concern and ask the adult what their initial views and wishes are. Some professional referrers report feeling uncomfortable about doing this. They may fear there will be an impact on their relationship with the adult. It is not unusual to discuss referral and potential outcomes with the adult only to be told that the criteria for the Section 42 duty is not met and there will be no involvement from the local authority. Such situations need to be explored carefully with the referrer, as you will need to find out what the adult's expectation is and discuss the next steps the adult and referrer can take.

Decision making about the Section 42 duty

The Section 42 duty on the local authority exists from the point at which a concern is received (LGA, 2019a). The Care Act 2014 divides the duty into two parts: Sections 42(1) and 42(2). The first decision on receipt of a concern relates to Section 42(1) of the Act, meaning does the concern meet the criteria for continued action under Section 42?

 ESSENTIAL INFORMATION: LEGISLATION

Section 42 duty: Section 42(1)

Once a referral expressing concern is made, the local authority decision maker needs to gather enough information in order to ascertain whether there is:

Reasonable cause to suspect that an adult in its area (whether or not ordinarily resident there):

(a) has needs for care and support (whether or not the authority is meeting any of those needs);

(b) is experiencing, or is at risk of, abuse or neglect; and

(c) as a result of those needs is unable to protect himself or herself against the abuse or neglect or the risk of it. (Care Act 2014, Section 42(1)).

We have stressed 'reasonable cause to suspect' as the decision maker only needs to gather enough information to establish this.

Do look up any local authority records that contain relevant information and to return to the referrer to ascertain relevant current circumstances. Sometimes a concern can appear to be a repeat of a long-standing situation. A useful question to ask the referrer is '*Why refer now?*' What has changed in the adult's situation? What new risks have occurred? Why are existing approaches no longer working? There may have been a number of concerns about low impact risk when considered individually, but if considered together indicate an ongoing abusive situation with cumulative risk to the adult.

Part of information gathering should be talking with the adult to ascertain their views on the alleged abuse, how they are experiencing the harm, the risk to their safety and well-being and what they think will help to remove or mitigate those risks. It may be that it is unsafe to have these conversations at this point. The focus of any subsequent enquiry or action must therefore be to identify how and when the views of the adult will be ascertained. Conversation with an adult who does not have care and support needs will provide an opportunity for them to discuss their thoughts on preventing harm, any support they need to be safe and where they can get information about other options available to them.

If the criteria for further action under Section 42 are not met, there are a range of other routes that can be used to support the adult. If the adult appears to have care and support needs, but there is no indication of abuse at present, a care and support needs assessment (Care Act 2014, Section 9) or carer's assessment may be indicated to prevent harm. Do consider how and whether referrals into care management processes are followed up. Adults with urgent needs may be left on a waiting list: how will this impact on the potential for harm that you are trying to prevent?

In other instances the adult may have no care and support needs. Support and action may need to be considered using different routes. Decision-making teams need to be very clear about who to contact and how to refer to other services in the local area:

- Do you know how non-urgent referrals into mental health services are made in your area?
- If there are concerns about radicalisation into terrorism, how do you make an urgent or non-urgent referral into Prevent teams?
- If you have enough information from the adult or referrer about domestic abuse, can you complete a DASH assessment that will indicate if a referral should be made to a MARAC (see Chapter 7)? Do you have the contact details for local domestic abuse services?

If you have advised a referrer to contact a different service, do ask them to come back for further advice. If there is a risk of harm, do contact the referrer again to make sure they have been able to take matters forward with another service. Referrers can remain unclear about next steps, believing that now they have told the local authority, that their duty of care has somehow been transferred. This is not acceptable in any case, but particularly so if the risks discussed indicate that there may be a serious outcome if concerns are not addressed by other services.

It may be difficult to ascertain whether an adult is experiencing, or is at risk of, abuse or neglect and what their views are at this stage. The decision might be to initiate an enquiry under Section 42(2) in order to gather more information. If it is later established that the adult is able to protect themselves or is not experiencing abuse the enquiry ends and the Section 42 duty will cease.

 ESSENTIAL INFORMATION: LEGISLATION

Section 42 duty: Section 42(2)

If there is reasonable cause to suspect that the concern relates to an adult whose circumstances meet the criteria we have set out, the next decision is about whether an enquiry, or some other course of action, is needed.

'The local authority must make (or cause to be made) whatever enquiries it thinks necessary to enable it to decide whether any action should be taken in the adult's case (whether under this Part [of the Act] or otherwise) and, if so, what and by whom' (Care Act 2014, Section 42(2)).

A range of actions can be taken under Section 42(2), including a care and support needs assessment under Section 9 or under Section 11 of the Care Act. Section 11 applies if the adult refuses but is not capacitated to make this decision and it is in their best interests to be assessed, or the adult refuses an assessment under Section 9 of the Care Act, but is experiencing, or is at risk of, abuse or neglect. Section 19 of the Care Act can be used to support urgent need without a needs or financial assessment.

We will detail adult safeguarding enquiries further in Chapter 9.

Who has a duty to make decisions under Section 42?

Only the local authority can decide whether the criteria for use of the Section 42 duty exists and whether an enquiry needs to be undertaken. This decision cannot be made by the adult or their representative as it is a local authority statutory duty: only the local authority can decide. The decision can be informed by the adult, but it is not their decision.

The 'No Secrets' (Home Office and Department of Health, 2000) concept of 'significant harm' to an adult, which would mean that the harm to an adult reached a threshold for an adult safeguarding process, no longer exists within the Care Act 2014. Instead, if an adult meets the criteria for the Section 42 duty, any subsequent enquiry or further action needs to be proportionate to the impact of harm and degree of continued risk. It may well be that the harm that has been discussed with the adult appears to be a one-off occurrence with minimal harm to the adult, who does not think any actions need to be taken. After these enquiries are conducted, the Section 42 duty can be considered as ended.

An adult may be subject to the risk of actual and continual harm by a member of their family or a friend who they feel afraid of. The adult may be under duress from the source of harm but wish any enquiry to end. The local authority still has a Section 42 duty towards the adult and must decide whether the risk is harmful enough for enquiries to continue and/or a contingency plan to be made with the adult.

Multi-agency information gathering and decision making

Multi-agency information gathering and decision making can be more effective if a multi-agency safeguarding hub (MASH) is used. The first MASHs were developed in 2011 in response to the communication failures identified in serious case reviews about children and highlighted in the Munro Review of Child Protection (Munro,

2011). MASH models vary greatly: some are based on the co-location of the police and local authority social workers, sometimes with health or probation input; others may be virtual or regular meetings. They will have the following features in common:

- a core group of professionals working collaboratively within an integrated unit;
- the core group usually has access to many other organisations and agencies that might be able to contribute to a picture of an individual's situation;
- while intelligence gathering and information sharing are vital responsibilities of the MASH, the most effective models are those that are able to make timely and appropriate decisions about the information analysed; and
- joint risk assessments underpin the decision-making approach. Whatever model is developed, all MASH models require good leadership and clear governance to create a shared operational culture and focus on outcomes (Centre of Excellence for Information Sharing, 2017).

MASH models were often initiated with children's services with an adult MASH being bolted on. The outcomes of an adult MASH can be harder to demonstrate, although this may be because of the early stages of development of these MASHs or because of the lack of certainty about their core business, such as which group of adults needs to go to the MASH.

What gets in the way of making decisions about Section 42?

Decisions are not made in a vacuum; the context in which we make a decision is influential. We have discussed the influence of the culture of your organisation in Chapter 1, and the ambiguity of the legislation and guidance around the three criteria for use of the Section 42 duty in Chapter 3.

Decisions about whether the statutory duty applies, about what actions need to be taken to support the person through an enquiry, or as a result of enquiry, and indeed how long an enquiry will take, may be influenced by an awareness of how much resource is available. Dixon's research (2023) into how social workers assess and manage risk and uncertainty found that practitioners were aware of the impact their decisions had on the teams undertaking enquiries. They were at times criticised by senior or team management for sending through 'too many referrals' and, consequently, they were concerned that the referrals they sent through might not receive an adequate response.

Working arrangements in safeguarding decision-making teams are designed to cope with high volumes and fast decision making, often facilitated by electronic decision-making tools. The workflow is fast, and decision makers may have worked in the same team for a long period. Dixon (2023) describes a blunting of compassion and empathy that can lead to people becoming abstract sets of colour codes on the decision-making tool. SAR Stephen (Torbay and Devon Safeguarding Adults Partnership, 2023) found that pressure on long-term members of a decision-making team led to poor decision making about the use of the Section 42 duty under the Care Act with Stephen, a man with learning disabilities who was being exploited by a group of men and went on to be murdered by one of them. Stephen's social care provider made a number of referrals about his situation, as did other organisations, but a negative perception of the provider led to the risks he faced being unappreciated by decision makers.

Working at a fast pace can lead to bias about referrers or about the details of a referral. Dixon (2023) noted: 'A process common amongst social workers, is that they started with a hypothesis that emergency service referrals were inappropriate and then looked for evidence to disprove this ... it was notable that referrals by care home managers or nursing home managers were treated differently. These workers were viewed as liable to under-report safeguarding concerns' (p 75).

Flawed decision making as a result of discounting the perspectives of emergency services has been noted in Safeguarding Adults Reviews (SARs) (Hampshire SAB, 2022) while the attitudes towards social care providers have also resulted in poor decision making and planning to protect adults with care and support needs: 'The skills and knowledge of care providers must be respected and drawn upon in making plans. Care home 1 and 2 understood Kath well and at times were her confidants. Their views were not given the same weight as those of practitioners who saw Kath infrequently and may have relied on their historical knowledge of her to understand her views and wishes' (Plymouth Safeguarding Adults Board, 2023).

When working quickly we use mental shortcuts to classify and categorise people. If we do not use our professional curiosity, we risk overlooking relevant information and create stereotyped categorisations that are not in tune with reality. We are at risk of bias.

Confirmation bias: looking for or preferring evidence that supports or confirms a pre-held view and ignoring or filtering out contrary evidence. This can exaggerate any assumptions you have already made.

Conscious bias: those we are aware of, which relate to past experience or misinformed attitudes.

Numerous SARs have found bias against people who use substances (Alcohol Change UK, 2019) with notions of 'lifestyle choice' being used to justify not addressing high impact self-neglect. Is substance dependence, often developed to manage trauma, really a choice?

Unconscious bias: is usually quick and automatic. In the moment you may have little awareness that you are making assumptions or discriminating against someone because of your prejudices.

What can you do to avoid these factors? You need access to challenging and reflective supervision which promotes your professional curiosity. You need to engage in peer discussions from the perspective of curiosity: are there unwritten rules in this team? Is there a culture of respect for partners, and if not, what is informing this? As you can see from the SARs, a lack of respect between partners leads to negative outcomes for adults. You also need to make time for reflection, to explore your own thinking, biases and assumptions.

Concerns that do not meet the criteria for the Section 42 duty

What if the person does not have care and support needs? A local authority can decide to undertake a non-statutory (sometimes called 'other') enquiry if the adult does not have care and support needs and the Section 42 duty does not apply. A non-statutory enquiry has the same objectives as a Section 42 enquiry and the same focus on involving the adult and addressing risk with them. Because the Section 42 duty does not exist, the adult can decide that they do not want an enquiry and stop the process. The only exception might be if there is a vital interest or a public interest involved.

Local authorities appear to use non-statutory enquiries for a number of purposes. Some use this category to make enquiries about carers. During the first year of the COVID-19 pandemic, local authorities reported receiving high levels of safeguarding concerns about adults who did not have care and support needs but were at risk of multiple categories of abuse and neglect. They were supported without using Section 42 (LGA, 2021a). Others have reported using the category to cover enquiries following the death of an adult, or 'low level' abuse or 'poor quality care rather than safeguarding'. It is not clear that these latter uses meet the criteria for a non-statutory enquiry. If the purpose of the enquiry is to assess whether other adults are at risk of harm from the same circumstances as the adult who died, then surely this is a statutory enquiry. If any harm is experienced or there is a risk of harm to an adult with care and support needs from poor practice, this too is potentially a statutory rather than a non-statutory enquiry.

What if there is disagreement about the decision?

In Chapter 8 we discuss using routes to resolve professional differences or 'escalation routes'. One of the most common uses of these routes is to resolve disagreements about decisions made about the use of the Section 42 duty. A referrer has a duty of care towards the adult. The referrer will need to escalate their disagreement with the local authority's decision; for example, if the decision is that the Section 42 duty is not met but there are risks for the adult and any other proposed action will not mitigate those risks. Professional deference can mean that the referrer does not challenge the decision, but we must remember that the well-being of the adult is central to all safeguarding, including challenging colleagues in other organisations. The context for decision making we described earlier means that sometimes nuanced risk is missed. Challenge and debate between organisations can defend against this.

Quality and adult safeguarding

Decisions about what type of enquiry is to be carried out, what the focus will be and who is best to undertake the enquiry are discussed in Chapter 9. But for now, we will look at a common decision that must be made when an individual is using a provided service: is the concern about the quality of provision rather than adult safeguarding, and is it therefore a matter for quality improvement teams to follow up?

The Care and Support Statutory Guidance (DHSC, 2014) points out that adult safeguarding cannot be engaged in the quality assurance of services, that it is the responsibility of the provider, the commissioners of the service; for example, local authorities or the NHS, and the care regulator (in England, the Care Quality Commission (CQC)).

> Safeguarding is not a substitute for: providers' responsibilities to provide safe and high quality care and support, commissioners regularly assuring themselves of the safety and effectiveness of commissioned services [or] the Care Quality Commission (CQC) ensuring that regulated providers comply with the fundamental standards of care or by taking enforcement action (statutory guidance, Section 14.9)

Some local authorities have officers who support the promotion of quality in the services commissioned by the local authority. These quality assurance activities can range from visits to providers to check they are compliant with the contract they have agreed with the authority, collating information from various sources to identify themes and trends about quality, or actively working with providers to address concerns about the quality of provision. The range of activities engaged in is usually determined by the size of the resources available, and the relationship between quality assurance and adult safeguarding can depend on what response quality assurance officers can give. In areas where there is little or no quality assurance resource, adult safeguarding practitioners can find themselves engaged in activities that attempt to prevent harm by promoting quality. In areas where there is an effective quality assurance response, there is a risk that concerns that should be addressed via the Section 42 duty are not seen and adults are left at risk while a quality improvement programme progresses. The case example in the Reflective Activity illustrates this potential pitfall.

REFLECTIVE ACTIVITY

Case study: Doris Green

Doris Green had type 1 diabetes but during building work at the care home was seen walking about in bare feet. Care staff didn't appear to understand the impact a cut to her foot could have. You were told that only one member of staff had training in diabetic care and another person with diabetes was about to be admitted. The quality team visited the provider who agreed that the primary care diabetic specialist nurse could support them to source the right training for staff and would also speak to Doris's key worker. But no immediate action was taken to ensure that Doris was having her needs met, and was safe, while this improvement action was undertaken.

Reflective questions

- What relationship do you have with your local quality assurance (or contract compliance) team?
- What role can individual safeguarding practitioners play in establishing and maintaining a conversation about quality and safety in provided services?

Our thoughts are that safeguarding practitioners need to form working relationships with colleagues in quality and compliance teams and must support the assessment of individual risk while quality of service concerns are addressed. Joint visits and attendance at relevant meetings when there is a possibility of risk are all helpful.

Provided services can be found to be short-staffed, but the impact of this on the individuals using the service is not always considered: how does the absence of staff affect well-being? Each individual will have different needs and areas of vulnerability. These must be understood and actions taken to prevent harm to them. Enquiries can be made alongside improvement actions that will maintain the well-being of people using the service while poor practice is addressed. While safeguarding is not a substitute for the activities of providers, commissioners and regulators, those activities are also not a substitute for adult safeguarding. Risks to individuals or groups of adults can be assessed during any large-scale quality improvement work by using the model suggested in Chapter 7 for risk assessment in organisations. These risks can be monitored and reviewed on a regular basis as the improvement work continues.

Decisions about advocacy

Under the Care Act 2014, local authorities must make sure that an adult is able to be involved in their own safeguarding. The Act identifies that if an adult has 'substantial difficulty' in doing so, then the local authority has a duty to arrange independent advocacy.

It is important that this 'substantial difficulty' is not confused with a lack of mental capacity, even though the characteristics look similar. It may be hard to engage with an adult whose survival behaviours mean that the avoidance of services feels more comfortable. An adult may have substantial difficulty in being involved because their distress about a past experience of working with statutory services interferes with their ability to use or weigh information or they may be inexperienced in expressing their views and wishes or making decisions and communicating these. They might also be under such coercive control that they cannot use or weigh information. Past trauma may make it hard for practitioners to engage meaningfully with them. An advocate can support the adult to engage and to have control and choice in their lives. The Care and Support Statutory Guidance takes a broader view of who may have 'substantial difficulty' in being involved: 'an individual who is thought to have been abused or neglected may be so demoralised, frightened, embarrassed or upset that independent advocacy provided under section 68 to help them to be involved will be crucial' (DHSC, 2014, 7.28). All the factors that may impede an adult's involvement should be considered. Our focus must be on how much we can maximise the adult's involvement and what steps we need to take to do this.

It is important to note that the adult needs to consent to any person seen as appropriate to represent and support them, and that if they are unable to consent, the local authority must be satisfied that the person's appointment is in the adult's best interests. The person who is allegedly causing harm to the adult cannot act as their representative. In addition, the statutory guidance reminds us that the appropriate person may not be 'suitable' if they live far away or are unable to participate themselves for any reason (DHSC, 2014, 7.35). It is the local authority's decision whether the adult should be represented by an appropriate person, whether an advocate should be commissioned, or whether indeed both should happen if the appropriate person is able to carry out some of their obligations well but will struggle with others.

If an enquiry needs to be undertaken very urgently, it can begin without an advocate being appointed, but the duty to appoint an advocate under Section 68 still exists and an appointment must be made as soon as possible. Conversely, an advocate may have been appointed but an enquiry finds that there is someone who can act as the appropriate representative; in this case, the advocate can simply hand over to them.

The Care and Support Statutory Guidance (DHSC, 2014, 7.9) advises that if a person lacks capacity to make decisions and has been represented by an Independent Mental Capacity Advocate (IMCA), then the same advocate should be used to avoid the person having to instruct and get to know a new advocate.

REFLECTIVE ACTIVITY

Reflective questions about advocacy

- Are you clear about your duty to arrange an advocate?
- Have you been able to create a relationship with your local advocacy services?

- • Do you know what their experience has been of providing advocacy to involve adults in their own safeguarding?
- • What challenges and barriers do advocates experience?

Who should undertake the enquiry?

A local authority has a legal duty to make an enquiry under Section 42 of the Care Act, but it can ask, or 'cause', another organisation to make enquiries regarding a specific and individual case: 'The local authority must make (or cause to be made) whatever enquiries it thinks necessary to enable it to decide whether any action should be taken in the adult's case … and, if so, what and by whom' (Care Act 2014, Section 42(2)).

Remember that a local authority cannot delegate its duty under Section 42, but it can cause an enquiry on the basis that another organisation is the most appropriate service or has the expertise or the duty to do so. Care Act Section 6 (6c) duty to cooperate does not apply if undertaking an enquiry would be incompatible with the organisation's duties or would have an adverse effect on its functions. The local authority must give the organisation making the enquiry on its behalf a clear idea of what it is expected to do, it must support the organisation and must assure the quality of the enquiry when returned.

Who can be caused to make an enquiry?

Table 8.1 gives a short list of organisations that either have the role and responsibility for certain types of enquiry or may know the adult so well that they are able to use their relationship to broach sensitive areas of the adult's life with them. In complex cases there may be several activities going on; for example, an assessment of the adult's care and support needs, a criminal investigation, and a health assessment. Think about when and how these activities take place. Could there be joint visits with other professionals? Check that the well-being of the adult is being supported through all enquiries; for example, while a police investigation may need to take precedence, ensuring that the adult has practical support to maintain their well-being is paramount and must be considered at all times.

Decisions about what happens as a result of an enquiry

The key decisions about how an enquiry is conducted and what it focuses on should be made with the involvement of the adult. Although the local authority is the decision maker regarding whether or not there should be an enquiry, all other decisions need to be shared and the adult's views and wishes taken into account. Key aspects of the involvement of adults in enquiries are considered further in

Table 8.1: Organisations that may be able to undertake a Section 42 enquiry

Enquiry activities	Organisation that may be able to enquire
Establishing the views, wishes and desired outcomes of the adult	The most appropriate person in the situation, the professional who knows the adult best and who the adult trusts. This could be a social worker, or could be a nurse, occupational therapist, care worker, provider manager, housing support worker, PCSO, community psychiatric nurse or GP.
	Remember: If the adult has substantial difficulty in being involved in the enquiry, an appropriate person should be identified to represent them, and if there is no appropriate person, an independent advocate must be instructed.
Care and support needs assessment under Section 9 or 11 of the Care Act 2014	Social worker or similar social care staff
Assessment of health, including mental health needs	Appropriate health worker such as GP, district nurse, psychiatrist or community psychiatric nurse
Allegations that a crime has been committed	Police
Anti-social behaviour – this can range from noisy neighbours, which is a civil matter, through to hate crime and threatening behaviour, criminal matters	Non-criminal: landlord, if breach of tenancy agreement, environmental health or the local authority anti-social behaviour team Criminal: police
Bogus calls, internet or post scams, rogue traders	Trading Standards and/or the police
Breach of health and safety legislation and regulations	CQC if this occurs in a regulated setting, the Health and Safety Executive if in a non-regulated setting
Incident in an NHS setting or health funded care	An incident of harm may well meet the criteria for a serious incident investigation by health colleagues
Breach of terms of employment and/or disciplinary procedures	The person's employer
Misuse of enduring or lasting power of attorney or misconduct of a court-appointed deputy	Office of the Public Guardian (OPG), Court of Protection (COP) or the police
Person making decisions about the care and well-being of an adult who does not have mental capacity to make decisions about their safety are made without authority or are not in the best interests of the adult	OPG or COP
Misuse of appointee-ship	Department for Work and Pensions

Chapter 9. The crucial element that informs the adult's involvement is the mutual exploration of the outcomes the adult hopes for as a result of the enquiry. How do they want their lives to change? What is important to them? What would improve their quality of life?

These desired outcomes strongly influence the decisions made at the end of the enquiry. The statutory guidance reminds us that:

'What happens as a result of an enquiry should reflect the adult's wishes wherever possible, as stated by them or by their representative or advocate. If they lack capacity, it should be in their best interests if they are not able to make the decision and be proportionate to the level of concern.' (DHSC, 2014, 19.2)

An adult may decide that they want no further action taken. The adult's decision may need to be overridden and further enquiries and actions continue if the adult's 'vital interests' or European Convention on Human Rights (ECHR) Article 2 Right to Life are at continued risk or there is a public interest; for example, a criminal offence has taken place, which may put others at risk, or regulatory enforcement action needs to be taken by the CQC or other relevant regulator. The adult should be informed that this is happening.

In these circumstances, we may need to continue to share information about the adult without their consent. The statutory guidance states that:

> If the adult has the mental capacity to make informed decisions about their safety and they do not want any action to be taken, this does not preclude the sharing of information with relevant professional colleagues. This is to enable professionals to assess the risk of harm and to be confident that the adult is not being unduly influenced, coerced or intimidated and is aware of all the options. This will also enable professionals to check the safety and validity of decisions made. It is good practice to inform the adult that this action is being taken unless doing so would increase the risk of harm. (DHSC, 2014, 14.92)

Decisions made by other organisations

Decisions made by other organisations will influence how enquires are undertaken, the outcomes of enquiries and how adults are protected. In Chapter 6 we talked about the importance of building relationships with other organisations, and understanding their role, responsibilities and powers. Although local authorities have duties under the Care Act 2014, local authority adult safeguarding practitioners are reliant on other organisations using their powers to effect change via criminal justice or enforcement action in the lives of adults at risk.

Criminal justice

While it is useful for all practitioners to have some grasp of criminal law, it is ultimately police colleagues who will be able to identify that a crime has been committed. Below we set out a simplified summary of police decision-making processes. Do use this as a basis to ask your police colleagues for a more detailed description when needed. Depending on the type of crime that has allegedly been committed, the factors that go into decision making can be complex and are underpinned by a wide range of legislation and police operational procedures.

The police may decide to carry out an initial investigation. Securing forensic evidence is important at this point after any victims have been identified and assisted. 'The first chance to obtain material may be the last. Identifying these actions during the initial investigation stage produces the most effective outcome. A delay in protecting, preserving or gathering material may result in evidence being contaminated or lost' (College of Policing, 2023). If further investigation of the facts needs to be undertaken, the case may be passed on to another investigating officer who must make a clear plan for further investigation. Once the police have concluded their investigations, they will refer the case to the Crown Prosecution Service (CPS) for advice on how to proceed in all but the most minor and routine cases. The CPS makes the decision on whether a suspect should be charged, and what that charge should be.

Where a person is suspected of committing an offence, the Police and Criminal Evidence Act 1984 Code of Practice, Code C (PACE, 1984, p 41, 10A) requires there to be 'some reasonable, objective grounds, based on known facts or information, which are relevant to the likelihood that the offence has been committed and the person to be questioned committed it' (PACE, 1984, p 41, 10A) before the person can be charged. Once the person is charged with an offence, the CPS and police are jointly responsible for the prosecution of the case. The CPS will read the case file and the two tests laid down in the Code for Crown Prosecutors – the *evidential test* and the *public interest test* – must be applied in every case.

In the evidential test the prosecutor must decide whether or not there is enough evidence against the defendant for a realistic prospect of conviction. If there is not a realistic prospect of conviction, the case must not go ahead, no matter how important or serious it may be. It is the duty of every crown prosecutor to make sure that the right person is prosecuted for the right offence.

The public interest test is applied after the crown prosecutor decides that there is a realistic prospect of conviction. A prosecution is less likely to be needed if, for example, a court would be likely to fix a minimal or token penalty, or the loss or harm connected with the offence was minor and the result of a single incident (CPS, 2019b). The interests of the victim are an important factor when considering the public interest. Crown prosecutors will always take into account the consequences for the victim and any views expressed by the victim or victims' family.

If the crown prosecutor decides that a prosecution should not go ahead, the case will be stopped, usually by what is called 'discontinuance'. If a prosecutor decides not to bring charges against a suspect, discontinues proceedings or offers no evidence in a case, there is a right to appeal under the victims' Right to Review scheme (CPS, 2020).

Care Quality Commission

The CQC has both civil and criminal enforcement powers. The CQC's civil powers focus on reducing the risk to people who use regulated services and their criminal powers are used to hold registered persons to account for serious failures. In some cases, both civil and criminal enforcement powers are used at the same time. It can appear to take time for the CQC to take action to use its enforcement powers. The CQC has to base its actions on evidence and will need evidence from third parties, such as adult safeguarding services, to begin to compile a portfolio of evidence that can be used to take legally compliant enforcement action. The CQC uses an enforcement decision tree to guide its decision making on the use of enforcement powers (CQC, 2024). The decision tree has four stages:

1. initial assessment;
2. legal and evidential review;
3. selection of the appropriate enforcement action; and
4. final review.

Initial assessment is triggered when the CQC becomes aware of a possible breach of law or regulation that may warrant civil and/or criminal enforcement action. Sources of information to evidence this include notifications by providers, safeguarding concerns, instances of whistleblowing, reportable incident or coroners' reports, complaints, information from the public, and concerns identified during a CQC inspection. At this stage the CQC may carry out an inspection, may gather more evidence or may refer the concern to another public body. The CQC may also progress straight to Stage 2 of the decision tree and consider what enforcement action to take.

Legal and evidential review involves an assessment of the legal and evidential basis to determine whether there is sufficient evidence to substantiate a breach of the legal requirements by a registered person. CQC colleagues and their managers can carry out this function. If the CQC considers that the evidence demonstrates an identifiable breach of a legal requirement and the evidence is sufficient and robust to prove the breach, the case will continue to the next stage.

Selection of the appropriate enforcement action is made using two criteria: the seriousness of the breach and evidence of multiple and/or persistent breaches, to decide which enforcement powers can be used. The CQC takes progressively stronger action in proportion to the seriousness of the breach and the potential impact on people using a service as well as the number of people affected. The CQC also takes stronger action where a service is carried out in an inappropriate way without effective management of risk. Depending on the seriousness of the breach, recommendations for civil action can range from cancellation of registration of the service, which closes the service, to a requirement notice for a minor breach with no serious consequences.

Criminal enforcement action is considered in every case where the CQC proposes civil enforcement or identifies a specific incident of suspected avoidable harm. Decisions about the most appropriate criminal enforcement action to take are made in consultation with CQC legal services and must follow the two-stage test as set out in the Code for Crown Prosecutors, mentioned earlier, meaning that the evidential and public interest tests apply. This action is usually considered when a regulation has been breached and an adult has experienced serious and avoidable harm. In April 2015, the CQC assumed responsibility for prosecuting providers for all health and safety related incidents, taking over from the Health and Safety Executive and local authorities.

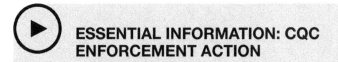

ESSENTIAL INFORMATION: CQC ENFORCEMENT ACTION

Shrewsbury and Telford Hospital NHS Trust

Mohammed Ismael Zaman (known as Bolly) attended the Royal Shrewsbury Hospital to receive dialysis on 18 October 2019. When a patient receives dialysis, their connection lines must always be visible; however, this did not happen in this case. The trust also failed to ensure that their staff were adequately trained to follow best practice guidelines regarding the connection lines being secured to his bed, which may have resulted in them becoming disconnected. He was found by staff bleeding heavily from a disconnected line, resuscitation was attempted but was unsuccessful. Sadly, Bolly died.

Max Dingle was admitted to the Royal Shrewsbury Hospital on 27 April 2020 due to shortness of breath and a high temperature. On 28 April 2020, he was assessed as requiring a specialist bariatric bed. On 3 May 2020, Max was found trapped in the bariatric bed and died shortly afterwards. The trust failed to train staff in the setting up of bariatric beds and this led to the entrapment of Max.

Shrewsbury and Telford Hospital NHS Trust did not take all reasonable steps to ensure that safe care and treatment was provided, resulting in the most serious avoidable harm possible to two patients and the exposure of harm to other patients at the Royal Shrewsbury Hospital. The trust was ordered to pay a total of £1,375,712.

▶ KEY MESSAGES

- **Be clear about what decision is being made and who can make it. If a local authority has a duty to decide, it does not need the consent of the adult involved but must make the decision based on reasonable and proportionate information gathering and without assumptions.**

- It is important to seek the views of adults regarding the decisions to be made, to act on the duty to arrange advocacy if an adult will have 'substantial difficulty' in being involved and to consider the best interests of an adult who is unable to inform the decision.

- It is important to understand the decision-making processes of organisations who have powers that they can use to protect adults. We need to have some understanding of the checks, balances and procedures those organisations use in exercising their legal powers.

KNOWLEDGE REVIEW

- WHAT are the local authorities' duties related to adult safeguarding under the provisions of the Care Act 2014? What can impede decision making about how those duties are used?

- IN what circumstances should you arrange advocacy? What should you bear in mind when considering an appropriate person to represent an adult?

- UNDER what circumstances can you cause another organisation to undertake an enquiry?

- WHAT are the two basic principles that both the CPS and the CQC must bear in mind when considering prosecutions?

FURTHER READING

- More resources on decision making about the Section 42 duty can be found at: www.local.gov.uk/making-decisions-duty-carry-out-safeguarding-adults-enquiries-resources [Accessed 12 July 2024].

- This article gives a thoughtful view on what advocacy can mean to older people in the context of adult safeguarding and explores the role of the advocate and meaning of advocacy post the Care Act 2014: Lonbay, S. and Brandon, T. (2017) 'Renegotiating Power in Adult Safeguarding: The Role of Advocacy', *The Journal of Adult Protection*, 19(2): 78–91.

- To read Torbay and Devon Safeguarding Partnership SAR Stephen (2023) go to: www.devonsafeguardingadultspartnership.org.uk/document/sar-stephen/ [Accessed 7 June 2024].

9

Adult safeguarding enquiries

Chapter aim

In this chapter we will look in detail at some of the essential components of an enquiry, whether single or multi-agency, with an emphasis on practical approaches to involve adults and work with other organisations. Do review the learning from previous chapters to remind yourself about aspects of making relationships, working with risk and decision making. We will focus on resolution and recovery in more detail in Chapter 10.

This chapter includes:

- The essential components of an enquiry

- Single and multi-agency enquiries

- Involving adults in enquiries and using advocacy

- Supporting other organisations during the enquiry

- Making safeguarding plans

- The importance of escalation

The essential components of an enquiry

The Care Act 2014 statutory guidance describes a set of objectives to be achieved in an enquiry, no matter how short or complicated and no matter whether there is one, or several, organisations involved.

 ESSENTIAL INFORMATION: LEGISLATION

Objectives of a Section 42 enquiry

The objectives of an enquiry into abuse or neglect are to:

- establish facts;
- ascertain the adult's views and wishes;
- assess the needs of the adult for protection, support and redress and how they might be met;
- protect from the abuse and neglect, in accordance with the wishes of the adult;
- make decisions as to what follow-up action should be taken with regard to the person or organisation responsible for the abuse or neglect;
- enable the adult to achieve resolution and recovery.

DHSC, 2014, 14.94

An enquiry does not progress through distinct linear stages but is fluid or dynamic in nature. It is important to address the objectives of an enquiry listed above in whatever order meets the needs of the adult. Enquiries must be proportionate to the impact of harm or risk of harm and interfere as little as possible in the adult's life. Our focus is on whether the adult or others are being harmed or are at risk of harm, and if action needs to be taken to help. The statutory guidance describes the proportionate nature of enquiry: 'An enquiry could range from a conversation with the adult, or if they lack capacity, or have substantial difficulty in understanding the enquiry their representative or advocate, prior to initiating a[n] ... enquiry under Section 42, right through to a much more formal multi-agency plan or course of action' (DHSC, 2014, 14.77). We will explore these essential components in the case studies below.

Single and multi-agency enquiries

The majority of enquiries will involve conversations with the adult. Some enquiries stop there; a series of conversations may be all that is needed to respond proportionately to the risk of harm. Even with a conversation-based enquiry there will often be colleagues from other organisations involved as with the example of Ron Wise below.

Enquiries that involve a number of organisations must also involve the adult, and a person-centred, Making Safeguarding Personal (MSP) approach still applies.

REFLECTIVE ACTIVITY

Case study: Ron Wise and a 'conversation' enquiry

Ron Wise's support worker referred a concern about an 'old friend' taking up residence in Ron's flat and potentially exploiting him. Ron lives in a supported living flat in sheltered accommodation and has learning disabilities.

Ron told the support worker that he did not want this man to stay with him but felt sorry for him. You telephoned Ron, who invited you over to the flat. He told you that he had sorted the situation out himself but would welcome a chat. You visited Ron, and he told you that the old friend left to stay with other friends. He did not want him back; he said that he did not feel threatened by him and did not give him money but the friend ate all Ron's food and made him feel uncomfortable. Ron thought that the friend would return. He wanted to think through a strategy for saying 'no', which he could rehearse with his support workers.

You devised a strategy with Ron that included the following practical steps: Ron will not buzz people through to the flat before hearing who they are, he will tell the friend or any other unwelcome visitor that he cannot see them and will end the conversation quickly. He will be clear with visitors that he does not have people to stay, and he will alert his support workers if he needs support to tell a visitor to leave.

Ron's support worker arrived and Ron updated him as to what was agreed. This turned into a wider conversation about how hard Ron found it to stand up for himself. Ron and the support worker identified other opportunities when Ron could practise doing this, beginning with being assertive with his support worker.

Reflective questions

- How could a similar scenario result in a further enquiry?
- What further factors might you see?

Our thoughts are that we would need to undertake a further enquiry if there were signs that the friend was trying to undermine Ron's ability to self-determine: signs of deliberate exploitation. In this case, Ron may say that the friend threatened or demeaned him or demanded that he would move into the flat or become Ron's 'carer'. We may then also consider any public risk. If the friend sounds exploitative and travels between various addresses, are others at risk? We might want to find out more about this friend. Is he known to the police?

In these scenarios Ron will remain in control of how he protects himself, but we would need to review his outcomes with him, including whether he wants to make any complaint to the police about the friend's exploitative behaviour. Ron might want to get to know the local Police Community Safety Officer (PCSO) and we should also consider any other protective and preventative factors in Ron's life. It will be important to arrange return visits to review the safeguarding plan with Ron as needed.

The course of action to be followed is sometimes difficult to predict and can emerge as the enquiry progresses, new facts emerge, circumstances change or the outcomes the adult is seeking alter.

Multi-agency enquiries

A common feature noted in Safeguarding Adults Reviews (SARs) (Preston-Shoot et al, 2024b) is the absence of multi-agency meetings as part of an enquiry. Multi-agency meetings are key in sharing information, assessing risk and agreeing shared risk management strategies. Taking a multi-agency approach to an enquiry will overcome silo-working and ensure good coordination between all the organisations and practitioners involved. Multi-agency meetings will be essential throughout the course of the enquiry and afterward, as part of support to a safeguarding plan. Meetings should not be 'one-off' events convened during a crisis. The actions agreed as part of an enquiry must be followed up and there must be a lead agency who can do this. In the case of an enquiry under Section 42, the lead agency will be the local authority safeguarding practitioner or team. A lead agency is essential to successful multi-agency working:

> Even where risk management strategy meetings have taken place, interventions involving multiple agencies remain complex and dynamic, with an individual's circumstances sometimes changing rapidly. One notable shortcoming identified by SARs was the absence of a coordinating agency with a lead professional who could be relied upon to know how other agencies were involved, and act as a conduit of information and consultation on multi-agency strategy. In many of the cases featured in the SARs, no one agency was familiar with the whole picture. (Preston-Shoot et al, 2024b, p 103)

REFLECTIVE ACTIVITY

Case study: Lucille Randall – A multi-agency coordinated enquiry

Concerns about **Lucille** have been referred to the local authority adult safeguarding team by the housing provider tenancy support team. Lucille came over to the UK from Barbados in the 1960s to work as a nurse and is now in her mid-80s. She was an active member of the community, regularly attending church and visiting friends in her block of flats. Since her cousin moved in with her as her carer, Lucille has not been seen around and neighbours report being turned away at the door when they visit. The tenancy support officer called to see Lucille but a middle-aged woman answered, introducing herself as Lucille's cousin and saying that Lucille was too ill to receive visitors. Information gathering via Section 42(1) reveals that Lucille is on regular medication and has frequent appointments with the diabetes nurse, but she has not been seen at her GP surgery for several weeks. You telephone Lucille but a woman answers and tells you again that Lucile is too ill to come to the phone. On further questioning she tells you that she is Lucille's daughter, and that Lucille has seen a doctor who has told her to keep away from people.

You will need to plan this enquiry using a multi-agency meeting. If you go around to the flat, you are likely to also be refused entrance. Consider whether there is a practitioner from another organisation that can visit with you; the GP or nurse, for example, who could not be refused admission on the grounds that Lucille is ill. We may get a chance to speak with Lucille's cousin/daughter too and understand any motivation for preventing people seeing Lucille. Together you can be more assertive about seeing Lucille. What will the next steps be if your assertive attempts to get in fail? We need to be proportionate in our approach and respect Lucille's right to privacy, but at the moment it appears that Lucille's cousin/daughter is refusing entrance. The GP or community nurse can explain at the meeting the implications of Lucille not seeing the diabetes nurse or getting medication: how imminent and impactful is the risk to her? What do the neighbourhood police know about the situation, and in the light of information about risk, what is their view on a second joint visit should the first plan fail? Our first aim is to see Lucille alone and ascertain her wishes. We will need to consider our questions for Lucille and her 'carer' and what the sequence of events should be in light of any concerns about her medical status. As well as discussing an engagement plan with all the organisations involved and gathering information about risk, we will need to agree a multi-agency communication plan. Lucille needs to be seen as soon as possible and events could move quickly.

Reflective questions
• Who else could you involve in the multi-agency planning meeting?
• What other plans could you make within a multi-agency meeting?

Our thoughts are that we will need to work closely together to see Lucille and we will need to do this quickly. Multi-agency work results in good problem solving. While the principles of proportionality and protection must be balanced, at the moment we need to work quickly to see Lucille and make sure she is well.

The beginning of the enquiry

Taking time to plan even the shortest of enquiries is important. At this stage of the enquiry, we need to take time to plan our conversation with the adult and to think through how we will explain adult safeguarding and the concerns about them. Find out if there is information in your organisation that will help you talk about adult safeguarding with the adult and those around them.

During your conversation with the adult, you will ask for their perspective on the concern by asking them, 'What happened?' Missing this step can have disastrous consequences. For example, Mr Short was alleged by a hospital worker to have disclosed that he was regularly sexually assaulted by night-care staff. The police were contacted and an emergency planning meeting convened. Mr Short was interviewed by a police officer and social worker. He was very embarrassed. He explained that he disliked the night staff attending to his personal needs and so made jokes about it. Mr Short had been joking, but this had been misunderstood by the concerned health worker.

Talking with the adult also gives you an opportunity to seek their consent to you asking other agencies for information about them. If the adult refuses their consent, you may have to accept this, but you can share information without their permission if there is a risk to their 'vital interests' (General Data Protection Regulations, Article 6(1)(d); see European Parliament, 2016) or you believe that they are under duress or being controlled by another person, there are others at risk or a 'serious crime' has been committed as discussed in Chapter 8.

Lastly, you will ask the adult what thoughts they have about what they want to happen next. They may wish you to do nothing, but remember the duty to enquire is still there. You may need to decide to continue with the enquiry. If you do need to continue, it is important to tell the adult why you are continuing without their consent and that you will keep them informed as much, or as little, as they wish and that they can still be involved at a later date if they change their mind. The adult may have an initial set of thoughts about what they want to happen next, what kind of life they want and who is important to them. Being harmed, being visited by a social worker and talking about harm may all be stressful for the adult. It can be helpful to go back after the adult has had time to think through what has happened. Being rushed is not empowering, and potentially life-changing decisions take time to make.

What if the adult is prevented from seeing you by another person?

The first essential step when faced with this dilemma is to try to understand why the adult is being prevented from seeing you. We list some common scenarios, but remember that each situation is unique:

• People may try to keep social workers away from the adult because of previous poor experiences, including having children taken into care or being sectioned under the Mental Health Act, or they may have a general mistrust of statutory services.

- People may misunderstand the intention of social workers, fearing that the adult will be 'put into a home', or the house they live in will be sold immediately to pay care fees. They may not understand what we mean by adult safeguarding and what this entails.
- People may prevent access to the adult because they are afraid that some aspect of their own behaviour that they are defensive about will be identified such as substance dependence or other addictions, mental health difficulties, learning disability or dementia.
- Obstructing may be an aspect of coercive control, the behaviour that underlies domestic abuse. The adult is deliberately isolated and their life strictly controlled.
- The obstructer may know that there are serious problems but want life to stay as it always has been. This can be true of adult children who are now neglecting a frail or incapacitated parent, but do not wish to acknowledge that changes must be made, or they may be protective family members who wish to keep a disabled person 'safe' and away from the possibility of change.

Norrie et al (2018) carried out a study of social workers and service user representatives in three English local authorities, capturing their perspectives about the options they used to respond to the obstruction of entry to older adults. The majority of the social workers interviewed reported that their first action was to try to 'negotiate with the obstructive third party' (p 1079). They tried to develop a rapport with the person obstructing or 'hindering' in order to understand the context for the refusal of access. Social workers also carried out as many checks as possible on the person obstructing, to understand on what basis they lived with the adult or whether they had a history of domestic abuse or addiction. These factors are important to understand in order to plan the negotiation. If an engagement and negotiation approach failed, the social worker might become more assertive, using professional, rather than legal, authority to emphasise the importance of seeing the adult alone and unhindered. Social workers also talked about 'pursuing creative routes' (p 1080). They might plan to meet the adult outside of the home in the day centre they attended, via a GP appointment or in another public place. They might try to get another family member to facilitate a meeting. These options and the 'neutral person' options (see below) must always be risk assessed to explore the possibility of further serious harm to the adult because they have met with a professional and disclosed harm.

People who have previously had a bad experience of working with social workers or are fearful of statutory services may be able to relate to a more neutral figure – for example an advocate – to help them understand the concerns and possible outcomes of adult safeguarding. You could also consider if someone from a different organisation is more likely to be able to enter the premises and carry out an initial conversation with the adult.

Consider:

- Would a colleague from a partner agency have more success in gaining access to the adult?

- Is there someone who can be considered as 'neutral' by the person who is obstructing access?
- Is there a care provider or district nurse who regularly visits the adult?

Remember that you need to initially brief and continue to support the person who will talk with the adult, and plan for any increased risk to the adult from this approach. Examples of a 'neutral person' include: primary health care professionals including GPs, nurses, community occupational therapists, or other services who know the adult including home care or voluntary sector organisations. Neutral agencies may include Trading Standards, Victim Support, fire and rescue, the RSPCA, advocates including Independent Mental Capacity Advocates (IMCAs) or family solicitors.

REFLECTIVE ACTIVITY

Case study: Mrs Swift

Mrs Swift lives in a sheltered housing complex. She is 92 years old. Her son Nigel moved in after his partner threw him out after violence against her and her children. A concern was received from the Ambulance Trust after they were called to the flat: Nigel had pushed Mrs Swift during an argument between them and had later disconnected the oxygen she relied on to help her cope with breathing difficulties.

Mrs Swift used the lifeline alarm after he had left the flat. Mrs Swift did not want to be taken to hospital and did not want Nigel to know she had told anyone about him. She seemed to the ambulance staff to be afraid of Nigel but determined to 'stand by him', explaining that he had a difficult childhood with a violent father. She does not want a social worker involved; she says that Nigel hates them as they tried to take his children away.

You make some initial enquiries about Nigel and discover that there are recorded concerns about threatening behaviour towards his mother. The police tell you that he was arrested a year ago after assaulting his partner but not charged. Nigel does not venture far from the flats and the GP surgery tells you that he attends appointments with Mrs Swift. The sheltered housing 'floating' warden tells you that Nigel should not be living in the flat and he has frightened Mrs Swift's friends away as well as stopping her attending local clubs as he does not think she is 'safe' outside the flat.

Nigel does not want to help Mrs Swift with her personal care, however, and for the moment a carer goes in every morning and two carers assist Mrs Swift to use the shower twice a week. You want to engage with Mrs Swift to see if she is well and what her views are on taking matters forward. There is not only a risk to Mrs Swift's safety but also a risk that Nigel may stop the home care agency seeing her as he is controlling all other external connections she has.

Reflective question

- How are you going to engage with Mrs Swift without endangering her safety and well-being further?

Our thoughts are that there are a number of options to consider: we need to engage the home care agency and seek their knowledge about the situation and whether they can assess Mrs Swift's immediate safety as well as trying to ascertain her thoughts about the situation. Are there any opportunities for them to speak with Mrs Swift alone? When Mrs Swift does attend the GP surgery, could Nigel be assertively told to remain outside on a pretext?

Planning an enquiry

After ascertaining the views and wishes of the adult, there may be further enquiry planning, especially if more than one organisation is to be involved. Good planning will make sure that the adult can benefit from the assistance of the right services, and that the activities of those services are coordinated and supported by the local authority. The statutory guidance describes some of the activities that may take place during an enquiry:

- Using the wishes of the adult at risk ascertained during the early part of the enquiry, discuss what further enquiries and/or actions they think are required.
- Enable the adult to understand what options might be and how their wishes might be realised.
- Support the adult at risk to gain confidence and self-esteem to enable self-protection, especially in complex domestic circumstances, involving the police, NHS and others as required.
- Consider actions such as disciplinary, complaints or criminal investigations or work by contracts managers and the CQC to improve care standards.
- Consider both civil and criminal justice approaches that are also available as ways to improve well-being, including therapeutic or

family work, mediation and conflict resolution, peer or circles of support.

(Adapted from Care and Support Statutory Guidance, DHSC, 2014, 14.105)

As well as the organisations listed in the statutory guidance, we would add colleagues from third sector organisations, housing providers, care and support providers, community safety colleagues and many other organisations who are or can work with adults at risk of abuse.

Planning is best seen as a process and not a single event. The process begins, as described, with ascertaining the adult's views and wishes, their 'desired outcomes'. The rest of the planning process can be undertaken in various ways, depending on complexity, via virtual or face-to-face meetings or meetings with individual practitioners.

Regular face-to-face or virtual meetings can seem time-consuming to those participating, but are effective mechanisms for gathering information, enabling problem solving, agreeing detailed enquiry processes and sharing decision-making. If organisations are anxious about the risk to the adult, then a meeting, preferably face to face, will help to share anxiety as people plan together. Planning via the telephone can be a pragmatic solution when only one other organisation is involved, with the local authority acting as coordinator in a straightforward enquiry. It is important that the busy nature of everyday work is not allowed to get in the way of face-to-face planning when it is needed. Face-to-face or virtual multi-agency meetings may no longer be part of the business culture of some organisations, but adult safeguarding should challenge these cultures, remembering to use the principles of proportionality and partnership at all times. While simple plans may mean a short conversation, plans that involve several strands of enquiry or that may create risks for the adult or others must be fully discussed and explored. More time and resources will be needed if badly made plans do not prevent further harm: adults will be referred back for more intervention or could be left in an abusive situation. Better to spend time working together to resolve a situation of risk now than spend time working with the aftermath of a lack of proportionate action. Planning an enquiry can involve a range of considerations, which we now set out.

What facts do we need to ascertain? What is the focus of the enquiry?

Ideally, the focus of the enquiry is what the adult wishes the enquiry to focus on. As we have argued in Chapter 7, adults are experts in their own lives and about their needs for protection, redress and recovery. We also need to remember the balance between protection, prevention and proportionality; we should not be gathering facts that have no relevance to the concern. However, there are situations where the focus may be on facts that the adult finds hard to understand. For many adults, their supporters and, sometimes, practitioners, the facts that need to be understood to prevent harm or protect the adult and others are outside our life experience.

Examples may include: coercive control in domestic abuse; high-risk violent behaviour; coercive control that is used to enact exploitative disability hate crime or sexual exploitation of individuals or groups; the psychological mechanisms which internet and other scammers use to keep people 'hooked' into being scammed; the plausible reasons given by practised confidence tricksters to gain money and resources; exploitation via cuckooing or other gang-related activity; and human trafficking. These complex areas require careful exploration with the adult together with partnership planning and working together from a range of organisations.

How the adult is and will be involved

What are the adult's views, wishes and outcomes, and how will these be updated and continue to be understood? How will the adult's wishes inform the enquiry?

Are there services or people the adult thinks should be involved? Are there services or people the adult does not want to be approached? How will this affect the enquiry? Are there evidenced reasons to override this wish?

Does the adult have significant difficulty in being involved? Is there someone appropriate they want to represent them? If not, has advocacy been commissioned? If the adult has been assessed as not having the mental capacity to make decisions about outcomes, who is representing them and how will they be involved? How will we observe the adult's best interests at all times? How will we monitor the adult's well-being as the enquiry progresses?

Known risks

Is there a need for an interim safeguarding plan to promote the well-being of the adult or adults involved while enquiries are undertaken? How will risk be assessed with the adult or their representative, and how will any risks that may arise because an enquiry is in progress be addressed?

Assessments needed

Is an assessment of the adult's care and support needs under Section 9 of the Care Act 2014 needed? Or an assessment of their mental capacity regarding specific decisions about the concerns expressed, their safety or involvement in the process?

If there are a range of enquiries – for example, a police investigation of a potentially criminal act, or a medical assessment, or care and support needs assessment – how will these be coordinated in a way that is least disruptive to the adult, makes best use of the practitioner's expertise, and maximises the best outcome negotiated with the adult? How will the information be shared and coordinated? How will those undertaking the enquiry be supported? As new facts emerge or circumstances change, the enquiry plan will need to be changed. A lead practitioner or manager from the local authority who is coordinating the enquiry plan will ensure that the plan continues to respond to emerging needs, risks, the adult's wishes and changing circumstances.

REFLECTIVE ACTIVITY

Case Study: Mrs Swift Enquiry Plan

After planning with you and their manager, **Mrs Swift's** two regular home carers spoke with her while they were supporting her to shower two days after the ambulance referral. She is bruised from being pushed but otherwise physically OK. Mrs Swift says she has had enough; she loves Nigel but is afraid of him. He is shouting at her more and drinking alcohol heavily. Now the shock of his behaviour towards her has worn off, she has decided that she wants him to leave, and for him to get some help. Mrs Swift is aware that she is in breach of her tenancy. She wanted to help Nigel but matters seem to be getting worse. Mrs Swift does not want the police to prosecute Nigel but wants some peace from him for now. She wants someone to help her to tell him to go. After getting this report, you convene an enquiry planning meeting with the housing association landlord, the police, the home care agency and a social worker.

Reflective questions

- What is your assessment of the risk of further harm to Mrs Swift?
- How urgently should a response be made?
- What avenues are open to support Mrs Swift, taking account of her currently expressed wishes and the risk of creating further risk or damaging her quality of life?

Our thoughts are that the risk of Mrs Swift being harmed are high and imminent given Nigel's previous and current behaviour and the escalation of his drinking alcohol. Mrs Swift wants to have a break from him, and for him to 'get help'. A joint visit (from both (a) the landlord to explain breach of tenancy and the need to leave that same day to Nigel and (b) a social worker to support Mrs Swift and explain the options to her) may help, but the police will need to be on stand-by should this fail.

Involving adults in enquiries and using advocacy

Adult safeguarding enquiries are intended to empower those whose human rights they seek to uphold, but the experience of adult safeguarding risks being disempowering, and can lead to adults feeling singled out, considered separately from their relationships and networks and judged and intruded on. They may fear that the adult safeguarding process takes them to a point of no return, over which they have little control (Sherwood-Johnson et al, 2013). The safeguarding process can reduce the resilience of the adult and the systems around them. An adult's resilience can be promoted through a sense of belonging to a network of secure relationships, a sense of self-esteem and of self-efficacy, the feeling of control and competence to influence their situation (Bloom, 1996; Gilligan, 1997). In order to counter the risk of reducing the adult's resilience, it is important that they are supported to be involved in the adult safeguarding process.

 ESSENTIAL INFORMATION: PRACTICE GUIDANCE

Practical steps to take to involve people in enquiry processes

Conversations

Follow the guidance in Chapter 4 to engage, creating a relationship with the adult and their identified networks. Talk with the people the adult suggests can help. Make sure you keep the adult, or their representatives, updated as to how the enquiry plan is progressing. As discussed in Chapter 7, gather facts and assess risk together.

Information

Make sure you understand how you will communicate with the adult. Do have accessible information to leave with them, including how they can contact you and anyone else who will be a contact during the enquiry. Discuss timescales, what is realistic and acceptable to the adult, what can be done quickly, what will take more time.

Meetings

Make sure meetings are accessible to the adult and their supporters. Start by talking with the adult about what arrangements will be best for them. It may be preferable to hold meetings at the adult's house or in a place in which they feel comfortable and most able to participate. Some adults have access to good internet and feel most comfortable online. The adult can bring supporters or a representative or may have an advocate. They may not wish to attend the meeting but have their views represented by another either verbally or in writing. A shorter meeting may be more manageable for everyone, including the adult. You may need to build in breaks and hold the meeting at a time when the adult is most able to participate and/or their representative is available. The meeting must be conducted at the adult's pace. The adult could work with you to set the agenda for the meeting. Consider how the meeting will be conducted to ensure maximum participation, listening and responding to the adult's contribution.

Advocates instructed by the local authority

It is important to understand what type of advocate may be able to support and represent the adult. There are several roles with 'advocate' in their job title, but it should not be presumed that all specialist advocates are able to advocate on behalf of adults regarding adult safeguarding. Care Act advocates commissioned by the local authority will be able to meet the requirements of advocacy within adult safeguarding. This is 'instructed advocacy', as the adult has the mental capacity to make decisions relevant to the concern.

If the adult has substantial difficulty because they do not have the mental capacity to make the relevant decisions, then an IMCA is the appropriate advocate. Many advocacy organisations who provide Care Act advocates also provide IMCAs and it is helpful and reasonable that the adult is represented by the same advocate for different aspects of their needs. IMCAs are specialist advocates trained to support decision making and act as 'non-instructed' advocates. They can act as the voice of the adult, making sure that their wishes, views and beliefs are represented and that their rights are secured. IMCAs use a range of approaches to inform their understanding of the adult's perspective. These include a rights–based model that focuses on the adult's human rights, a witness observer model where the advocate spends time with the person observing how they interact with others and the environment around them, and a person–centred model, which focuses on getting to know the person and what is important in their life.

Advocates that cannot be instructed by the local authority

The adult may have access to an Independent Mental Health Advocate (IMHA). An IMHA is a specialist advocate and can act as an instructed or non-instructed advocate depending on the adult's capacity to instruct. The right to an IMHA was introduced in 2007 under amendments to the Mental Health Act 1983. The IMHA's role is to help people to understand their legal rights under the MHA 1983 (2007). Advocating in an adult safeguarding situation is not part of the IMHA's role, unless that situation is related to the care and treatment the adult is receiving under a mental health section, such as neglect or ill treatment in a mental health hospital or other premises. IMHAs may offer to advocate and, especially if they have a relationship with the adult, are helpful, but they are under no legal obligation to do so.

Independent Domestic Violence Advocates (IDVAs) have a distinct role in domestic abuse situations. Their purpose is to address the safety of victims at high risk of harm from partners, ex-partners or family members in order to secure their safety and the safety of any children in the situation. IDVAs work with adults from the point of crisis to assess their level of risk, discuss the range of suitable options and develop safety plans. These plans will include actions from the Multi-Agency Risk Assessment Conference as well as sanctions and remedies available through the criminal and civil courts, housing options and services available through other organisations. IDVAs support and work over the short to medium term to get an adult on the path to long-term safety (SafeLives, 2014a,b). It may well be that an IDVA will accompany and support an adult through adult safeguarding relating to domestic abuse, but their role is to work with the adult to address domestic abuse concerns and create safety plans; they cannot be involved in the adult's need for advocacy regarding other aspects of well-being.

What do advocates do?

The Care and Support Statutory Guidance describes advocates as having two roles:

1. they need to *provide support* to the adult to assist them in understanding the safeguarding process; and
2. *representation*, particularly in ensuring that the individual's voice is heard and the safeguarding process takes account of their views wherever appropriate. (DHSC, 2014, 7.50–7.52)

Studies of advocates in adult safeguarding in England (Lonbay and Brandon, 2017) and Scotland (Sherwood-Johnson, 2016) identify four areas of activity:

1. **Creating a supportive relationship**. Understanding the adult, their preferences, needs, strengths, circumstances and also, in non-instructed advocacy, their past wishes and views.
2. **Enabling communication**. Making sure the adult can understand the procedures and their rights within these. Taking steps to ensure that the adult is involved and that their views and wishes are central to the process.
3. **Supporting the adult to participate in meetings**. Considering options together, planning with them what they want to say and do.
4. **Acting as the adult's memory**. Keeping notes, asserting their needs and wishes, making sure the adult is not being persuaded against their interests or being rushed, going over what happened afterwards.

Advocates need time to get to know the adult and to form a relationship of trust with them. It is important to remember that the advocate is doing their best to represent the adult. They are independent of all organisations and cannot be swayed by the concerns of the practitioners involved. Representing or supporting the adult's wishes is about empowering them to have as much control as possible during a time when they have lost so much control. Sometimes we might experience relationships with advocates as oppositional or uncomfortable. We need to reflect on how we would feel if the adult themselves was being assertive and challenging; the advocate is doing this on their behalf.

REFLECTIVE ACTIVITY

Case study: Mrs Swift and her advocate

The enquiry plan was only partially successful in achieving the aim of giving **Mrs Swift** a space free of Nigel and his frightening behaviour. It was Mrs Swift's decision as to whether he left the flat or not and whether she continued to breach her tenancy. Mrs Swift told Nigel that she wanted him to leave but, given he had nowhere to go, would allow him 'a few more days' to visit the housing point of access and get himself sorted out. This extended into a week. Fortunately, Nigel did not forbid the home carers coming in who he perceived as a 'neutral party' and so Mrs Swift's well-being could be ascertained and the multi-agency group around her could stay vigilant of her safety.

Nigel continued to drink heavily and fell into the path of a motorcyclist on his way back from the supermarket. He was taken to hospital and admitted as he had a head injury and fractured leg. The police reported this to the social worker who went straight round to see Mrs Swift. Mrs Swift was very distressed, she felt the social worker was pressuring her, she felt she couldn't think straight, that she wasn't being listened to, and wanted everyone to leave her alone. Mrs Swift was in a dilemma: she loved her son, but also did not want to lose her tenancy or spend her life in fear of him. She had no other family or friends to whom she could turn.

Reflective question
· What can you do to support Mrs Swift during this crucial time?

Our thoughts are that, because of the deep dilemmas in her life and absence of neutral support, she is experiencing significant difficulty in being involved in the enquiry, weighing up information, and being listened to. You could talk with her about having a neutral person, a Care Act advocate, to support her to think through her wishes and to make sure that her views are listened to.

> ### How did Mrs Swift's story end?
>
> The initial approach to support Mrs Swift to tell Nigel to leave was not fully successful. A further meeting was being planned when events changed Mrs Swift's circumstances and brought matters to a head. In situations where there are a range of risky behaviours, this sometimes happens and a good monitoring and multi-agency communication plan will help all involved to respond effectively to crises and opportunities.
>
> Mrs Swift and her advocate were able to work well together. Their relationship formed the basis for extensive conversations about Mrs Swift's feelings and wishes and Nigel's options. Nigel was discharged to a ground-floor room in a bed and breakfast. Mrs Swift visited him when she wanted to, armed with cake and details of the local Alcoholics Anonymous group. She sees her grandchildren again as Nigel's ex-partner is no longer suspicious of her. Her locks are changed as she does not want Nigel to live with her again; and as her life begins to feel good, she is feeling stronger.

Supporting other organisations during the enquiry

Remember the local authority retains the enquiry duty. It must set clear terms of reference for any enquiry, giving the organisation making the enquiry on its behalf a clear idea of what it is expected to do. The local authority must assure the quality of the enquiry when it is returned. It is also good practice to give the name of a contact who can support the organisation at any point during the enquiry.

While adult safeguarding practitioners in local authorities have had training and ongoing support in using the MSP approach, many private, voluntary and independent-sector health and social care providers have had no or little training. Many providers will already be using person-centred, creative and preventative approaches and find that asking adults about outcomes and redress is second nature. Some providers are not so confident about involving adults or their representatives. Their concerns may range from worrying about upsetting people or losing the trust and confidence of those using the service, through to seeing safeguarding as a disciplinary or regulatory matter that is dealt with by managers and owners, not the adults who use the service or their representatives or indeed the frontline staff who work with them. It does not help when employing organisations are asked by the local authority to undertake an 'investigation' rather than an 'enquiry', as an investigation will mean a disciplinary process to the organisation, a process without the objectives of an enquiry.

Lawson (2017) has written guidance on good practice and MSP for a range of organisations including housing, police, commissioners and health and care providers. Telling agencies what MSP is and how to use person-centred approaches is only a beginning. While commissioners and regulators must promote such approaches, we also need to share our knowledge and training about involving people with our provider colleagues. Our case-auditing experience shows an emerging picture of a 'two-tier' use of MSP approaches. If an adult is living in their own home, they are more likely to be involved in their own safeguarding than an adult living in a care setting. There may be several underlying reasons for this, but a clear trend is that we are more likely to ask a provided service to undertake an enquiry in a care home. That provider may not have had training or support to use an MSP approach, while community organisations may be more practised in using enabling approaches to care and support.

ESSENTIAL INFORMATION: PRACTICE GUIDANCE

When causing another organisation to make an enquiry: Dos and Don'ts

1. **Do** set clear terms of reference in writing: be clear on what you want the organisation to enquire about. What needs to be understood or what risks need to be considered?

2. **Do** detail how you expect the organisation will involve the adult in the enquiry. Be clear and specific: 'Speak with Mrs Jones and ask her what impact this incident has had on her. How does she feel now? What would help her recover? What would improve her quality of life? What does she think is now the best way forward?' **Don't** say 'use a Making Safeguarding Personal approach' as the provider may not be clear what this is. Make sure that an advocate is instructed by the local authority if needed to support the adult.

3. **Do** be clear about who the organisation should report to; give their contact details. Make sure the organisation knows who will support them if they have questions or make an unexpected discovery (for example, that a crime has been committed).

4. **Do** negotiate the timescale for return of the enquiry report. You can follow up a few days beforehand to make sure all is well. **Don't** let matters drift; instead, set new timescales and find out what barriers or challenges are being experienced. Remember it is a local authority duty to make sure the enquiry is undertaken.

5. **Do** quality assure the report. Has the enquiry been objective and thorough? Has it addressed the terms of reference? Has the adult or their representative been involved? Has the conclusion of the enquiry been evidenced? Has any further

need for protection been determined and actioned? What recommendations are made? If you cannot accept the quality of the enquiry, you can ask the organisation to undertake further work with a new negotiated timescale, or you can undertake a further enquiry yourself.

Local authorities are increasingly giving template forms to organisations caused to undertake enquiries. These can be useful, for setting out expectations and timescales as well as the expectation that the adult will be involved in the enquiry.

Making safeguarding plans

Safeguarding planning often occurs as part of the enquiry, but if the situation is complex a plan may not be agreed until the end of the enquiry. As we have already discussed, the process of enquiry and planning can be fluid; it may be possible to make plans rapidly or it may take some time to do so. The imminence of harm, the decision-making pace the adult needs, the outcomes they seek and the need for input from a range of organisations can all influence when and how safeguarding plans are made.

Essential components of a safeguarding plan

The statutory guidance tells us that 'Once enquiries are completed, the outcome should be notified to the local authority which should then determine with the adult what, if any, further action is necessary and acceptable. It is for the local authority to determine the appropriateness of the outcome of the enquiry' (DHSC, 2014, 14.110). In addition, 'The local authority must determine what further action is necessary. Where the local authority determines that it should itself take further action (for example, a protection plan), then the authority would be under a duty to do so' (DHSC, 2014, 14.107).

The local authority's Section 42 duty continues as plans are made and monitored. The local authority is the lead agency in decision making about whether a safeguarding plan is needed and what actions should be part of the plan. Once it decides that a plan is needed, the local authority has a duty to put a protection plan in place.

The statutory guidance notes that:

> if the adult has the capacity to make decisions in this area of their life and declines assistance, this can limit the intervention that organisations can make. The focus should therefore be on harm reduction. It should not however limit the action that may be required to protect others who are at risk of harm. The potential for 'undue influence' will need to be considered if relevant. If the adult is thought

to be refusing intervention on the grounds of duress then action must be taken. (DHSC, 2014, 14.108)

What kinds of action can be taken if we believe that another person is preventing the adult making their own decisions? It is important not to collude with this type of control by closing the case and ending contact with the adult. We need to find opportunities to continue to work with the adult, and to understand if coercive control is manifested in this situation, and how we can support the adult to be able to make their own decisions, using the law, including inherent jurisdiction as necessary. (See Mr Meyers's case in Chapter 4 on inherent jurisdiction.)

When an adult does not have the mental capacity to make decisions about their own safety, the principles of best-interests decision making must be observed. As discussed in Chapter 4, we must look for and use the least restrictive option that will keep the adult safe while restricting their rights and freedoms as little as is possible. We must consider the adult's human rights (as considered in Chapter 2), in particular, the ECHR Article 2 right to life, Article 3 freedom from inhuman or degrading treatment, Article 5 right to liberty and Article 8 right to private and family life, and how these will be supported within a safeguarding plan.

The statutory guidance summarises what should be noted within a plan:

- what steps are to be taken to assure their safety in future;
- the provision of any support, treatment or therapy including ongoing advocacy;
- any modifications needed in the way services are provided (for example, same gender care or placement; appointment of an OPG deputy);
- how best to support the adult through any action they take to seek justice or redress;
- any ongoing risk management strategy as appropriate; and
- any action to be taken in relation to the person or organisation that has caused the concern. (DHSC, 2014, 14.111)

Plans will be as unique as the adult they are used to protect, taking account of the adult's views, wishes and outcomes and containing creative solutions to ensure that the adult has the best quality of life along with the most reliable resources to support them. Some safeguarding plans are simple; for example, the plan (earlier in this chapter) made with Ron Wise that involved Ron, his social worker and his support worker. Some plans involve several organisations, are complicated or have a number of actions that need to be taken jointly or in a specific order, as with Mrs Swift. Plans may involve more than one organisation and have a degree of risk attached, for the adult and/or for the practitioners involved. Safeguarding plans that are not simple are best formulated at a face-to-face meeting where the adult, their supporters and all of the organisations involved can share ideas and anxieties, and plan creatively together.

The principles of empowerment and proportionality must guide the decisions made. Adults have autonomy and having their expertise valued and wishes respected and acted on can promote the adult's self-esteem and reduce the possibility of harm and exploitation in the future. Options that increase the adult's capability to protect themselves must be considered. As well as practical steps, this might include therapeutic work that helps the adult recover from past and present abuse or trauma.

A plan agreed by the adult and those closest to them will be more effective in preventing further harm; if the adult and their informal supporters are involved in problem solving, they are likely to be able to continue to problem solve together in the future (Taylor and Tapper, 2017). We can work with the adult and their supporters through best-interests meetings, family meetings or by engaging individuals in a family separately.

Statutory children's services in England are using family group conferences (FGCs) as an empowering and effective approach to enabling problem solving within the 'system' around the child. Three quarters of local authorities in England and Wales currently run or commission FGCs for children in their area (Family Rights Group, 2019) but Manthorpe and Rapaport (2020) were only able to identify ten local authorities across the UK who were using the approach for adults. Awareness of the usefulness of the approach is developing, but resource limitations appear to be preventing the development of FGCs in adult safeguarding. In the meantime, FGC practitioners (Family Group Conferencing for Adults, 2024) continue to develop and research the approach.

ESSENTIAL INFORMATION: PRACTICE GUIDANCE

Family group conferences

Family group conferences are not to be confused with family meetings and are a specific approach to family decision making. They have distinct features:

- The process begins with preparation. An FGC facilitator visits and prepares all participants, identifying and addressing the concerns of the participants, any long-standing relationship difficulties and any potential risk factors. The adult decides who they want to be at the meeting, and where and when it will take place. This process can take weeks but completing this first stage is essential, as each participant must fully understand why the FGC is being called, what will happen there and what their role is. The adult decides how they want to be supported through the meeting: this can be by an advocate or maybe someone they have a close and trusting relationship with. The facilitator is neutral; they are independent of all agencies and professionals involved. They are skilled and experienced in facilitating and coordinating FGCs.
- The meeting has three stages. The first is information sharing: the adult, their family and friends and the professionals involved are facilitated to share information about the concern. The emphasis is on problem solving, not blame, and on the strengths in the room. The second part of the meeting is 'private family time'. The adult, their family and friends and, if applicable, the adult's

advocate meet without the professionals and neutral facilitator present and make a Family Action Plan. This is presented to the referrer of the concern in the third part of the meeting for discussion facilitated by the coordinator. Once finalised, arrangements for monitoring and review of the plan are agreed. FGCs can be used as consultation and information gathering to inform a best-interests decision and are useful when there is disagreement between family members or between family members and professionals.

Reflective questions

- In which situations would you find an FGC useful?
- Are there elements within the approach that you may be able to use in practice now?
- Can you share your awareness of the FGC approach to inspire colleagues to request that your local authority invests in an FGC project?

Safeguarding planning with individuals and families

White (2017, pp 111–121) notes some key questions to consider when creating a safeguarding plan:

- How can safety be promoted without damaging the adult's human rights, or the benefits they gain from the situation?
- Are there ways of supporting the adult to change the situation to reduce risk while still respecting their choice and promoting the quality of life they want?
- What could go wrong? What contingencies are needed?
- Does everyone involved have a joined-up understanding of the adult's situation, what is important to them and what the risks are?

It is important to think through the adult's desired outcomes from the adult safeguarding process alongside their views on how their overall well-being can be maintained or improved. The adult's thoughts on recovery and resolution should also be discussed, and options presented to them to achieve this if they are unsure of what may be available. We will explore recovery and resolution further in Chapter 10. This process should not be rushed. Many adults complain that they feel rushed by the safeguarding timescales and efficiency of the enquiry officer. Adults need time to think through what they wish to happen, and for this reason it is recommended that the adult's desired outcomes are reviewed at the beginning, middle and end of the adult safeguarding process. This will also give you time to talk through with the adult what outcomes are and are not possible.

There are occasions when the adult's outcomes are not possible; for example, to close a care home or arrest someone who has not committed a crime. There are also situations when to meet the adult's outcomes would cause an unacceptable risk of harm to the adult or other adults or children. The duty of care to safeguard the adult will always need to be balanced with their right to self-determination. These situations need careful negotiation with the adult and others involved, and all decisions should be discussed and explained to the adult in a way they can understand.

Remember that an adult may have had years of experience of living with an abusive partner or adult child and developed strategies in the past for dealing with the abuse that are no longer working, as frailty or illness changes relationships and abilities. An adult may value a relationship with the person who is now harming them and may decide that some elements of abuse are preferable to losing the valued relationship. Others may be very afraid of the person harming them and fear taking any action that may increase the person's abusive behaviour towards them. They may be experiencing coercion and/or control. Other adults may be clear that they want action to be taken on their behalf and want the police or regulator to be involved. The adult's previous experiences may affect how they view the harm and what they feel will support them to either self-protect or be protected.

The policies and procedures produced by the West Midlands Adult Safeguarding Editorial Group (2024) describe a range of potential actions that serve as a useful prompt in considering creating a safeguarding plan. We have extended and described these in the Essential Information boxes.

 ESSENTIAL INFORMATION: PRACTICE GUIDANCE

Actions to promote the safety and well-being of an adult

- Provision of care and support services to promote safety and well-being (for example, homecare, telecare).
- Security measures such as door locks and entry devices, personal alarms, telephone or pager, CCTV. Telephone nuisance call blocking, mail preference services, changing telephone numbers or email addresses.
- Installing smoke alarms or other anti-fire equipment.
- Formalised arrangements for monitoring safety and well-being (for example, 'keeping in touch' plans, usually used where an adult with capacity will not accept any other form of support).
- Putting a flag on organisation systems with documented and agreed actions to be taken when the organisation is alerted.
- Activities including personal development and awareness raising that increase a person's capacity to protect themselves, support or activities that increase self-esteem and confidence.
- Ongoing advocacy services to make sure the adult is in control of their life or a particular aspect of it. Reducing isolation using befriending services, creating

'circles of support'. Linking the adult up with local crime prevention organisations via the PCSO or Neighbourhood Watch.

- Support through the criminal justice system: IDVA or Independent Sexual Violence Advocate, Intermediary Service.
- Prevention Orders: domestic abuse, forced marriage. Civil injunctions.
- Guardianship order under the MHA to require residence or access to be given to residence.
- Application to the Court of Protection (COP) for a single decision or court-appointed deputy.
- Application to the High Court under inherent jurisdiction if the adult is prevented from exercising their free will by another.
- For redress: application for criminal injuries compensation or Civil Law; suing for damages.
- For recovery: support to recover from crime; Victim Support.

Useful organisations that can inform and contribute to the plan:

- health services;
- housing providers;
- domestic abuse support services;
- Trading Standards;
- fire and rescue;
- police; and
- access to support for people who are victims of modern slavery/human trafficking via the National Referral Mechanism.

(Adapted from West Midlands Adult Safeguarding Editorial Group, 2024)

In addition to actions that promote the safety and well-being of the adult, there may be actions we can take to prevent further harm by an individual or organisation.

ESSENTIAL INFORMATION: PRACTICE GUIDANCE

Actions to prevent further abuse or neglect by a person or an organisation

- Meeting with an individual who poses a risk of harm and negotiating changes to their behaviour.

- Family group conferencing to agree changes to harmful behaviour.
- Carrying out a carer's assessment and providing services to decrease risk of harm or changing the support services provided to an adult to decrease carer stress.
- Changing the support given to an adult who has care and support needs and is a source of harm to other adults.
- Criminal prosecution.
- Application for a court order; for example, a restraining contact or an anti-social behaviour order.
- Application to the COP to change or remove a lasting power of attorney; application to the Department of Work and Pensions to change or cancel appointee-ship.
- Enforcement action by the CQC, including cancellation of registration.
- Prosecution by Trading Standards.
- Referral to the relevant registration body (for example Nursing and Midwifery Council, Health and Care Professionals Council, General Medical Council).
- Training needs assessment, supervision (of employee/volunteer) or disciplinary action following an internal investigation.
- Organisational review and action plans to address poor management or leadership, staffing levels, policies/procedures, working practices, organisational culture.

(Adapted from West Midlands Adult Safeguarding Editorial Group, 2024)

Safeguarding plans can be ineffective, and even increase the risk to the adult, if they are not carefully monitored and reviewed. Other services may believe that an adult is living in a safe situation 'because there is a plan in place' without stopping to review the impact of changes in the adult's life with the adult and those close to them. How this will be done, when and by whom needs to be set out in the safeguarding plan. Some useful questions to consider when setting out how the plan will be reviewed are:

- Does the adult feel safer? If they are concerned, who will they contact and how?
- When will you both agree that the need for the plan has ended?
- If the adult cannot tell you themselves, how will you assess the success of any plan? Who will tell you and how often?

If there is a safeguarding plan, the impact of existing risk on the adult's well-being must be considered with the adult at every review. The term 'disguised compliance' is sometimes used to describe cooperation on the part of those supporting the adult which does not result in any actual change. A focus on what has demonstrably improved or changed in the adult's life can help to protect against lack of compliance by those supporting the adult.

New concerns should result in a new assessment of risk and review of any plan, together with a consideration of whether another enquiry is needed.

The Section 42 duty ends when the adult safeguarding plan is no longer required, such as when the adult is no longer at risk of abuse or neglect, or risks have reduced to the level that the adult wishes to live with and that present no risk to their 'vital interests' (ECHR Article 2 rights) or risk to others (public interest). The adult must inform the decision to end a safeguarding plan and a review of the plan will be the best way of achieving this. When the safeguarding plan is no longer needed it is important to let other organisations still working with the adult, and the referrer if appropriate, know that the plan has ended so that they do not assume that the adult has supports in place, and also let them know they must refer to adult safeguarding should they have new concerns in the future; something that should be done even if a plan is in place.

The importance of escalation

It is important to understand what to do if partnerships with other agencies or within your own agency go wrong. Common scenarios include disputes about decision making, poor practice, organisations not completing the actions they have committed to do as part of an enquiry or safeguarding plan, or organisations who have agreed to progress a 'caused' enquiry failing to do so. Your local Safeguarding Adults Board (SAB) will have an escalation policy that has been agreed by all SAB partners. It is worth having a copy of this and discussing the principles with your colleagues.

Gloucestershire SAB have used restorative practice principles to inform their escalation procedure. The procedure is intended to promote a quick and straightforward means of resolving professional disagreements while ensuring that the safety of the adult remains the most important consideration and that disagreements do not detract from this. Gloucestershire have been using restorative approaches to improve the effectiveness of meetings, communications and problem solving, and to promote shared responsibility and accountability. In common with other escalation pathways, escalation begins with practitioner-to-practitioner challenge; if not resolved, then manager-to-manager challenge; and ultimately, in Gloucestershire, to a SAB Resolution Panel that will make a decision binding on all parties.

 ESSENTIAL INFORMATION: PRACTICE GUIDANCE

Principles to use in professional disagreements

- Respond positively to feedback: it is not personal, it's about an adult; issues have been raised because there are concerns about the level of risk/lived experiences for an adult(s). Being able to positively accept challenge is equally as important as being able to rise to a challenge.

- Seek to resolve any professional disagreements at the lowest possible level as part of everyday working practice and within the timescales laid out in guidance.
- Encourage others to challenge or question your own practice to ensure healthy challenge becomes part of all of our professional and learning cultures.
- Wherever possible, discussions should take place face-to-face or by telephone. Try to avoid the use of email alone to raise a challenge. However, it is good practice to follow up your conversation by email to document the discussions that took place.
- The tone of challenge should be one of respectful enquiry, not criticism. Be curious and remain curious until you understand and accept the reasons behind the decision that has been made or an alternative decision has been reached.
- Challenge should always be evidence based and solution focused.
- Be persistent and keep asking questions.
- Discuss your concerns with the named/designated safeguarding lead within your organisation or through supervision arrangements.
- Always keep a written record of actions and decisions taken in line with your own organisation's information governance and record-keeping policies.
- Remember, you are acting in the best interests of the adult and they must always remain central to your discussions and decision making.

(Gloucestershire Safeguarding Adults Board, 2024)

▶ KEY MESSAGES

- Enquiries are fluid, rather than a defined set of linear activities, that meet a set of objectives as specified in the Care and Support Statutory Guidance in a proportionate, person-centred way.

- There are many reasons why you might be prevented from meeting with an adult. You will need to understand these in order to plan your approach to the person obstructing or hindering.

- Enquiries, no matter how short, need to be planned. Enquiries that involve several organisations are best planned in a face-to-face or virtual meeting.

- Care Act advocates and IMCAs can be instructed (commissioned) to represent the adult and can make sure the adult is involved in their own safeguarding through creating relationships, enabling communication, supporting the adult in meetings and acting as their 'memory'.

- A range of organisations can be 'caused' to make an enquiry, but this must be compatible with the agencies' existing duties and must cause no adverse effect to the agencies' exercise of their existing functions.

🗺 KNOWLEDGE REVIEW

- WHAT factors would cause you to consider moving from an enquiry focused on a conversation with the adult into a more extended enquiry into the abuse or neglect?

- WHAT approaches can you use to gain access to an adult if a third party appears to be preventing this? If these approaches fail, in what circumstance would you consider the use of legal powers?

- WHAT should you expect from different types of advocate?

- WHAT are your duties, and your role and responsibility, in relation to 'caused' enquiries?

- WHAT are the crucial elements in ensuring the success of a safeguarding plan?

- WHEN might you need to use an escalation pathway? What will your first step be?

🗺 FURTHER READING

- We recommend Emily White again, for her reflections on Making Safeguarding Personal through the enquiry process: White, E. (2017) 'Assessing and Responding to Risk', in A. Cooper and E. White (eds) *Safeguarding Adults Under the Care Act 2014: Understanding Good Practice*, London: Jessica Kingsley, pp 110–27.

- You can find out more about family group conferences from: Taylor, M. and Tapper, L. (2017) 'Participative Practice and Family Group Conferencing', in A. Cooper and E. White (eds) *Safeguarding Adults Under the Care Act 2014: Understanding Good Practice*, London: Jessica Kingsley, pp 57–73. Also have a look at the work being done by the Family and Group Conferencing for Adults Research and Practice Network at www.communitycatalysts.co.uk/fgcforadults/ [Accessed 12 July 2024].

- Guidance on gaining access to an adult at risk is available from SCIE. See SCIE (Social Care Institute for Excellence) (2018) 'Gaining Access to an Adult Suspected to Be at Risk of Neglect or Abuse'. Available from: www.scie.org.uk/safeguarding/adults/practice/gaining-access [Accessed 12 July 2024].

10

Recovery and resolution

Chapter aim

In this chapter we will explore the resources and methods needed by adults at risk and by practitioners to move on from adult safeguarding work. We illustrate a range of approaches to recovery and resolution for adults at risk, including mediation and restorative justice, together with access to counselling and supportive interventions or victim support organisations.

This chapter includes:

- What do recovery, resolution and restoration mean to adults and those working with them?

- The impact of harm on adults

- Counselling and therapeutic approaches

- Mediation

- Restorative justice

- Criminal justice

- Compensation

The statutory guidance stipulates that a Section 42 enquiry should consider how the adult will recover from the harm and/or achieve a resolution of the experience, and that plans for recovery and resolution should be part of ongoing discussion and planning after the enquiry is completed (DHSC, 2014, 14.95 and 14.106). This element of adult safeguarding is often neglected. There may be many reasons for this omission such as stretched resources meaning that practitioners do not look beyond initial protection work, or perhaps practitioners are unsure how to support an adult's recovery or resolution of matters between people. The long-term impact of harm on the well-being of adults at risk may not be adequately considered, and services that might assist adults to recover are unknown.

REFLECTIVE ACTIVITY

Throughout the chapter, reflect on what you would expect to happen after you were assaulted or harmed in any way:

- What support would you expect?
- How are your expectations about your own well-being mirrored in how you support adults to recover from and resolve the impact of harm on their lives?
- What challenges or barriers can you identify in your own thinking about recovery and resolution for adults? What assumptions or biases are there in your thinking?

Our thoughts are that prioritising recovery and resolution can act as preventative measures for future abuse as well as improving well-being and outcomes for the adult overall. If you do not think recovery and resolution would be important to your well-being, reflect on this: why do you not need or deserve this?

What do recovery, resolution and restoration mean to adults and those working with them?

The term 'recovery' can denote a return to one's previous condition of well-being before harm occurred. 'Resolution' is a more ambiguous term, implying that a difficulty or dispute is finished or agreed; a problem solved. For adults who continue to live in potentially harmful circumstances, this may not always be possible, but it is always worth asking the questions, 'How would you like matters to be resolved?' or 'When would you feel that the problem has ended?' Although not mentioned in the statutory guidance, the term 'restoration' is also worth thinking about: the act of being restored, gaining something back that was lost. All these terms have assumed more than their actual meanings within adult safeguarding, largely because of the potentially empowering effect on adults of support to recover, and the impact on the adult's self-esteem and confidence in being actively involved in restorative approaches. Craig (1998) describes the potential impact of engagement in mediation for older people:

> Mediation promotes self-esteem through the experience of having one's point of view heard and valued, and in the ability to resolve matters oneself. Mediation can be seen as valorising for anxious older people who experience achievement through the mediation process of helping them construct improvements in their relationships. It also encourages self-protection as they become assertive and confident in communication. (p 178)

The immediate actions we take after harm is disclosed will support recovery, but for many, recovery is a long-term endeavour. Recovery from the immediate impact of abuse can be focused on practical measures as well as giving advice or listening and reassuring, whereas long-term recovery work focuses on addressing the trauma of abuse in order to enable the adult towards recovery and restoration in its fullest sense. Previous trauma will be compounded by being abused and the adult may experience an intensification or return to survival behaviours. Pritchard (2013) distinguishes between recovery and healing in her work, 'recovery is immediately after something; healing is long-term' (p 19). Pritchard derives much of her practice wisdom from listening to adults; participants in her 'Beyond Existing' therapeutic support groups describe 'recovery' as attending to their physical needs and immediate emotional reactions to abuse, but 'healing' as the promotion of long-term change that will address their psychological state and ultimately result in the restoration or development of self-esteem, confidence, being at peace with oneself, and being free of the emotions relating to the harm.

What immediate actions are needed to promote recovery in the short term?

Adults may be left without food, heating or accommodation, or be unsafe or physically injured. Activities to restore the adult's basic needs will include:

- organising food, heating, money;
- receiving medical attention for injuries;
- finding suitable clothing;
- moving accommodation;
- changing locks, making premises secure;
- changes to care and support plans or changes in the provider or staff supporting them;
- meeting immediate emotional needs, shock and distress, the need for reassurance; and
- making sure the adult can talk with someone who will listen and if needed can give advice on recovery activities.

The impact of harm on adults

All adults who have been abused will have emotional distress caused by the abuse, and for some this is made more complex by the stirring up of emotions and memories of previous harm. Feelings of loss, shame and anger, and the trauma of being abused, will not only cause the adult's enjoyment of life to diminish but may affect their relationships with others and their physical health. Support to recover is not a case of one size fits all. We must ask the adult what they think will help them in the short and longer term. The facts you have ascertained during the enquiry may have revealed historical abuse and long-term harm. You may need to include the impact of these historical experiences in talking with the adult about recovery. Remember that the adult may be re-traumatised by an expectation that they recount the details of historical abuse. It is not important for you to know exactly what happened in the past but to understand the impact over the life course of those experiences. Each adult will have a different reaction to being abused. For some there will be weeks or even months of distress, which might manifest in physical decline or illness or in behavioural changes.

For a few adults there will be long-term consequences. These may include symptoms that can be described as post-traumatic stress disorder (PTSD) or other long-term mental health issues.

 ESSENTIAL INFORMATION: PRACTICE GUIDANCE

Post-traumatic stress disorder symptoms to be aware of

PTSD may be 'acute' (symptoms are experienced for less than three months), 'chronic' (symptoms are experienced for more than three months) or have a 'delayed onset' (occurring at least six months after the traumatic event).

Impacts can be:

- **Physical**, including heart symptoms, exhaustion, exacerbation of aches and pains, digestive disorders, acute sensitivity to noise and light, sudden sounds; some research indicates risk of development of serious illness in frail or older adults.
- **Emotional**, including hypervigilance (looking out for danger all the time), anxiety including panic attacks, depression, being angry or fearful, easily moved to tears, insomnia. Avoidance reactions which include inability to remember some aspects of the trauma, avoidance of certain people or places, feeling numb or empty, feeling life is no longer interesting, there are no exciting possibilities to look forward to, there is no 'future'. The adult may numb their feelings; for example, they are unable to be as affectionate or loving as previously, or to experience deep feelings of sadness or happiness.
- Some experience the traumatic event in terms of **flashbacks**, nightmares or re-experiencing acute emotions associated with the event or constant rumination about the harm.
- In order to cope with this, some adults may develop **drug or alcohol issues**, self-harm or have/act on suicidal feelings. The adult may fear being alone, but also fear crowds, lose trust in others or be suspicious of intentions.

(Adapted from NICE, 2018b)

It is important to explore with the adult the impact that abuse has had and put their reactions into context. Adults and those close to them may feel very distressed for weeks or months after being harmed. Do make sure that there are opportunities for the adult to talk if they wish and to be listened to. Encourage them to experience whatever feelings arise and take steps to reduce social isolation if the adult wishes you to do so.

There are few research studies on the long-term impact of harm on adults with care and support needs, but research on the impact of abuse on the general adult population applies to all adults, whether or not they have care and support needs. Some researchers identify that the circumstances of adults with care and support needs will increase the risk of long-term damage to emotional and physical well-being. Rowsell et al (2013) claim that trauma resulting from the violation of a caregiver's duty to provide protection and attachment security to a more vulnerable person is associated with a higher risk of developing PTSD.

Psychological harm may be more pronounced for individuals who have had long-term frequent experiences of harm or witnessing abuse; for example, adults who spent their childhood or young adulthood in settings where their human rights were not respected, who were bullied or assaulted, or who are living in domestic or institutional settings where they are frequently harmed. Disabled people are more likely to report that domestic abuse led to them experiencing anxiety, depression or panic attacks than adults without a disability, and domestic abuse can negatively impact a woman's ability to manage her primary physical disabilities, leading to the onset of debilitating secondary conditions (Public Health England, 2015).

Bows (2018) describes the physical and emotional effects on older people of sexual violence. Physical effects included genital and other injuries (including broken bones related to frailer skin and bodies), which create long-term health conditions and exacerbate existing health conditions. Older survivors of sexual violence experienced a decline in health that included heart attacks, PTSD, urinary incontinence and other life-damaging effects. The practitioners within Bows' research felt these symptoms were worse for older people because they had fewer opportunities to develop or use supportive networks through employment or social relationships.

Both the physical and emotional effects of sexual violence are thought to result in a number of lifestyle changes for older survivors, leading to social isolation (Lachs and Pillemer, 2004); older survivors are more likely to develop agoraphobia, altered relationships with family or friends, and disengagement from support organisations. Bows (2018) notes that the type and nature of sexual violence to older women is similar to that of younger women; however, 'there is still a poverty of research examining the effects of sexual violence on older people, their support needs and coping strategies, and experiences of accessing support services' (p 1072).

Rowsell et al (2013) have researched how symptoms of PTSD manifest in adults who have profound learning disabilities and simple communication skills:

Marked increases were reported in the frequency and severity of a range of emotional, physiological and behavioural symptoms of psychological distress in men and women with severe intellectual disabilities following alleged abuse. Over time, there was some alleviation in the victims' difficulties, but their psychological functioning remained severely compromised. (p 263)

The responses of the 18 people in the research were similar to those in the general population. However, unlike members of the general population, the research subjects had no access to services specialising in the treatment of PTSD. The very limited recovery made by the group two years after being abused is attributed to the lack of recognition of their distress and lack of specialist services to address their PTSD.

In common with the rest of the population, some adults may continue to experience distress years after the harm has ceased. An understanding of PTSD is useful in understanding what the impact of harm might be, and the reasons for changes in how the adult feels and behaves after being harmed. There are steps we can take to make sure that we are considering the impact of abuse on adults and, as discussed in the next section, can explore options with them to support recovery. The first step is developing an awareness of the symptoms of damage caused by abuse.

We need to be aware of our own and others' assumptions and prejudices about the impact of abuse on adults. For example, these assumptions may be informed by stereotypes (Bows, 2018) caused by ageist attitudes that think of older people as asexual and outside the accepted boundaries of concern as survivors of sexual violence (Bows and Westmarland, 2017) or think that people who are cognitively impaired do not experience the impact of trauma. Adults with memory impairment are sometimes described as having no memory of the abuse and therefore being unharmed. The subsequent changes in behaviour, as described in the Vera Jones story in Chapter 5, may go unnoticed. Recognition of the need for recovery work with people who live in care homes or other communal settings can be lost when services focus on remedying the situation through changes in staff and management and do not consider the impact on individuals.

The absence of recognition of PTSD or other post-abuse physical and mental health conditions has implications for the long-term recovery of adults and may also limit any thoughts of attempting to gain compensation for the significant and life-changing effects of abuse. Attempts to support the adult to regain well-being will be unsuccessful unless the distress they have experienced is addressed. There is growing evidence that given good support, an individual's quality of life can actually improve post-abuse. Weiss (2014) argues that successful growth after trauma for older people rests on avoiding a sense of rejection, receipt of social support (particularly for emotional comfort) and having a sense of participation in society.

A full awareness of the impact of abuse on adults means that safeguarding plans must always consider a longer-term plan about how the adult will be supported to fully recover in accordance with their wishes of a best-interests decision.

Counselling and therapeutic approaches

A significant amount of work is needed to recognise the impact of harm on adults, to identify existing specialist services that can help and to promote the creation of services that can address the full range of recovery needs of adults at risk of harm. You need to be aware of the options for recovery open to adults and to actively support the adult to access these as wished.

What actions can we take now?

- Explore with adults the options to help them recover from harm. If your service is closing down the case, make sure you work with the adult to identify who they will talk with to discuss their emotional and physical well-being at monthly intervals for the first six months to a year. Discuss what the adult's thoughts are on getting help and support and the options open to them to pursue. If the adult is part of a group living setting where harm has occurred, consider how recovery support can be arranged for all individuals within the group as necessary.
- Identify services in your area that offer counselling or therapeutic responses to address the needs of all adults, or who could do so if support to enable access was offered. Keep this information handy to use when discussing options with adults. Options may include NHS services that can be accessed through the adult's GP (specialist counselling, PTSD support including cognitive behavioural therapy, other mental health supports), or via a Community Learning Disabilities Team (CLDT).
- There may be support available via local services set up to support adults who have been sexually abused or have experienced domestic abuse. Domestic abuse services in your area may offer a version of The Freedom Programme suitable for women who have a learning disability. The Freedom Programme (2018) can be offered on a one-to-one basis or as very small group sessions to women with a learning disability who are currently in an abusive relationship. Sessions help participants make sense of and understand what has happened to them. There may be a programme in your area. You can also identify national agencies who may be able to help. Respond offer support services and psychotherapy for people with learning disabilities traumatised by abuse (Respond, 2024). Victim Support (2019) may be able to put you in touch with local services as well as offering support via a volunteer to the adult.
- Adults living in group settings may benefit from regular opportunities to meet and talk through their current well-being with an advocate or similar as well as using more specific services to address their individual recovery needs. Make sure that recovery is on the agenda of all planning meetings related to organisational abuse. Changing the culture of an organisation, increasing the use of person-centred and human rights-based approaches, can help to identify how

individual adults are experiencing the impact of previous and current abuse, and give opportunities to address specific needs.

- It is worth highlighting any gaps in provision for recovery to commissioners in both the local authority and the clinical commissioning group. Keep raising your own and your colleagues' awareness of the impact of harm and of useful responses; reflect on and challenge any discriminatory assumptions you and others make about the impact of abuse on adults and how their recovery needs should be addressed.

Mediation

Recovery can involve not only personal recovery but the recovery of relationships or of a valued previous way of life, or the recovery of confidence and self-esteem from being actively involved in making decisions about how future relationships will progress. Mediation approaches promote the resolution of problems between people. Mediation skills are used in a range of processes useful to plan protection and recovery including family group conferences and restorative justice. Mediation is a process in which an impartial third party (the 'mediator') meets with those in conflict to help them to reach agreement on the issues that divide them and is most effective when the issues being addressed are open to resolution through the modification of perceptions, attitudes or behaviour. Mediators avoid taking sides, making judgements or giving guidance and should have had recognised training in mediation, and be able to demonstrate active listening skills. Mediation in adult safeguarding is under-researched in the UK although some researchers (Craig, 1998; Bagshaw et al, 2015) have explored the potential impact of mediation schemes on outcomes for older people.

Civil or non-restorative justice mediation can be used in a variety of settings, from family disputes to disputes between neighbours or people who live in the same care home or supported accommodation. Practitioners who want to use mediation skills in everyday practice will need mediation training. Do also consider that if you have been involved in an enquiry about harm, you may well not be seen as a neutral party by the source of harm or others in the situation, and you may have your own feelings about the rights and wrongs of the situation.

Potential strengths of mediation

Mediation is concerned with equalising power relations between people and should be an empowering experience for the adult, enabling their voice to be heard and understood by others in the situation and promoting their self-determination as decisions are agreed by the adult and others directly involved. Resolution may be supported via the mediation principle of solving problems and reaching understanding or agreement rather than blame.

Further harm may be prevented if problems between people can be resolved and relationships promoted. Mediation may support an adult's desired outcome regarding retaining or improving relationships with those who have harmed them. Mediation helps people communicate: sometimes harm occurs because people do not understand the other's perspective or there has been miscommunication.

The approach should **not** be considered if:

- The adult or others do not have the mental capacity to participate.
- There is violence or risk of violence in the relationship.
- The process of mediation is likely to increase harm.
- There are imbalances of power that cannot be balanced by the intervention of a neutral mediator. The relationship between an adult and a professional who has a duty of care towards them cannot be open to mediation because of that duty of care owed to the adult and the inherent power imbalance in the situation. In these cases, other approaches may help, such as a genuine apology and an assisted discussion on future plans.

REFLECTIVE ACTIVITY

Case study: mediation between Agnes Milton and her grandson

Agnes Milton cared for her grandson, Kevin, after his mother emigrated to Australia with her new partner. Kevin was 15 at the time and is now 19 years old. He had not wanted to emigrate and leave his friends and school, and was very close to his grandmother. Agnes was referred to adult safeguarding via her church. Agnes asked the priest to contact adult safeguarding as Kevin was disturbing her sleep with rowdy friends, taking odd sums of money from her purse and was 'disrespectful' in his attitude.

Agnes has Parkinson's disease and has just started having carers to support her with her personal care as she is struggling to do this independently. Her health is suffering from lack of sleep, and she is worried that the small instances of theft may indicate that Kevin has a problem with drugs or drink. At his age Agnes thought her grandson should be 'grateful' she had given him a roof over his head, but he had shouted at her that he wanted to go to Australia and make his own life. Agnes wanted help to 'clear the air, and sort things out' with this much-loved but upsetting young man.

Reflective question
- Would mediation be an appropriate approach to support Agnes and Kevin to resolve their differences?

> *Our thoughts* are that there appears to be no risk of violence in the relationship or risk of increasing harm by taking an approach to enable both grandmother and grandson to discuss their different perspectives, hopes and wishes and make plans for their future relationship.

Face-to-face mediation meetings are most productive, but if the adult is not ready to face a person they are afraid of, or very angry with, then 'shuttle mediation' – when the neutral mediator relays the thoughts, feelings and wishes between parties – may be useful. A Care Act advocate can be commissioned to support an adult who may have substantial difficulties in participating in the mediation process, but who has the mental capacity to make the decision to do so.

REFLECTIVE ACTIVITY

Case study: shuttle mediation in Whitegulls supported living

Pete Grainger and Jason Dodge once lived in the same care home and disliked each other. Pete moved to a supported living flat in a complex for people with learning disabilities three years ago. He was an active member of the complex and organised the film night and enjoyed regular pub visits with others who lived at Whitegulls. Jason moved in a month ago and was pleased to see Pete.

Pete was shocked to see Jason and has either avoided meeting him, so missing out on social activities, or been rude when they inadvertently meet in the communal areas. Jason has started to tell others that he will 'get Pete back' for this. It is hard to know how to move things forward as neither man will discuss their previous relationship, but it has caused a bad feeling throughout the complex and there is a risk that matters will deteriorate and one will harm the other in some way. Neither Jason nor Pete are happy about the situation.

Reflective questions
- Could mediation help?
- What approach would you use?

Our thoughts are that a mediator needs to meet with Pete and Jason separately. If one or the other is not ready to meet together then a 'shuttle mediation' approach would be a good starting point in trying to get the other to see the predicament from the other's point of view and start to move forward.

Restorative justice

Restorative justice (RJ) is a form of mediation used when a crime has been committed. It is also sometimes referred to as restorative practice and has much in common with all mediation approaches although there is an additional emphasis on the identified offender understanding the impact of the harm they have caused. Victims of crime are entitled to be actively informed about restorative justice services in their area and what restorative justice can offer:

> Restorative Justice offers you an opportunity to be heard and sometimes to have a say in the resolution of offences. This can include agreeing activities for the offender to do as part of taking responsibility for their actions and to repair the harm that they have done. Restorative Justice can provide a means of closure and enable you to move on, while providing an opportunity for offenders to face the consequences of their actions and to understand the impact that it has had upon other people. (Code of Practice for Victims, Section 7.2 (MoJ, 2020, p 34))

Restorative justice is voluntary. Both the victim of crime and the offender must agree to engage with the process, which is managed by a trained RJ facilitator. Any risk to the victim's physical or psychological well-being is carefully considered and, if there are any doubts about the safety of a meeting, 'shuttle mediation' is used. The offender must have already admitted the offence, although an RJ process can take place before a trial and after sentencing, potentially when the offender is in prison. Practitioners need to work with RJ facilitators to make sure that the adult is able to engage as fully as they wish and that their specific needs are considered. The practitioner may give information to inform the RJ risk assessment with the adult's consent. Advocacy may need to be commissioned to support the adult, and as RJ can be seen as recovery and resolution from adult abuse, this will be a Care Act advocate commissioned by the local authority as part of the Section 68 duties.

REFLECTIVE ACTIVITY

Case study: restorative justice after a hate crime

Wendy Young has been the target of harassment by young people in her local area for the past year. She has learning disabilities and uses hearing aids. A group of young people regularly shouted at her in the street, three of them really 'targeted' her, continually knocking at her door and shouting in her face when she opened it, pushing notes through her door threatening her, and following her in the local Co-op making loud comments about her. The police arrested and cautioned the three youths, which appeared to have deterred two of them. However, one young woman, Rosalyn, continued a campaign against Wendy and has now been arrested again and charged with criminal damage after breaking a window and using 'threatening or abusive words or behaviour likely to cause harassment, alarm or distress'. Wendy was approached by the police about the possibility of a restorative justice meeting with Rosalyn, and after talking it through with her mother and social worker, decided to agree to this.

Reflective questions

- What support might Wendy need?
- Are there any risks to Wendy from using this approach?
- What might be the benefits?

Our thoughts are that we need to find out from Wendy how she feels about meeting Rosalyn and the way the RJ facilitator will work with her:

- Does she have confidence in the RJ facilitator?
- Are there any access issues the facilitator and police need to consider?

It is Wendy's choice whether she wishes to do this or not, and she stands to gain a great deal in terms of self-esteem and confidence should the RJ meeting go well.

What happened?

Rosalyn began the meeting in the local community centre by giving an account of the incidents when she abused Wendy. After each incident account, Wendy told Rosalyn how frightened she had been. Wendy's mother supported her and with her permission told Rosalyn how long it had taken Wendy to feel safe in her own home and what damage she felt she had done to Wendy's confidence; she had ruined her quality of life. Rosalyn gave a long and sincere apology to Wendy and handed over an agreed amount to compensate for the breakage of the window. Wendy thanked her for this and Rosalyn told her that she had nothing further to fear; she would never frighten Wendy again and would stop her friends from doing so.

Criminal justice

Some adults will feel a sense of resolution through the prosecution and sentencing of the person who harmed them. This route to resolution can be uncertain. When supporting the adult to engage with criminal justice agencies, it will be important for all those involved to keep a sense of realism about what might happen. Some cases do not pass the evidential test for prosecution and will not go forward to court. Others may result in a prosecution but not the type of sentence that the adult hoped for. Make sure that police colleagues explain the stages of criminal justice decision making as outlined in Chapter 8. Do keep other options, RJ or civil action, on the table. For some adults or their families, the 'day in court' is the only pathway that will demonstrate to them that the harm caused to them has been taken seriously, but do continue to be honest and realistic about the steps that must be taken before this happens, and what alternatives there may be.

Experiences of the criminal justice system can help or hinder an adult's recovery from harm. Where there is a potential for criminal prosecution it is important to ensure that counselling or therapeutic support provided to the adult will not interfere with criminal processes and evidence. This should be discussed as part of the safeguarding planning processes and where needed guidance can be obtained from the Crown Prosecution Service (CPS) about an individual's case. Court proceedings will involve discussions of the harm and can reactivate traumatic memories and feelings; you may need to arrange extra support.

Special measures

There are a range of formal measures that can be taken to support the adult through the criminal justice system. Remember that these measures are intended to increase the adult's ability to give their 'best evidence', not to provide emotional support. Introduced under the Youth Justice and Criminal Evidence Act 1999, these special measures apply to witnesses in criminal proceedings who may be intimidated or vulnerable and include any witness whose quality of evidence is likely to be diminished because they:

- are suffering from a mental disorder (as defined by the Mental Health Act 1983);
- have a significant impairment of intelligence and social functioning; or
- have a physical disability or are suffering from a physical disorder. (CPS, 2021).

The CPS (2021) 'eligibility for special measures' guidance notes that 'some disabilities are obvious, some are hidden. Witnesses may have a combination of disabilities. They may not wish to disclose the fact that they have a disability during initial and subsequent needs assessments ... different witnesses on the autistic spectrum may have very different needs from each other.' People who have been allegedly trafficked or subject to sexual assault are considered 'intimidated witnesses'.

It is vital that the need for special measures is identified early so that arrangements can be planned. The practitioner may need to make sure that an assessment of the adult's needs has been initiated by the police or prosecuting solicitors to establish whether special measures are needed. The court may not grant the application, however. It will only do so if it is satisfied that the special measures will enable the witness to give their best evidence.

Special measures can include changes to the environment in which the adult gives evidence:

- use of screens to shield the witness;
- a live link to enable the witness to give evidence during the trial from outside the court through a televised link to the courtroom;
- evidence given in private exclusion from the court of members of the public and the press (except for one named person to represent the press); and
- video recorded interviews and removal of wigs and gowns by judges and barristers.

Special measures can also provide support to communication before and during court hearings; an intermediary may be appointed by the court to assist the witness to give their evidence at court. They can also provide communication assistance in the investigation stage; approval for admission of evidence so taken is then sought retrospectively. The intermediary is allowed to explain questions or answers so far as is necessary to enable them to be understood by the witness or the questioner but without changing the substance of the evidence. Other aids to communication may be permitted to enable a witness to give their best evidence whether through a communicator or interpreter, or through a communication aid or technique, provided that the communication can be independently verified and understood by the court. This can include computers, voice synthesisers, symbol boards and books.

Adults may also be distressed when details revealed in court are reported in the local or national press. Courts can impose restrictions on reporting the details of adult witnesses using Section 46 of the Youth Justice and Criminal Evidence Act 1999. The court must be satisfied that the quality of the witness evidence or cooperation with the preparation of the case is likely to be diminished because of fear or distress in connection with being identified by the public as a witness. The court must balance the 'interests of justice' against the public interest and must not impose unreasonable restrictions on reporting the proceedings. Our experience is that such orders are rarely made; adults at risk are not protected from press interest with sometimes distressing consequences. The Mental Capacity Act 2005 did not include any legislation regarding the protection from media interest of people who lack mental capacity and full details of their harm can be published in the media.

Compensation

Some of the adults who lived at Winterbourne View (South Gloucestershire SAB 2012) were awarded compensation by the Department of Health who also commissioned Respond to offer therapeutic services to 19 people who were harmed there (BBC News, 2013). We are not aware of other compensation awards to adults who have experienced harm through organisational abuse, and consideration of whether and how an adult can claim compensation is not part of usual considerations during safeguarding enquiry or planning.

The failure to appreciate the symptoms of trauma can impede compensation claims (Rowsell et al, 2013) as lasting harm to the person's well-being must be evidenced. Compensation could be used to pay for specialist recovery support or to fund measures to improve the adult's damaged quality of life and well-being. There are two options for an adult or their representative to consider regarding compensation. First, a civil claim through a solicitor. The purpose of civil claims is to recognise a wrong by awarding 'damages' or compensation for injury. The adult can claim compensation for damages against the person who abused them, or their employer, or the organisation for which they were working at the time. The abuse should be reported as a crime to the police before any civil action is taken. Compensation claims relating to abuse are sometimes settled out of court so avoiding court action and the risk of adverse publicity and hardship to all involved. A compensation claim should be registered at court within three years of abuse occurring, although this can sometimes be extended by the court in certain circumstances (for example, historical child abuse).

The second route to compensation is through the Criminal Injuries Compensation Authority (CICA). CICA is a body set up by the government to compensate victims of any crime of violence. It makes financial awards to those who have suffered physical and psychological injury caused by a criminal offence committed against them. The adult must claim within two years of the abuse and must be able to demonstrate that they reported the matter to the police and cooperated with police investigations. The injury must be diagnosed and evidenced by the relevant medical professional (MoJ, 2012). Victim Support services will help adults and their representatives to access CICA and provide emotional support if discussing the crime in order to make a compensation claim is distressing.

▶ KEY MESSAGES

- **Being abused and harmed can be distressing and cause trauma reactions for any person, no matter what their circumstances or degree of cognitive impairment. There is little research on this matter, but the studies that have been carried out suggest that the risk of long-term damage to physical or emotional health is increased for many adults at risk.**

- **It is important to be aware of the impact of harm and to reflect on any bias or prejudice you may have that prevents you from understanding the short- and long-term effects of trauma.**

- You must research the options for recovery for adults in your area and highlight gaps in provision to commissioners.

- There are special measures available for people to give evidence in court. Adults who have experienced abuse by an organisation or who have suffered physical and psychological injury caused by a criminal offence committed against them may be entitled to compensation.

KNOWLEDGE REVIEW

- WHAT current and historical circumstances might affect an adult's ability to recover from harm?

- WHAT are the indicators of PTSD? What other effects can being abused have on those who have been harmed?

- WHAT approaches to recovery and resolution are informed by mediation practices?

- WHAT are the two main sources of compensation for adults harmed by abuse?

FURTHER READING

If you want to know more about restorative justice, a good handbook to start with is: Liebmann, M. (2007) *Restorative Justice: How It Works*, London: Jessica Kingsley.

References

ACE Hub Wales (2022) 'Trauma-Informed Wales: A Societal Approach to Understanding, Preventing and Supporting the Impacts of Trauma and Adversity'. Available from https://traumaframeworkcymru.com/ [Accessed 24 March 2024].

ADASS (Association of Directors of Adult Social Services) (2017) 'Making Safeguarding Personal'. Available from www.adass.org.uk/making-safeguarding-personal-publications [Accessed 6 January 2019].

Age UK (2011) 'Safeguarding the Convoy'. Available from www.campaigntoen dloneliness.org/wp-content/uploads/Safeguarding-the-Convoy.-A-call-to-act ion-from-the-Campaign-to-End-Loneliness.pdf [Accessed 12 May 2019].

Alcohol Change UK (2019) 'Learning From Tragedies: An Analysis of Alcohol-Related Safeguarding Adults Reviews Published in 2017'. Available from https://alcoholchange.org.uk/publication/learning-from-tragedies-an-analy sis-of-alcohol-related-safeguarding-adult-reviews-published-in-2017 [Accessed 7 June 2014].

Alzheimer's Society (2020) 'The Impact of COVID 19 on People Affected by Dementia'. Available from www.alzheimers.org.uk/sites/default/files/2020-08/The_Impact_of_COVID-19_on_People_Affected_By_Dementia.pdf [Accessed 9 January 2024].

Aspinwall-Roberts, E., Fleming, V., Khatri, R. and Jones, P.A. (2022) '"They Don't Want Them to Have Capacity": Multi-Agency Operationalisation of the Mental Capacity Act 2005 in England With Adults Who Self-Neglect'. *Health and Social Care in the Community*, 30(6): 4395–4404.

Association for the Prevention of Torture (2017) 'What Is Torture?' Available from: www.apt.ch/en/what-is-torture/ [Accessed 5 January 2019].

Bachman, C. and Gooch, B. (2018a) 'LGBT in Britain: Health Report'. Available from: www.stonewall.org.uk/lgbt-britain-health [Accessed 7 January 2019].

Bachman, C. and Gooch, B. (2018b) 'LGBT in Britain: Trans Report'. Available from: www.stonewall.org.uk/lgbt-britain-trans-report [Accessed 7 January 2019].

Bagshaw, D., Adams, V., Zannettino, L. and Wendt, S. (2015) 'Elder Mediation and the Financial Abuse of Older People by a Family Member', *Conflict Resolution Quarterly*, 32(4): 443–80.

Baker, D. (2017) 'Mental Capacity Act and Adult Safeguarding', in A. Cooper and E. White (eds) *Safeguarding Adults Under the Care Act 2014: Understanding Good Practice*, London: Jessica Kingsley, pp 128–46.

Barnett, D. (2018) *Self Neglect and Hoarding. A Guide to Safeguarding and Support* Jessica Kingsley: London and Philadelphia.

BASW (British Association of Social Workers) (2014) 'Code of Ethics for Social Workers: Statement of Principles', October. Available from: www.basw.co.uk/about-basw/code-ethics [Accessed 11 August 2018].

BBC News (2013) 'Winterbourne View Victims to Receive Compensation', 27 November. Available from: www.bbc.co.uk/news/uk-england-bristol-25127564 [Accessed 10 May 2019].

Beckett, C., Maynard, A. and Jordan, P. (2017) *Values and Ethics in Social Work* (3rd edn), London: Sage.

BIHR (British Institute of Human Rights) (2013) 'Mental Health Advocacy and Human Rights: Your Guide'. Available from: www.bihr.org.uk/mental-health-advocacy-and-human-rights-your-guide [Accessed 19 November 2018].

BIHR (British Institute of Human Rights) (2022) The British Institute of Human Rights' Response to the Government Consultation on Human Rights Act Reform: 'A Modern Bill of Human Rights'. Available from: www.bihr.org.uk/media/grljjokd/update-1.pdf?id=3247 [Accessed 7 June 2024].

Bishop, E. (2012) 'Where Social Workers Are Going Wrong on the Mental Capacity Act', *Community Care*, 30 October. Available from: www.communityc are.co.uk/2012/10/30/where-social-workers-are-going-wrong-on-the-men tal-capacity-act/ [Accessed 11 August 2018].

Bloom, M. (1996) *Primary Prevention Practices*, Thousand Oaks, CA: Sage.

Bonnick, H (2019) *Child to Parent Violence and Abuse: A Practitioner's Guide to Working with Families*. Shoreham by Sea: Pavilion Publishing and Media Ltd.

Bows, H. (2018) 'Practitioner Views on the Impacts, Challenges, and Barriers in Supporting Older Survivors of Sexual Violence', *Violence Against Women*, 24(9): 1070–90.

Bows, H. (2019) 'Domestic Homicide of Older People (2010–15): A Comparative Analysis of Intimate-Partner Homicide and Parricide Cases in the UK', *The British Journal of Social Work*, 49: 1234–53.

Bows, H., Bromley, P. and Walklate, S. (2023) 'Practitioner Understandings of Older Victims of Abuse and Their Perpetrators: Not Ideal Enough', *The British Journal of Criminology*, 63: 1–18.

Bows, H. and Westmarland, N. (2017) 'Rape of Older People in the United Kingdom: Challenging the "Real Rape" Stereotype', *British Journal of Criminology*, 57(1): 1–17.

Braye, S., Orr, D. and Preston-Shoot, M. (2011) 'Conceptualising and Responding to Self-Neglect: The Challenges for Adult Safeguarding', *The Journal of Adult Protection*, 13(4): 182–93.

Braye, S., Orr, D. and Preston-Shoot, M. (2015) 'Self-Neglect Policy and Practice: Research Messages for Practitioners'. Available from: www.scie.org.uk/files/self-neglect/policy-practice/self-neglect_practitioners_briefing.pdf [Accessed 10 December 2018].

Braye, S. and Preston-Shoot, M. (2017) 'Learning from SARs: A Report for the London Safeguarding Adults Board'. Available from: www.croydonsab.co.uk/wp-content/uploads/2019/01/learning-from-sars.pdf [Accessed 6 June 2024].

Burke, B. and Harrison, P. (2016) 'Exploring the Political and Ethical Dimensions of Social Work Practice with the "Other"', in C. Williams and M.J. Graham (eds) *Social Work in a Diverse Society: Transformative Practice with Black and Minority Ethnic Individuals and Communities*, Bristol: Policy Press, pp 39–56.

Burke, C. (2006) *Building Community Through Circles of Friends*, Foundation for People with Learning Disabilities, London: Mental Health Foundation.

Burton, V. and Revell, L. (2018). 'Professional Curiosity in Child Protection: Thinking the Unthinkable in a Neo-Liberal World', *British Journal of Social Work*, 48: 1508–1523.

Cambridgeshire and Peterborough Domestic Abuse and Sexual Violence Partnership (2021) Older People DASH. Download form www.cambsdasv.org.uk/web/make_a_referral/593292 [Accessed 5 April 2024]

Centre of Excellence for Information Sharing (2017) 'Multi-Agency Safeguarding Hubs'. Available from: http://informationsharing.org.uk/download/502/ [Accessed 6 February 2019].

College of Policing (2023) 'Investigation Process'. Available from www.college.police.uk/app/investigation/investigation-process [Accessed 20 February 2024].

Collingbourne T. (2014) 'The Care Act 2014: A Missed Opportunity?' *European Journal of Current Legal Issues*, 20(3). Available from: http://webjcli.org/article/view/365/464 [Accessed 4 January 2019].

Commissioner for Older People in Northern Ireland (2014) 'Protecting Our Older People in Northern Ireland: A Call for Adult Safeguarding Legislation', June. Available from: www.copni.org/media/1299/final-protecting-our-older-people-_-a-call-for-adult-safeguarding-legislation.pdf [Accessed 3 January 2019].

Conservative Party (2010) 'Invitation to Join the Government of Britain: Conservative Party Manifesto 2010'. Available from: https://conservativehome.blogs.com/files/conservative-manifesto-2010.pdf [Accessed 5 January 2019].

CPS (Crown Prosecution Service) (2019a) 'So-Called Honour-Based Abuse and Forced Marriage: Guidance on Identifying and Flagging Cases'. Available from www.cps.gov.uk/legal-guidance/so-called-honour-based-abuse-and-forced-marriage-guidance-identifying-and-flagging [Accessed 20 March 2024].

CPS (Crown Prosecution Service) (2019b) 'Reporting a Crime; Decision to charge'. Available from www.cps.gov.uk/reporting-crime [Accessed 20 December 2019].

CPS (Crown Prosecution Service) (2020) 'Victims Right to Review Service', July. Available from: www.cps.gov.uk/legal-guidance/victims-right-review-scheme [Accessed 7 February 2018].

CPS (Crown Prosecution Service) (2021) 'Legal Guidance Special Measures'. Available from: www.cps.gov.uk/legal-guidance/special-measures [Accessed 12 April 2024].

CPS (Crown Prosecution Service) (2022a) 'Disability Hate Crime and Other Crimes Against Disabled People: Prosecution Guidance', August. Available from: www.cps.gov.uk/legal-guidance/disability-hate-crime-and-other-crimes-against-disabled-people-prosecution-guidance [Accessed 14 January 2024].

CPS (Crown Prosecution Service) (2022b) 'Domestic Abuse Guidelines for Prosecutors'. Available from: www.cps.gov.uk/legal-guidance/domestic-abuse-guidelines-prosecutors [Accessed 10 June 2024].

CPS (Crown Prosecution Service) (2023) 'CPS Economic Crime Strategy 2025 – Two Year Progress Report'. Available from www.cps.gov.uk/publication/cps-economic-crime-strategy-2025-two-year-progress-report [Accessed 10 June 2024].

CQC (Care Quality Commission) (2022) 'The Impact of COVID-19 on the Use of Deprivation of Liberty Safeguards'. Available from www.cqc.org.uk/publications/major-reports/impact-covid-19-use-deprivation-liberty-safeguards [Accessed 12 April 2024].

CQC (Care Quality Commission) (2023) 'Our Updated Human Rights Approach'. Available from www.cqc.org.uk/about-us/our-updated-human-rights-approach [Accessed 6 June 2024].

CQC (Care Quality Commission) (2024) 'Enforcement Decision Tree', January. Available from: www.cqc.org.uk/sites/default/files/20170217_enforcement_decision_tree.pdf [Accessed 7 April 2024].

Craig, G. and Clay, S. (2017) 'Who Is Vulnerable? Adult Social Care and Modern Slavery', *The Journal of Adult Protection*, 19(1): 21–32.

Craig, Y. (1998) 'Intergenerational Mediation: Its Potential for Contributing to the Prevention of Elder Abuse', *Journal of Social Work Practice*, 12(2): 175–80.

Davies, E. (2019), 'What is Discriminatory Abuse?', Ann Craft Trust. Available at: www.anncrafttrust.org/what-is-discriminatory-abuse/ [Accessed 21 February 2024].

Davison, S., Rossall, P. and Hart, S. (2015) 'Financial Abuse Evidence Review, Age UK', November. Available from: www.ageuk.org.uk/globalassets/age-uk/documents/reports-and-publications/reports-and-briefings/money-matters/financial_abuse_evidence_review-nov_2015.pdf [Accessed 10 December 2023].

Department for Constitutional Affairs (2007) 'Mental Capacity Act 2005 Code of Practice'. Available from: www.gov.uk/government/publications/mental-capacity-act-code-of-practice [Accessed 30 March 2024].

DH (Department of Health) (2011) 'Adult Safeguarding: Statement of Government Policy', May. Available from: www.gov.uk/government/publications/adult-safeguarding-statement-of-government-policy [Accessed 5 January 2024].

DH (Department of Health) (2012) 'Consultation on New Safeguarding Power'. Available from: www.gov.uk/government/consultations/consultation-on-a-new-adult-safeguarding-power#history [Accessed 3 January 2019].

DH (Department of Health) (2013) 'Statement of Government Policy on Adult Safeguarding', May. Available from: https://assets.publishing.service.gov.uk/government/uploads/system/uploads/attachment_data/file/197402/Statement_of_Gov_Policy.pdf [Accessed 9 September 2019].

DH (Department of Health) (2015a) 'Mental Health Act 1983: Code of Practice.' Available from: https://assets.publishing.service.gov.uk/media/5a80a774e5274a2e87dbb0f0/MHA_Code_of_Practice.PDF [Accessed 11 July 2024].

DH (Department of Health) (2015b) 'Care and Support: What's Changing?', September. Available from: www.gov.uk/government/publications/care-and-support-whats-changing/care-and-support-whats-changing [Accessed 4 October 2018].

DHSC (Department of Health and Social Care) (2014, last updated March 2024) 'Care and Support Statutory Guidance'. Available from: www.gov.uk/government/publications/care-act-statutory-guidance/care-and-support-statutory-guidance [Accessed 26 March 2024].

DHSC (Department of Health and Social Care) (2018) 'Modernising the Mental Health Act: Increasing Choice, Reducing Compulsion – Final Report of the Independent Review of the Mental Health Act 1983', December. Available from: https://assets.publishing.service.gov.uk/government/uploads/system/uploads/attachment_data/file/762206/MHA_reviewFINAL.pdf [Accessed 5 January 2019].

DHSC (Department of Health and Social Care) (2021) 'Reforming the Mental Health Act'. Available from: www.gov.uk/government/consultations/reforming-the-mental-health-act/reforming-the-mental-health-act [Accessed 14 March 2024]

Dixon, J. (2023) *Adult Safeguarding Observed: How social workers assess and manage risk and uncertainty*. Bristol: Policy Press.

Dybicz, P. (2004) 'An Inquiry into Practice Wisdom', *Families in Society*, 85(2): 197–203.

European Court of Human Rights (2022) *Guide on Article 8 of the European Convention on Human Rights*. Council of Europe.

European Parliament (2016) 'Regulation (EU) 2016/679 of the European Parliament and of the Council of 27 April 2016 on the Protection of Natural Persons with Regard to the Processing of Personal Data and on the Free Movement of Such Data, and Repealing Directive 95/46/EC (General Data Protection Regulation)', *Official Journal of the European Union*. Available from: http://eur-lex.europa.eu/legal-content/EN/TXT/PDF/?uri=CELEX:32016R0679&from=EN [Accessed 12 March 2024].

Family Rights Group (2019) 'Family Group Conferences and Lifelong Links'. Available from: https://frg.org.uk/involving-families/family-group-conferences [Accessed 15 March 2024].

Flacks, S. (2012) 'Deviant Disabilities: The Exclusion of Drug and Alcohol Addiction from the Equality Act 2010', *Social & Legal Studies*, 21(3): 395–412.

Francis, R. (2013) 'Report of the Mid Staffordshire NHS Foundation Trust Public Inquiry', 3 vols. Available from: www.gov.uk/government/publications/report-of-the-mid-staffordshire-nhs-foundation-trust-public-inquiry [Accessed 2 January 2019].

Frost, L. (2016) 'Exploring the Concepts of Recognition and Shame for Social Work', *Journal of Social Work Practice*, 30(4): 431–46.

Furedi, F. (2011) 'Changing Societal Attitudes and Regulatory Responses to Risk-Taking in Adult Care', Joseph Rowntree Foundation, September. Available from: www.jrf.org.uk/report/changing-societal-attitudes-and-regulatory-responses-risk-taking-adult-care [Accessed 12 December 2018].

Ghaye, T. (2008) *Building the Reflective Healthcare Organisation*, Oxford: Blackwell.

Gilligan, R. (1997) 'Beyond Permanence? The Importance of Resilience in Child Placement Practice and Planning', *Adoption and Fostering*, 21(1): 12–20.

Gloucestershire Safeguarding Adults Board (2024) 'Escalation of Professional Differences Guidance', May. Available from: www.gloucestershire.gov.uk/media/voyovoag/gsab-escalation-protocol-jan-2024.pdf [Accessed 4 April 2024].

Government Equalities Office (2013) 'Disability: Equality Act 2010 – Guidance on Matters to be Taken into Account In Determining Questions Relating to the Definition of Disability (HTML)'. Available from www.gov.uk/government/publications/equality-act-guidance/disability-equality-act-2010-guidance-on-matters-to-be-taken-into-account-in-determining-questions-relating-to-the-definition-of-disability-html#fn:2 [Accessed 19 February 2024]

Graham, M. and Cowley, J. (2015) *A Practical Guide to the Mental Capacity Act 2005: Putting the Principles of the Act into Practice*, London: Jessica Kingsley.

Greer, J. (2016) *Resilience and Personal Effectiveness for Social Workers*, London: Sage Publications Ltd.

Heath, H. and Phair, L. (2009) 'The Concept of Frailty and Its Significance in the Consequences of Care or Neglect for Older People: An Analysis', *International Journal of Older People Nursing*, 4(2): 120–31.

Heath, H. and Phair, L. (2011) 'Frailty and Its Significance in Older People's Nursing', *Nursing Standard*, 26(3): 50–5.

HM Government (2018) 'Discrimination: Your Rights'. Available from: www.gov.uk/discrimination-your-rights [Accessed 6 January 2019].

Holmes, D. and Smale, E. (2018) *Mind the Gap: Transitional Safeguarding – Adolescence to Adulthood*. Dartington: Research in Practice.

Holt, A. (2017) 'Parricide in England and Wales (1977–2012): An Exploration of Offenders, Victims, Incidents and Outcomes', *Criminology & Criminal Justice*, 17: 568–87.

Home Office (2011) 'Prevent Strategy', June. Available from: www.gov.uk/government/publications/prevent-strategy-2011 [Accessed 11 December 2018].

Home Office (2015) 'Controlling or Coercive Behaviour in an Intimate or Family Relationship: Statutory Guidance Framework', December. Available from: https://assets.publishing.service.gov.uk/government/uploads/system/uploads/attachment_data/file/482528/Controlling_or_coercive_behaviour_-_statutory_guidance.pdf [Accessed 7 January 2019].

Home Office (2018) 'Criminal Exploitation of Children and Vulnerable Adults: County Lines Guidance', September. Available from: https://assets.publishing.service.gov.uk/government/uploads/system/uploads/attachment_data/file/741194/HOCountyLinesGuidanceSept2018.pdf [Accessed 12 July 2019].

Home Office (2022) 'Domestic Abuse Statutory Guidance'. Available from: https://assets.publishing.service.gov.uk/media/62c6df068fa8f54e855dfe31/Domestic_Abuse_Act_2021_Statutory_Guidance.pdf [Accessed 22 March 2024].

Home Office (2023) 'Hate Crime England and Wales Second Edition'. Available from: https://www.gov.uk/government/statistics/hate-crime-england-and-wales-2022-to-2023/hate-crime-england-and-wales-2022-to-2023 [Accessed 10 January 2024].

Home Office and Department of Health (2000) 'No Secrets: Guidance on Developing and Implementing Multi-Agency Policies and Procedures to Protect Vulnerable Adults from Abuse'. Available from: www.gov.uk/government/publi cations/no-secrets-guidance-on-protecting-vulnerable-adults-in-care [Accessed 1 October 2018].

Home Office and Foreign and Commonwealth Office (2023) 'Forced Marriage Unit Statistics 2022'. Available from: www.gov.uk/government/statistics/for ced-marriage-unit-statistics-2022/forced-marriage-unit-statistics-2022#vict ims-with-mental-capacity-concerns [Accessed 20 March 2024].

House of Commons Library (2024) 'Hate Crime Statistics'. Available from: https:// researchbriefings.files.parliament.uk/documents/CBP-8537/CBP-8537.pdf [Accessed 20 February 2024].

House of Lords (2014) 'Select Committee on the Mental Capacity Act 2005 Report of Session 2013–14 Mental Capacity Act 2005: Post-Legislative Scrutiny'. Available from: https://publications.parliament.uk/pa/ld201314/ldselect/ldme ntalcap/139/139.pdf [Accessed 30 August 2018].

Hubbard, R. and Stone, K. (2022) *The Best Interests Assessor Practice Handbook*, Bristol: Policy Press.

Ingram, R. (2013) 'Locating Emotional Intelligence at the Heart of Social Work Practice', *British Journal of Social Work*, 43(5): 987–1004.

Johns, R. (2014) *Using the Law in Social Work* (6th edn), London: Learning Matters/Sage.

Joseph Rowntree Foundation (2024) 'The Essential Guide to Understanding Poverty in the UK'. Available from: www.jrf.org.uk/uk-poverty-2024-the-essent ial-guide-to-understanding-poverty-in-the-uk [Accessed 9 January 2024].

Kemshall, H., Wilkinson, B. and Baker, K. (2013) *Working with Risk: Skills for Contemporary Social Work*, Cambridge: Polity Press.

Kidd, J. and Manthorpe, J. (2017) 'Modern Slavery – The Adult Safeguarding Interface', *The Journal of Adult Protection*, 19(3): 158–66.

Kings Fund (2024) 'Illustrating the Relationship between Poverty and NHS Services.' Available from: www.kingsfund.org.uk/insight-and-analysis/long-reads/ relationship-poverty-nhs-services [Accessed 6 June 2024].

Lachs, M. and Pillemer, K. (2004) 'Elder Abuse', *The Lancet*, 364(9441): 1263–72.

Lammy, D. (2004) 'Mental Capacity Bill: The Parliamentary Under-Secretary of State for Constitutional Affairs Written Statement', *Hansard*, House of Commons, 18 June. Available from: https://api.parliament.uk/historic-hansard/written-sta tements/2004/jun/18/mental-capacity-bill [Accessed 1 October 2018].

Landman, R.A. (2014) '"A Counterfeit Friendship": Mate Crime and People with Learning Disabilities', *The Journal of Adult Protection*, 16(6): 355–66.

Law Society (2024) 'Human Rights Act Reforms and the Bill of Rights Bill'. Available from: www.lawsociety.org.uk/topics/human-rights/human-rights-act-reforms/ [Accessed 7 June 2024].

Lawson, J. (2017) 'The "Making Safeguarding Personal" Approach to Practice', in A. Cooper and W. White (eds) *Safeguarding Adults Under the Care Act 2014: Understanding Good Practice*, London: Jessica Kingsley, pp 20–39.

Lawson, J. (2018) 'Briefing on Working with Risk for Safeguarding Adults Boards, ADASS/LGA', Local Government Association, Ref. 25.90, November. Restricted.

Learning Disability England (2022) 'Policy Briefing: Coronavirus and People with Learning Disabilities in England'. Available from www.learningdisabilityengland. org.uk/wp-content/uploads/2021/03/Covid-research-Policy-Brief-England-FINAL.pdf. [Accessed 9 January 2024].

Liebmann, M. (2007) *Restorative Justice: How It Works*, London: Jessica Kingsley.

Local Government Association (LGA) (2019a) 'Making Decisions on the Duty to Carry Out Safeguarding Adults Enquiries: Suggested Framework to Support Practice, Reporting and Recording'. Available from: www.local.gov.uk/making-decisions-duty-carry-out-safeguarding-adults-enquiries [Accessed 9 June 2024].

Local Government Association (LGA) (2019b) 'Myths and Realities of Making Safeguarding Personal'. Available from: www.local.gov.uk/sites/default/files/documents/25.144%20MSP%20Myths_04%20WEB.pdf [Accessed 19 February 2024].

Local Government Association (LGA) (2020) 'Understanding What Constitutes a Safeguarding Concern and How to Support Effective Outcomes: Suggested Multi-Agency Framework to Support Practice, Recording and Reporting'. Available from: www.local.gov.uk/publications/understanding-what-constitutes-safeguarding-concern-and-how-support-effective-outcomes [Accessed 9 June 2024].

Local Government Association (LGA) (2021a) 'COVID-19 Adult Safeguarding Insight Project – Second Report (July 2021)'. Available from: www.local.gov.uk/publications/covid-19-adult-safeguarding-insight-project-second-report-july-2021 [Accessed 10 March 2024].

Local Government Association (LGA) (2021b) 'COVID-19 Adult Safeguarding Insight Project – Third Report (December 2021)'. Available from: www.local.gov.uk/publications/covid-19-adult-safeguarding-insight-project-third-report-december-2021 [Accessed 9 January 2024].

Local Government Association (LGA) (2022) 'Making Safeguarding Personal'. Available from: www.local.gov.uk/our-support/our-improvement-offer/care-and-health-improvement/making-safeguarding-personal [Accessed 19 February 2024].

Lonbay, S. and Brandon, T. (2017) 'Renegotiating Power in Adult Safeguarding: The Role of Advocacy', *The Journal of Adult Protection*, 19(2): 78–91.

Lord Laming (2003) 'The Victoria Climbie Inquiry. Report of an Inquiry by Lord Laming. Parliamentary Command Paper'. Available from: https://assets.publishing.service.gov.uk/media/5a7c5edeed915d696ccfc51b/5730.pdf [Accessed 18 February 2024].

Maclean, S. (2010) *The Social Work Pocket Guide to Reflective Practice*, Lichfield: Kirwan Maclean Associates.

Making Every Adult Matter (MEAM) (2024) 'About Multiple Disadvantage'. Available from: https://meam.org.uk/multiple-needs-and-exclusions/ [Accessed 10 January 2024].

Manthorpe, J. and Martineau, S. (2019) 'Mental Health Law Under Review: Messages from English Safeguarding Adults Reviews', *The Journal of Adult Protection*, 21(1): 46–64.

Manthorpe J. and Rapaport J. (2020) *NIHR SSCR Methods Review 26: Researching Family Group Conferences in Adult Services*, London: NIHR School for Social Care Research.

Manthorpe, J., Martineau, S., Norrie, C. and Stevens, M. (2016) 'Parliamentary Arguments on Powers of Access: The Care Bill Debates', *The Journal of Adult Protection*, 18(6): 318–28.

Marshall, H. and Sprung, S. (2018) 'An Exploration of the Mental Capacity Act – Ten Years on – The Key Learning Areas for Health Care Professionals', *Nursing: Research and Reviews*, 8: 29–38.

Marsland, D., Oakes, P. and White, C. (2015) 'Abuse in Care? A Research Project to Identify Early Indicators of Concern in Residential and Nursing Homes for Older People', *The Journal of Adult Protection*, 17(2): 111–25.

Martineau, S., Cornes, M., Manthorpe, J., Ornelas, B. and Fuller, J. (2019) *Safeguarding, Homelessness and Rough Sleeping: An Analysis of Safeguarding Adults Reviews*. London: Kings College London.

Mason, B. (1993). 'Towards Positions of Safe Uncertainty'. *Human Systems*, 4: 189–200.

Mason, K. (2023) 'Harassment and Slurs or Epistemic Injustice? Interrogating Discriminatory Abuse Through Safeguarding Adult Review Analysis'. *The Journal of Adult Protection*, 25(5): 254–65.

Mason, K., Biswas Sasidharan, A., Cooper, A., Shorten, K. and Sutton, J. (2022), 'Discriminatory Abuse: Time to Revive a Forgotten Form of Abuse?' *The Journal of Adult Protection*, 24(2): 115–25.

Mason, K., Cornes, M., Dobson, R., Meakin, A., Ornelas, B. and Whiteford, M. (2017/18) 'Multiple Exclusion Homelessness and Adult Social Care in England: Exploring the Challenges Through a Researcher-Practitioner Partnership.' *Research, Policy and Planning*, 33(1): 3–14.

McCarthy, M. (2017) '"What Kind of Abuse Is Him Spitting in My Food?": Reflections on the Similarities between Disability Hate Crime, So-Called "Mate" Crime and Domestic Violence Against Women with Intellectual Disabilities', *Disability & Society*, 32(4): 595–600.

McKay, M., Davis, M. and Fanning, P. (2009). *Messages: The Communications Skills Book* (3rd ed.), Oakland, CA: New Harbinger.

McNichol, A. (2016) 'DoLS Checks "Exposing Care Failings Missed by Other Assessments"' *Community Care*, 14 September. Available from: www.community care.co.uk/2016/09/14/dols-checks-exposing-care-failings-missed-assessme nts/ [Accessed 16 September 2019].

MENCAP (2012) 'Death by *Indifference*: 74 Deaths and Counting – A Progress Report 5 Years On', February. Available from: www.mencap.org.uk/sites/default/files/2016-08/Death%20by%20Indifference%20-%2074%20deaths%20and%20c ounting.pdf [Accessed 6 December 2018].

Migration Advisory Committee (2022) 'Recruitment and Retention in Adult Social Care: A Qualitative Study'. Published by UK Government. Available from: www.gov.uk/government/publications/recruitment-and-retention-in-adult-social-care-a-qualitative-study/recruitment-and-retention-in-adult-soc ial-care-a-qualitative-study-accessible [Accessed 3 January 2024].

MoJ (Ministry of Justice) (2012) 'Criminal Injuries Compensation Scheme', London: TSO. Available from: https://assets.publishing.service.gov.uk/governm ent/uploads/system/uploads/attachment_data/file/808343/criminal-injuries-compensation-scheme-2012.pdf [Accessed 5 March 2024].

MoJ (Ministry of Justice) (2018) 'Multi-Agency Public Protection Arrangements: MAPPA Guidance'. Available from: https://mappa.justice.gov.uk/connect.ti/ MAPPA/view?objectId=5682416 [Accessed 3 February 2019].

MoJ (Ministry of Justice) (2020) 'Code of Practice for Victims of Crime', October. Available from: https://assets.publishing.service.gov.uk/government/uploads/ system/uploads/attachment_data/file/476900/code-of-practice-for-victims-of-crime.pdf [Accessed 10 March 2024].

MoJ (Ministry of Justice) (2021) 'Consultation on Human Rights Reform: A Modern Bill of Rights'. Available from www.gov.uk/government/consultati ons/human-rights-act-reform-a-modern-bill-of-rights [Accessed 19 February s2024].

Munro, E. (2011) 'Munro Review of Child Protection: A Child-Centred System', May. Available from: www.gov.uk/government/publications/munro-review-of-child-protection-final-report-a-child-centred-system [Accessed 6 February 2019].

National Crime Agency (2017) 'County Lines Violence, Exploitation & Drug Supply', November. Available from: https://nationalcrimeagency.gov.uk/who-we-are/publications/234-county-lines-violen-ce-exploitation-drug-supply-2017/file [Accessed 5 December 2019].

National Crime Agency (2020) 'Beware Fraud and Scams During Covid-19 Pandemic Fraud'. Available from https://nationalcrimeagency.gov.uk/news/ fraud-scams-covid19 [Accessed 19 January 2024]

NHS Digital (2018) 'Safeguarding Adults England 2017–2018'. Available from: https://files.digital.nhs.uk/33/EF2EBD/Safeguarding%20Adults%20Col lection%202017-18%20Report%20Final.pdf

NHS Digital (2023) 'Safeguarding Adults Collection (SAC), Annual Report, England 2022–23'. Available from: https://digital.nhs.uk/data-and-information/ publications/statistical/safeguarding-adults/2022-23 [Accessed 26 March 2024].

NICE (National Institute for Health and Care Excellence) (2018a) 'NICE Guideline [NG108] Decision Making and Mental Capacity'. Available from: www.nice.org. uk/guidance/ng108/chapter/Recommendations#assessment-of-mental-capacity [Accessed 10 October 2018].

NICE (National Institute for Health and Care Excellence) (2018b) 'Post-Traumatic Stress Disorder: NICE Guideline [NG116]'. Available from: https://www.nice. org.uk/guidance/ng116 [Accessed 9 May 2019].

Norfolk Safeguarding Adults Board (2021) 'Professional Curiosity Guidance'. Available from: www.norfolksafeguardingadultsboard.info/protecting-adults/working-with-adults-at-risk/professional-curiosity/ [Accessed 2 anuary 2024].

Norrie, C., Stevens, M., Martineau, S. and Manthorpe, J. (2018) 'Gaining Access to Possibly Abused or Neglected Adults in England: Practice Perspectives from Social Workers and Service-User Representatives', *British Journal of Social Work*, 48(4): 1071–89.

Northern Ireland Department of Health (2015) 'Adult Safeguarding Prevention and Protection in Partnership Policy', Available from: www.health-ni.gov.uk/sites/default/files/publications/dhssps/adult-safeguarding-policy.pdf [Accessed 11 December 2018].

O'Reardon, M. (2022) 'Social Workers and Safeguarding Adult Reviews (SARs) – an Exploration of the Stories that are Told and the Narratives they Hold'. *Journal of Adult Protection*, 25(1): 20–32.

Office for Health Improvement and Disparities (2022) 'Guidance: Vulnerabilities: Applying All Our Health'. Available from: www.gov.uk/government/publications/vulnerabilities-applying-all-our-health/vulnerabilities-applying-all-our-health#core-principles-for-health-and-care-professionals [Accessed 17 March 2024].

Office of National Statistics (ONS) (2022) 'Deaths of Homeless People in England and Wales: 2021 Registrations'. Available from: www.ons.gov.uk/peoplepopulationandcommunity/birthsdeathsandmarriages/deaths/bulletins/deathsofhomelesspeopleinenglandandwales/2021registrations [Accessed 7 June 2024].

PACE (Police and Criminal Evidence Act) (1984) 'Codes of Practice Code C'. Available from: https://assets.publishing.service.gov.uk/government/uploads/system/uploads/attachment_data/file/729842/pace-code-c-2018.pdf [Accessed 5 February 2024].

People First (2022) 'Human Rights Act Reform Consultation Briefing'. Available from: www.peoplefirstltd.com/articles/british-institute-of-human-rights-the-rights-removal-bill [Accessed 19 February 2024].

Plymouth Safeguarding Adults Board (2019) 'Creative Solutions Forum: Terms of Reference', March. Available from: https://plysab.proceduresonline.com/pdfs/csf_terms_ref.pdf [Accessed 17 March 2024].

Preston-Shoot, M. (2017) 'What Difference does Legislation Make? Adult Safeguarding through the lens of Serious Case Reviews and Safeguarding Adult Reviews: A Report for the South West Region Safeguarding Adults Boards'. South West ADASS. Available from: https://somersetsafeguardingadults.org.uk/wp-content/uploads/SW-SCRs-SARs-Report-Final-Version-2017.pdf [Accessed 11 July 2024].

Preston-Shoot, M. and Taylor, G. (2022) 'Learning from Safeguarding Adults Reviews and Fatality Reviews' in Cooper, A and Preston-Shoot, M. *Adult Safeguarding and Homelessness*, London: Jessica Kingsley, pp 174–94.

Preston-Shoot, M. and Ward, M. (2021) 'How to Use Legal Powers to Safeguard Highly Vulnerable Dependent Drinkers in England and Wales', Alcohol Change. Available from: https://alcoholchange.org.uk/publication/how-to-use-legal-powers-to-safeguard-highly-vulnerable-dependent-drinkers [Accessed 11 July 2024].

Preston-Shoot, M., Braye, S., Stacey, H. and Doherty, C. (2024a) 'Second National Analysis of Safeguarding Adult Reviews. Final Report: Stage 1 Analysis. Case Characteristics; Nature of the Abuse and Neglect; SAR Reviewing Process', Local Government Association; Association of Directors of Adult Social Care; Partners in Care and Health. Available from: https://www.local.gov.uk/publications/second-national-analysis-safeguarding-adult-reviews-april-2019-march-2023 [Accessed 5 August 2024].

Preston-Shoot, M., Braye, S., Stacey, H. and Doherty, C. (2024b) 'Second National Analysis of Safeguarding Adult Reviews. Final Report: Stage 2 Analysis. Analysis of Learning', Local Government Association; Association of Directors of Adult Social Care; Partners in Care and Health. Available from: https://www.local.gov.uk/publications/second-national-analysis-safeguarding-adult-reviews-april-2019-march-2023 [Accessed 5 August 2024].

Preston-Shoot, M., Braye, S., Stacey, H. and Doherty, C. (2024c) 'Second National Analysis of Safeguarding Adult Reviews. Final Report: Stage 3. Conclusions and Improvement Priorities', Local Government Association; Association of Directors of Adult Social Care; Partners in Care and Health. Available from: https://www.local.gov.uk/publications/second-national-analysis-safeguarding-adult-reviews-april-2019-march-2023 [Accessed 5 August 2024].

Pritchard, J. (ed.) (2013) *Good Practice in Promoting Healing and Recovery for Abused Adults*, London: Jessica Kingsley.

Pritchard-Jones, L (2019) 'The Care Act 2014 and the Mental Capacity Act 2005: Learning Lessons for the Future?' in S. Braye and M. Preston-Shoot (eds) *The Care Act 2014: Wellbeing in Practice,* Sage: London, pp 98–112.

Prochaska, J. and DiClemente, C. (1982) 'Transtheoretical Therapy: Toward a More Integrative Model of Change', *Psychotherapy*, 19(3): 276–88.

Public Health England (2015) 'Disability and Domestic Abuse: Risk, Impacts and Response'. Available from: https://assets.publishing.service.gov.uk/government/uploads/system/uploads/attachment_data/file/480942/Disability_and_domestic_abuse_topic_overview_FINAL.pdf [Accessed 5 May 2019].

Research in Practice (2020) *Professional Curiosity in Safeguarding Adults: Strategic Briefing*, Totnes: Dartington

Respond (2024) 'What We Do'. Available from: https://respond.org.uk/what-we-do/ [Accessed 20 March 2024].

RiPfA (Research in Practice for Adults) (2017) 'Coercive Control'. Available from: https://coercivecontrol.ripfa.org.uk/ [Accessed 3 January 2024].

RiPfA (Research in Practice for Adults) (2019) 'Webinars'. Available from: www.ripfa.org.uk/resources/training-and-events/webinars/ [Accessed 11 January 2024].

Roch, A., Morton, J and Ritchie, G. (2010) 'Out of Sight Out of Mind? Transgender People's Experience of Domestic Abuse'. Available from: www.scottishtrans.org/wp-content/uploads/2013/03/trans_domestic_abuse.pdf [Accessed 12 April 2024].

Rosengren, D.B. (2017) *Building Motivational Interviewing Skills: A Practitioners Handbook* (2nd edn), London: Guilford Press.

Rowsell, A.C., Clare, I.C.H. and Murphy, G.H. (2013) 'The Psychological Impact of Abuse on Men and Women with Severe Intellectual Disabilities', *Journal of Applied Research in Intellectual Disabilities*, 26(4): 257–70.

Ruck Keene, A., Butler-Cole, V., Allen, N., Lee, A., Kohn, N. et al. (2024) 'A Brief Guide to Carrying Out Capacity Assessments'. Available from: www.39essex.com/sites/default/files/2024-04/Mental%20Capacity%20Guidance%20Note%20-%20Relevant%20Information%20for%20Different%20Categories%20of%20Decision%20March%202024%20v2.pdf [Accessed 3 March 2024].

SafeLives (2014a) 'National Definition of IDVA Work'. Available from: www.safelives.org.uk/sites/default/files/resources/National%20definition%20of%20IDVA%20work%20FINAL.pdf [Accessed 28 February 2024].

SafeLives (2014b) 'Resources for IDVAs'. Available from https://safelives.org.uk/about-domestic-abuse/domestic-abuse-response-in-the-uk/ [Accessed 12 July 2024].

SafeLives (2016a) 'Older People's Care Referral Pathway Guidance'. Available from: www.safelives.org.uk/sites/default/files/resources/Older%20peoples%20Care%20pathway%20guidance%20notes.pdf [Accessed 28 January 2024].

SafeLives (2016b) 'Spotlight #2: Disabled People and Domestic Abuse'. Available from: www.safelives.org.uk/knowledge-hub/spotlights/spotlight-2-disabled-people-and-domestic-abuse [Accessed 3 January 2024].

SafeLives (2016c) 'Safe Later Lives: Older people and Domestic Abuse'. Available from: https://safelives.org.uk/sites/default/files/resources/Safe%20Later%20Lives%20-%20Older%20people%20and%20domestic%20abuse.pdf [Accessed 16 January 2024].

SafeLives (2021) 'Transgender Victims' and Survivors' Experiences of Domestic Abuse'. Available from: https://safelives.org.uk/sites/default/files/resources/Briefing%20-%20Transgender%20Victim-Survivors%27%20Experiences%20of%20Domestic%20Abuse%20Final.pdf [Accessed 12 July 2024].

SCIE (Social Care Institute for Excellence) (2018) 'Gaining Access to an Adult Suspected to Be at Risk of Neglect or Abuse'. Available from: www.scie.org.uk/safeguarding/adults/practice/gaining-access [Accessed 8 January 2024].

SCIE (Social Care Institute of Excellence) (2022) 'Understanding the Impact of COVID'. Available from: www.scie.org.uk/providing-care/commissioning/impact-on-citizens/ [Accessed 9 January 2024].

Scott, J., Weatherhead, S., Daker-White, G., Manthorpe, J. and Mawson, M. (2020) 'Practitioners' Experiences of the Mental Capacity Act: A Systematic Review', *The Journal of Adult Protection*, 22(4): 227–244.

Scottish Government (2022) 'Code of Practice for the Adult Support and Protection Act (Scotland) 2007 (Revised)'. Available from: www.gov.scot/publications/adult-support-protection-scotland-act-2007-code-practice-3/ [Accessed 10 January 2024].

Sherwood-Johnson, F. (2016) 'Independent Advocacy in Adult Support and Protection Work', *The Journal of Adult Protection*, 18(2): 109–18.

Sherwood-Johnson, F., Cross, B. and Daniel, B. (2013) 'The Experience of Being Protected', *The Journal of Adult Protection*, 15(3): 115–26.

Sicora, A. (2017) *Reflective Practice and Learning from Mistakes in Social Work*, Bristol: Policy Press.

Sin, C.H. (2013) 'Making Disablist Hate Crime Visible: Addressing the Challenges of Improving Reporting', in A. Roulstone and H. Mason-Bish (eds) *Disability, Hate Crime and Violence*, Abingdon: Routledge, pp 147–65.

Skills for Care (2014) 'Care Act Learning and Development Materials Glossary'. Available from: www.skillsforcare.org.uk/resources/documents/Developing-your-workforce/Care-Certificate/Glossary.pdf [Accessed 7 June 2024].

Social Workers Union (2024) 'Social Worker's Concerns not Dealt with by Authorities'. Available from: https://swu-union.org.uk/2024/04/social-workers-concerns-about-welfare-not-dealt-with-by-authorities/ [Accessed 6 June 2024].

South Gloucestershire Safeguarding Adults Board (2019) 'What Makes a Good Care Home'. Available from: https://sites.southglos.gov.uk/safeguarding/wp-content/uploads/sites/221/2015/07/What-Makes-a-Good-care-Home.pdf [Accessed 16 January 2024].

Stevens, M., Martineau, S., Manthorpe, J. and Norrie, C. (2017) 'Social Workers' Power of Entry in Adult Safeguarding Concerns: Debates over Autonomy, Privacy and Protection', *The Journal of Adult Protection*, 19(6): 312–22.

Stone, K., Vicary, V., Spencer-Lane, T. and Ince, G. (2020) *The Approved Mental Health Professional Practice Handbook*, Bristol: Policy Press.

Substance Abuse and Mental Health Administration (SAMHSA) (2014) *Concept of Trauma and Guidance for a Trauma Informed Approach*. SAMHSA Trauma and Justice Strategic Initiative July 2014. U.S. Department of Health and Human Services, Policy, Planning and Innovation. Available from: https://store.samhsa.gov/sites/default/files/sma14-4884.pdf [Accessed 11 July 2024].

Survivors Trust (2023) 'Sexual Assault Referral Centres'. Available from: https://thesurvivorstrust.org/sarc/ [Accessed 5 April 2024].

Szerletics, A. (2011) 'Vulnerable Adults and the Inherent Jurisdiction of the High Court', Essex Autonomy Project, September. Available from: https://autonomy.essex.ac.uk/resources/vulnerable-adults-and-the-inherent-jurisdiction-of-the-high-court/ [Accessed 10 March 2024].

Take Five to Stop Fraud (2024) Accessibility toolkit. Available at: https://www.takefive-stopfraud.org.uk/accessibility-toolkit/ [Accessed 3 July 2024].

Taylor, M. and Tapper, L. (2017) 'Participative Practice and Family Group Conferencing', in A. Cooper and E. White (eds) *Safeguarding Adults Under the Care Act 2014: Understanding Good Practice*, London: Jessica Kingsley, pp 57–73.

The Freedom Programme (2018) 'Facilitator Training: Learning Differences Training'. Available from: www.freedomprogramme.co.uk/learning-differences-training.php [Accessed 1 March 2024].

The Survivors Trust (2018) 'Find Support in Your Area'. Available from: https://thesurvivorstrust.org/support-in-your-area/ [Accessed 5 March 2024].

Thompson, L.J. and West, D. (2013) 'Professional Development in the Contemporary Educational Context: Encouraging Practice Wisdom', *Social Work Education*, 32(1): 118–33.

UK Parliament (2018) Science and Technology Select Committee. 'Evidence Based Early Years Intervention'. Available from: https://publications.parliament.uk/pa/cm201719/cmselect/cmsctech/506/50605.htm [Accessed 24 March 2024].

UK Parliament Committees (2023) 'House of Commons House of Lords Joint Committee on the Mental Health Bill'. Available from: https://committees.parliament.uk/publications/33599/documents/182904/default/ [Accessed 19 February 2024].

United Nations Human Rights (1984) 'United Nations Convention Against Torture'. Available from: www.ohchr.org/EN/ProfessionalInterest/Pages/CAT.aspx [Accessed 29 March 2024].

Victim Support (2019) 'How We Can Help'. Available from: www.victimsupport.org.uk/help-and-support/how-we-can-help [Accessed 10 March 2024].

Weiss, T. (2014) 'Personal Transformation: Posttraumatic Growth and Gerotranscendence', *Journal of Humanistic Psychology*, 54(2): 203–26.

Welsh Government (2018) 'Guidance: Safeguarding Adults at Risk of Abuse or Neglect'. Available from: www.gov.wales/safeguarding-adults-risk-abuse-or-neglect [Accessed 15 January 2024].

West Midlands Adult Safeguarding Editorial Group (2024) 'Adult Safeguarding: Multi-Agency Policy and Procedures for the Protection of Adults with Care and Support Needs in the West Midlands'. Available from: www.safeguardingwarwickshire.co.uk/images/downloads/West-Midlands-Policy-and-Procedure/WM_Adult_Safeguarding_PP_v30.pdf [Accessed 4 March 2024].

White, E. (2017) 'Assessing and Responding to Risk', in A. Cooper and E. White (eds) *Safeguarding Adults under the Care Act 2014: Understanding Good Practice*, London: Jessica Kingsley, pp 110–27.

White, A., Sheehan, R., Ding, J., Roberts, C., Magill, N. and Keagan-Bull, R. et al (2023) 'Learning from Lives and Deaths – People with a Learning Disability and Autistic People (LeDeR) Report for 2022', LeDeR Autism and Learning Disability Partnership, King's College London.

Williams, V.J., Boyle, G., Jepson, M.J., Swift, P., Williamson, T. and Heslop, P. (2012) 'Making Best Interests Decisions: People and Processes'. Available from: https://research-information.bris.ac.uk/en/publications/making-best-interests-decisions-people-and-processes(4a89b31f-2097-4483-9a3f-73d32a243ad5).html [Accessed 5 April 2024].

World Health Organisation (WHO) (2023) 'Statement on the Fifteenth Meeting of the IHR (2005) Emergency Committee on the COVID-19 Pandemic'. Available from: www.who.int/news/item/05-05-2023-statement-on-the-fifteenth-meeting-of-the-international-health-regulations-(2005)-emergency-committee-regarding-the-coronavirus-disease-(covid-19)-pandemic [Accessed 19 March 2024].

Statutes, case law and Safeguarding Adults Reviews

The Houses of Parliament set out the statutory legal framework for adult safeguarding practice. In the UK, law operates by the principle of precedent, which means that when judges interpret the statute created by Parliament, they must consider the decisions made by other courts concerning the same situations, and where a binding decision has been made by a higher court, that judgement must be used to guide decisions in lower courts.

Figure A1 shows the hierarchy of courts in which judgements relevant to adult safeguarding law practice are likely to be made.

The statutes list has been organised by date with the most recent first. The case law (or common law) has been arranged alphabetically by theme and then by date with the most recent first. It is first arranged by theme to assist readers to find cases relevant to any queries they may have. Some cases are relevant to more than one subject area so may appear under more than one heading. For example, the Supreme Court's decision in the *P v Cheshire West and Chester Council* and *P and Q (MIG and MEG) v Surrey County Council* cases is binding on all subsequent deprivation of liberty cases in England and Wales and has overridden all previous judgements made in these cases (for example, in the Court of Protection and the Court of Appeal).

Statutes

Domestic Abuse Act (2021). Available from: www.legislation.gov.uk/ukpga/2021/17/section/1/enacted [Accessed 20 February 2024].

Mental Capacity (Amendment) Act (2019). Available from: www.legislation.gov.uk/ukpga/2019/18/enacted/data.htm [Accessed 6 December 2019].

Children and Social Work Act (2017). Available from: www.legislation.gov.uk/ukpga/2017/16 [Accessed 24 February 2024].

Consumer Rights Act (2015). Available from: www.legislation.gov.uk/ukpga/2015/15/contents/enacted [Accessed 17 November 2018].

Serious Crime Act (2015). Available from: www.legislation.gov.uk/ukpga/2015/9/contents/enacted [Accessed 21 December 2019].

Care Act (2014). Available from: www.legislation.gov.uk/ukpga/2014/23/contents/enacted [Accessed 29 May 2019].

Social Services and Well-being (Wales) Act (2014). Available from: www.legislation.gov.uk/anaw/2014/4/contents [Accessed 25 June 2019].

Equality Act (2010). Available from: www.legislation.gov.uk/ukpga/2010/15/contents [Accessed 19 December 2018].

Figure A1: Court structure relevant to adult safeguarding

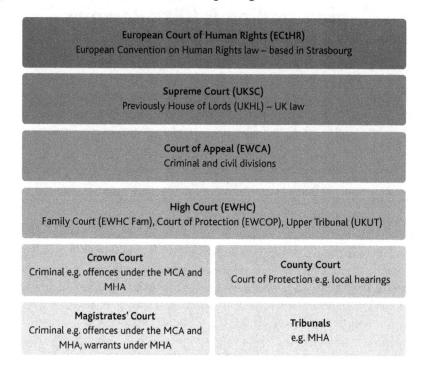

Adult Support and Protection (Scotland) Act (2007). Available from: www.legislat ion.gov.uk/asp/2007/10/contents [Accessed 25 June 2019].

United Nations Convention on the Rights of Persons with Disabilities (2006). Available from: www.un.org/development/desa/disabilities/convention-on-the-rights-of-persons-with-disabilities.html [Accessed 11 October 2018].

Mental Capacity Act (2005). Available from: www.legislation.gov.uk/ukpga/2005/9/contents [Accessed 1 May 2019].

Human Rights Act (1998). Available from: www.legislation.gov.uk/ukpga/1998/42/contents [Accessed 19 December 2019].

Police and Criminal Evidence Act (1984). Available from: www.legislation.gov.uk/ukpga/1984/60/contents [Accessed 16 September 2019].

Mental Health Act (1983, as amended 2007). Available from: www.legislation.gov.uk/ukpga/1983/20/contents [Accessed 10 December 2018].

Case law

Advocacy and representation

- *Re AJ (DOLS)* (2015) EWCOP 5. Available from: www.bailii.org/ew/cases/EWCOP/2015/5.html [Accessed 30 December 2017].

Consent to marriage

- *Southwark, (The London Borough of) v KA (Capacity to Marry)* [2016] EWCOP 20. Available from: www.39essex.com/information-hub/case/lb-southwark-v-ka-capacity-marry [Accessed 20 March 2024].

Deprivation of liberty

- *P v Cheshire West and Chester Council and another and P and Q v Surrey County Council* [2014] UKSC 19. Available from: www.bailii.org/uk/cases/UKSC/2014/19.html [Accessed 23 November 2018].

Imputability to the state

- *Staffordshire County Council v SRK* [2016] EWCOP 27. Available from: www.bailii.org/ew/cases/EWCOP/2016/27.html [Accessed 30 December 2018].

Inherent jurisdiction

- *Southend-on-Sea v Meyers* (2019) EWHC 399 (Fam). Available from: www.bailii.org/ew/cases/EWHC/Fam/2019/399.html [Accessed 5 April 2024].
- *Local Authority X v MM & Anor* (No. 1) [2007] EWHC 2003 (Fam). Available from: www.bailii.org/ew/cases/EWHC/Fam/2007/2003.html [Accessed 12 December 2018].

Mental capacity assessment, including salient points and causative nexus

- Executive dysfunction. *Warrington Borough Council v Y & Ors* [2023] EWCOP 27. Available from: www.courtofprotectionhub.uk/cases/warrington-borough-council-v-y-ors-2023-ewcop-27 [Accessed 20 March 2024].
- *PC v City of York Council* [2013] EWCA Civ 478. Available from: www.bailii.org/ew/cases/EWCA/Civ/2013/478.html [Accessed 30 March 2024].
- *CC v KK and STCC* [2012] EWCOP 2136. Available from: www.bailii.org/ew/cases/EWCOP/2012/2136.html [Accessed 30 March 2024].
- *Re E (An alleged patient): Sheffield City Council v E* [2004] 1 FLR 965. Available from: www.bailii.org/ew/cases/EWHC/Fam/2004/2808.html [Accessed 29 May 2019].

Risk and well-being

- *Local Authority X v MM & Anor (No. 1)* [2007] EWHC 2003 (Fam). Available from: www.bailii.org/ew/cases/EWHC/Fam/2007/2003.html [Accessed 23 January 2019].

- *London Borough of Croydon v CD* [2019] EWHC 2943. Available from: www.bailii.org/ew/cases/EWHC/Fam/2019/2943.html [Accessed 15 February 2024].

Safeguarding and Article 8

- *Essex County Council v RF & Ors* [2015] EWCOP 1. Available from: www.bailii.org/ew/cases/EWCOP/2015/1.html [Accessed 30 December 2018].
- *Milton Keynes Council v RR & Ors* [2014] EWCOP B19. Available from: www.bailii.org/ew/cases/EWCOP/2014/B19.html [Accessed 30 December 2018].
- *MK v Somerset County Council* [2014] EWCOP B25. Available from: www.bailii.org/ew/cases/EWCOP/2014/B25.html [Accessed 30 December 2018].
- *London Borough of Hillingdon v Steven Neary & Ors* [2011] EWCOP 1377. Available from: www.bailii.org/ew/cases/EWCOP/2011/1377.html [Accessed 22 May 2019].

Tort law

- *M'Alister (or Donoghue) (Pauper) appellant and Stevenson (respondent)*. Available from: www.bailii.org/uk/cases/UKHL/1932/100.html [Accessed 31 May 2019].

Safeguarding Adults Reviews

Devon Safeguarding Adults Board (2018) 'Safeguarding Adults Review: Adrian Munday (SAR Z)'. Available from: www.devonsafeguardingadultspartnership.org.uk/about/safeguarding-adult-reviews/torbay-and-devon-sars/sar-adrian-munday/ [Accessed 3 January 2024].

Hampshire Safeguarding Adults Board (2022) 'Thematic Review on Self-Neglect'. Available from: www.hampshiresab.org.uk/wp-content/uploads/Final-version-HSAB-Self-Neglect-Thematic-SAR-March-2022.pdf [Accessed April 5 2024].

Isle of Wight Safeguarding Adults Board (2019) 'SAR Howard'. Available from: www.iowsab.org.uk/wp-content/uploads/2019/01/2880-IoW-SAB-Howard-SAR-FINAL-FOR-PUBLICATION.pdf [Accessed 30 January 2024].

Lambeth Safeguarding Adults Board (2019) 'SAR Martin'. Available from: www.lambethsab.org.uk/about-the-board#SARS [Accessed 14 January 2024].

Plymouth Safeguarding Adults Board (2023) 'SAR Kath'. Available from: www.plymouth.gov.uk/sites/default/files/2023-12/Safeguarding-Adult-Review-Kath-v2.pdf [Accessed 4 April 2024].

Richmond and Wandsworth Safeguarding Adults Board (2020) 'SAR Jasmine'. Available from: https://sabrichmondandwandsworth.org.uk/media/1475/safeguarding-_adults_review_jasmine.pdf [Accessed 15 February 2024].

Salford Safeguarding Adults Board (2023) 'SAR Stanley'. Available from: https://safeguardingadults.salford.gov.uk/safeguarding-adult-board/safeguarding-adult-reviews-sar/published-sars-and-other-reviews/sar-stanley-2023/ [Accessed 10 January 2024].

Solihull Safeguarding Adults Board (2020) 'SAR Stephen'. Available from: www.safeguardingsolihull.org.uk/ssab/wp-content/uploads/sites/2/2021/09/Overview-Report-for-Stephen-SAR-1.pdf [Accessed 5 March 2024].

Somerset Safeguarding Adults Board (2018) 'Mendip House'. Available from: http://ssab.safeguardingsomerset.org.uk/wp-content/uploads/20180206_Mendip-House_SAR_FOR_PUBLICATION.pdf [Accessed 25 January 2024].

South Gloucestershire Safeguarding Adults Board (2012) 'Winterbourne View Hospital: A Serious Case Review'. Available from: https://sites.southglos.gov.uk/safeguarding/adults/i-am-a-carerrelative/winterbourne-view/ [Accessed 24 March 2024].

South Gloucestershire Safeguarding Adults Board (2018) 'Nightingale Homes'. Available from: http://sites.southglos.gov.uk/safeguarding/wp-content/uploads/sites/221/2018/10/SAR-Nightingale-Final-Oct-2018.pdf [Accessed 25 March 2024].

Teeswide Safeguarding Adults (2021) 'SAR Molly'. Available from: www.tsab.org.uk/wp-content/uploads/2022/06/Molly-Overview-Report-V5-Accessible-Version.pdf [Accessed 12 April 2024].

Torbay and Devon Safeguarding Adults Partnership (2023) 'SAR Stephen'. Available from: www.devonsafeguardingadultspartnership.org.uk/document/sar-stephen/ [Accessed 16 July 2024].

Index

References to figures appear in *italic* type; those in **bold** type refer to tables.